THOUSAND OAKS LIBRARY

NEWBURY PARK BRANCH

P9-DVR-367

DISCARDED

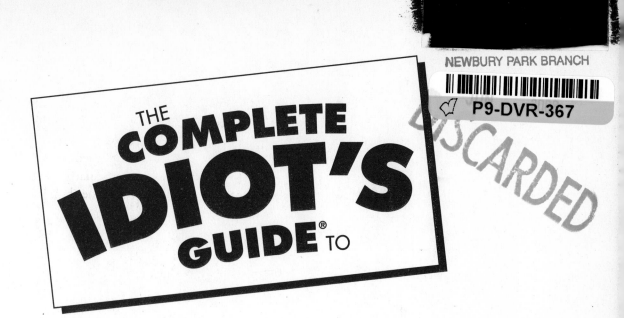

THE **COMPLETE IDIOT'S GUIDE**® TO

# Designing Your Own Home

COLLECTION MANAGEMENT

| | | |
|---|---|---|
| | | |
| | | |
| | | |
| | | |
| | | |
| | | |
| | | |

PROPERTY OF
**THOUSAND OAKS LIBRARY**
1401 E. Janss Road
Thousand Oaks, California

DISCARDED

NEWBURY PARK BRANCH

JUN 2005

THOUSAND OAKS LIBRARY

THOUSAND OAKS LIBRARY

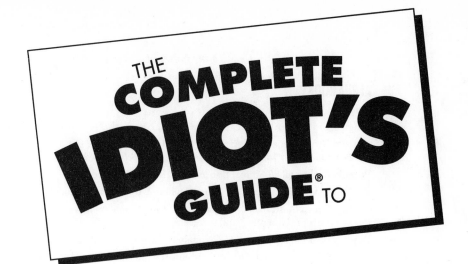

THE **COMPLETE IDIOT'S GUIDE**® TO

# Designing Your Own Home

*by Oreste Drapaca and Abigail R. Esman*

**ALPHA**

A member of Penguin Group (USA) Inc.

*To my sons, Sebastian & Tristan*

## ALPHA BOOKS

Published by the Penguin Group

Penguin Group (USA) Inc., 375 Hudson Street, New York, New York 10014, U.S.A.

Penguin Group (Canada), 10 Alcorn Avenue, Toronto, Ontario, Canada M4V 3B2 (a division of Pearson Penguin Canada Inc.)

Penguin Books Ltd, 80 Strand, London WC2R 0RL, England

Penguin Ireland, 25 St Stephen's Green, Dublin 2, Ireland (a division of Penguin Books Ltd)

Penguin Group (Australia), 250 Camberwell Road, Camberwell, Victoria 3124, Australia (a division of Pearson Australia Group Pty Ltd)

Penguin Books India Pvt Ltd, 11 Community Centre, Panchsheel Park, New Delhi—110 017, India

Penguin Group (NZ), cnr Airborne and Rosedale Roads, Albany, Auckland 1310, New Zealand (a division of Pearson New Zealand Ltd)

Penguin Books (South Africa) (Pty) Ltd, 24 Sturdee Avenue, Rosebank, Johannesburg 2196, South Africa

Penguin Books Ltd, Registered Offices: 80 Strand, London WC2R 0RL, England

## Copyright © 2006 by Abigail R. Esman

All rights reserved. No part of this book shall be reproduced, stored in a retrieval system, or transmitted by any means, electronic, mechanical, photocopying, recording, or otherwise, without written permission from the publisher. No patent liability is assumed with respect to the use of the information contained herein. Although every precaution has been taken in the preparation of this book, the publisher and authors assume no responsibility for errors or omissions. Neither is any liability assumed for damages resulting from the use of information contained herein. For information, address Alpha Books, 800 East 96th Street, Indianapolis, IN 46240.

THE COMPLETE IDIOT'S GUIDE TO and Design are registered trademarks of Penguin Group (USA) Inc.

International Standard Book Number: 978-1-59257-501-5 *728*
Library of Congress Catalog Card Number: 2006938596

09  08  07      8  7  6  5  4  3  2  1

Interpretation of the printing code: The rightmost number of the first series of numbers is the year of the book's printing; the rightmost number of the second series of numbers is the number of the book's printing. For example, a printing code of 07-1 shows that the first printing occurred in 2007.

*Printed in the United States of America*

**Note:** This publication contains the opinions and ideas of its authors. It is intended to provide helpful and informative material on the subject matter covered. It is sold with the understanding that the authors and publisher are not engaged in rendering professional services in the book. If the reader requires personal assistance or advice, a competent professional should be consulted.

The authors and publisher specifically disclaim any responsibility for any liability, loss, or risk, personal or otherwise, which is incurred as a consequence, directly or indirectly, of the use and application of any of the contents of this book.

Most Alpha books are available at special quantity discounts for bulk purchases for sales promotions, premiums, fund-raising, or educational use. Special books, or book excerpts, can also be created to fit specific needs.

For details, write: Special Markets, Alpha Books, 375 Hudson Street, New York, NY 10014.

**Publisher:** *Marie Butler-Knight*
**Editorial Director:** *Mike Sanders*
**Managing Editor:** *Billy Fields*
**Acquisitions Editor:** *Mike Sanders*
**Senior Development Editor:** *Phil Kitchel*
**Senior Production Editor:** *Janette Lynn*
**Copy Editor:** *Michael Dietsch*

**Cartoonist:** *Shannon Wheeler*
**Book Designer:** *Trina Wurst*
**Cover Designer:** *Bill Thomas*
**Indexer:** *Heather McNeill*
**Layout:** *Brian Massey*
**Proofreader:** *Mary Hunt*

# Contents at a Glance

**Appendixes**

# Contents

## Appendixes

# Introduction

The decision to design your own home is the kind of thing one comes up with in a moment of uninhibited inspiration, possibly followed by the thought—yours or someone else's—"are you kidding?"

But why should you be? Perhaps you've long wanted a custom home, but if it's going to be your home, designed for you, you should be the one to design it. Few things compare with the pride of achievement, the glorious sense of accomplishment, that come from having created something entirely yourself. And this, of course, gives you complete control of the project—no one is imposing his own taste on your dwelling place, or worrying about her reputation instead of your happiness. These alone are good reasons to take on a project like this single-handedly.

Or it may also be that you can't quite cover the added cost of an architect (though an architect *could* actually save you money in the long run). So you've browsed various commercial blueprints, the kind that allow you to mix and match, but ultimately, you've decided it made designing a house feel a little too much like ordering a pizza. Or maybe nothing you found, no matter how much you adjusted it, really quite became the house you want: the ones you like best might be designed for a wide lot, while yours is a long lot, or you might have an ocean view that can best be appreciated by changing a few rooms around, but then the layout no longer makes much sense.

And even those who may in fact prefer to work with an architect can benefit from learning about the process. Knowing more enables you to have some say in the design, and to have a better understanding of what you want *before* you meet with (or even select) your future architect.

This book, richly informed by the experience and expertise of an architect who has, over a 15-year career, designed buildings throughout the world, will prepare you for all of that. With step-by-step explanations and instructions augmented by insider tips and information, we will take you, in essence, from "are you kidding" to "no, I'm not"—and from there to a bemused and proud, "well, look at that: I did it!"—spoken, of course, as you walk through the front door that *you* selected, to the entryway that *you* created, of the home that *you* designed.

But what if you don't know a thing about beams or foundations, bay windows and dormers? What if right now, you don't even have much of an idea what it is you actually want? *What if you can't even draw?*

It's okay. We will get you there, and along the way you will learn about things you never knew you didn't know, and discover creative talents and inspiration you maybe never even knew you had.

## Where We're Going, And How We'll Get There

So here's a basic sketch—a floor plan, if you will—of how this book works, and the road that lies ahead.

xviii The Complete Idiot's Guide to Designing Your Own Home

**Part 1, "Starting Out,"** explores the why and how of designing your home—from the pros and cons of doing it yourself, to gathering ideas, to selecting and orienting your house on your site.

**Part 2, "Foundations,"** is art class 101, where we'll review how to make architectural drawings and models that will eventually make your now-intangible, possibly vague ideas, clear so that both you and your builder know what the house will look like when it's done.

**Part 3, "Your Money,"** covers working out what the project will cost, and the various experts who can help you get the most from your dollars, your time, or often enough, both.

**Part 4, "Getting to Work,"** is where the designing really starts, from sketching out the basic layout of your home to rendering the drawings and models we talked about back in Part 2. Here, too, you will learn about the kinds of materials you can use, and start making your selections: will it be a stone house with wooden floors? A wood house with stone floors? What kind of stone? What kind of wood? What about siding, cement, and what goes on your roof?

And because we believe in the importance of preserving the earth that serves, ultimately, as our real home—and in caring for the generations who will live here in the future—we'll talk about sustainable living options: how to make your home safe not just for you, but for the environment in which we live.

**Part 5, "Decisions, Decisions,"** takes you into the heart of the house—plumbing, electrical and heating systems, and the rooms you'll need the most—kitchens and baths. From the technical to the inspirational, this section will help you design a home that is as efficient as it is a joy to live in.

**Part 6, "The Entrancing Details,"** is where you begin personalizing your design, adding fireplaces, window elements, various built-ins and other special features, including a few you may not have even thought of yet. We'll also talk about lighting systems, which set the mood of every room—or even every moment—and make the most of your design. Finally, we'll get to the embellishments: your floor finishes, your wall coverings, and the special elements you'll add to the *outside* of your house, from driveways and spigots to terraces, gardens, and gazebos.

But there is more to being your own architect (or working alongside one) than just creating a design. You need to get this house built, which is what you'll learn about in **Part 7, "Making It Real."** You'll learn about cost estimates, finding a contractor, obtaining bids, arranging permits, and all the other little things you'll need to make that all-important step: from the design you've always dreamed about to the home where you will live.

## Landmarks

We've also created a system of symbols that will appear along the way. The point is to make things as clear as possible, and to alert you to important points we think warrant your attention (or are just interesting to know). Be on the lookout for the following:

### Architerms

Some of the vocabulary in this book may be new to you. We'll define various terms as they appear. You'll also find a more comprehensive glossary in an appendix at the end of the book.

### Flashpoint

These usually highlight important information or ideas discussed within a chapter. Flashpoints will also appear when we have a story to tell, something that will further inform you about architecture in general or the architectural design process.

### Design Tip

As you'd expect, Design tips are expert suggestions to guide your design or help you to make decisions along the way.

### Design Don't

These point out potential mistakes and caution you against any wrong moves.

## Acknowledgements

Oreste thanks the following:

Abigail Esman, for casting in words what I can only imagine, but not express.

Bob DiForio, patient agent.

Mike Sanders, patient editor.

Both my parents and all my grandparents, for insisting that I choose a profession, because that helps the progress of a civil society.

My U.S. family (my wife, Dr. Kimberly Busi, my mother-in-law Anita Busi, my sons Sebastian and Tristan, with Ula's help) supported me during time away from them and gave their opinions freely.

Several people helped me cross the Atlantic: Ion Ghika and family, Emil Voyles, and Mihai Radu.

Professionally, I had support and inspiration from several, among whom: the late Herbert Beckhart, Tim Culbert, professor Giuliano Fiorenzoli, Winslow Kosior, Mircea Ochinciuc, Christopher L. Olsen, Adrian Oprea, Douglas Platt, Christine Restaino, the late Frank Richlan, Harry C. Wolf III, the late Dan Zaharia.

—Oreste Drapaca

Abigail thanks Peter Madden, without whose friendship and guidance I could never have achieved the (re)design of my own home while writing this book; Lisa Ramaci, Barbara Divver, and Rosa and Aaron Esman, who made having that home possible; Bob DiForio, whose patience saw this book to completion; and the Drapaca family, who sacrificed so much time with Oreste, without whom this book never could have been.

—Abigail R. Esman

## Trademarks

All terms mentioned in this book that are known to be or are suspected of being trademarks or service marks have been appropriately capitalized. Alpha Books and Penguin Group (USA) Inc. cannot attest to the accuracy of this information. Use of a term in this book should not be regarded as affecting the validity of any trademark or service mark.

# Part 1

## Starting Out

Chances are, if you've picked up this book, you're looking for a new home. Not just that, but you're looking for your *own* new home—one tailored to your needs, your tastes, one you don't have to modify and rip apart and rebuild just to make it into some approximation of your dream house.

Enough of that. You just want the dream house already, period. It's possible, too, that you're thinking about hiring an architect to do the work for you. Even so, you'd like to gather together your own ideas, to have a sense of the process and your part of it, before you do. You may also already have bought a plot of land to build on. If not, you're looking, waiting to find that space that answers your desires, that ground that speaks your name.

In Part I, we will help you create that dream home, at least (for now) in your mind's eye—from the windows in the bedroom to the lingering sunset views.

# Why Design Your Own Home?

## In This Chapter

- ◆ Aesthetics and your custom home
- ◆ Building your home to be your castle
- ◆ Do-It-Yourself Pros and Cons

There was an old woman who lived in a shoe. Did you ever wonder why?

It surely wasn't practical: she had too many children. Was it for aesthetic reasons? Perhaps she had a shoe fetish—or, like many women, just loved shoes. One thing is likely: it was like no other house on the block.

Of course, it's possible she bought the house this way and didn't design it herself—but someone did, and that person's reasons were the same as yours: wanting a home that perfectly suited his or her taste, needs, and peculiarities—in short, a house that was unlike any other house in the world.

You have decided—or perhaps you are still deciding—to design your own home. This book was created to help you do just that, be it in the shape of a shoe, a castle, a gingerbread house, or the house you played in as a child. From first inspiration to the moment your builders reach for their hammers and nails, designing your own home is an adventure in discovery—about geology and landscape, balance and proportion, light and space and color, and, most exciting of all, about yourself.

## Aesthetics

Chances are, among the many reasons you have chosen to design your own house is the desire to live in a home that doesn't just suit your basic needs—X number of bedrooms, Y number of baths—but also represents something of you, of how you view yourself and how you want others to view you. You've always wanted a house with a porch just like your grandmother's porch, and turrets like the ones you saw once in a magazine, and rooms that speak to your tastes: large and spare and modern, or ornate and classical, with wooden floors or tile, with industrial steel staircases or sweeping marble ones.

Designing your own home makes this possible—and the savings in architects' fees (even if you decide to consult one from time to time) will help you come even closer to creating your dream home.

> ### Flashpoint
> Why design when you can redesign? Although predesigned plans are available on the web and elsewhere, they tend to be generic and average, targeted at everyone and, therefore, no one in particular. It's a bit like buying a frozen birthday cake and writing "Happy Birthday" on it yourself. Chances are you'll feel you've overcompromised or cheated yourself if you simply mix and match, or change a detail or two on the same design thousands of others have used, too. In the end, it defeats the purpose of designing a castle of your very own.

# Your Home Is Your Castle

Your home may be a castle, but is it *your* castle if it was designed for someone else or no one in particular, without your own special needs in mind?

A house, after all, is very personal: by designing it for yourself, you have the opportunity to plan much of your own life and where it will happen. In a custom-designed home, you get to decide everything: where the windows go, how high the stair treads rise, even the distance between the road and your front door. *You* choose whether the sunlight wakes you gently in the morning, or pours its first warm rays into the kitchen, set carefully far away on the other side of the house. (And there is something to deciding where the sun will rise and set that certainly makes one feel worthy of an imperial palace of a home.)

Or designing your own home could be a way of preserving aspects of the past: some people have re-created their childhood homes—sometimes in a "new and improved" version, and sometimes as authentically as their memories will allow. Your dream home is really just as close as your own imagination.

*Perhaps create a dream or source of inspiration, such as this castle found in Vaux-le-Vicomte, France.*

And if that weren't enough, a custom home caters not only to your wants, but to your needs. In the Netherlands, for instance, architectural standards were raised some years ago to accommodate the height of recent generations (on average, the Dutch are now the tallest people in the world). A Dutchman moving to Los Angeles, say, might therefore design a home with taller doorways and elevated countertops, or even placing electrical outlets not quite so close by the floor. These may seem like small details, but in combination, they add up to greater comfort, a sense of being, well, at *home* in your own home.

# Economic Pros—and Cons

The financial incentives for designing a home are based largely, of course, on the savings in architect's fees—tens of thousands of dollars that you can put into extra rooms, marble baths, a swimming pool—features usually beyond the budgets of homebuyers or most homebuilders. Essentially, your options expand, allowing you the option of spending your money where you want it to go: on your home.

You will, however, want to keep an eye on those savings: it may often be more cost-effective in the long run to have an architect close by, at least for consulting purposes. Doing it yourself can—and usually will—take longer; and you won't want to spend your carefully budgeted savings correcting errors that an architect, with many more years of experience and expertise, could have helped you to avoid. We will talk more about the potential benefits of working with consultants in Chapter 7.

# Before You Decide, Consider This ...

Let's be honest: architecture is a challenging and complex, if highly rewarding, enterprise. Professional architects, after all, undergo extensive training to master complex spatial concepts and the various components involved.

So right now, before you even start, forget any thoughts you may have had that this will be a simple, "Thin Thighs in 30 Days" endeavor: it won't. Designing a home can be a long process that seems almost incomprehensible at times, even—in the worst moments—insurmountable. Frustrations are inevitable as you face the disappointing reality that some ideas may not fit your budget, local zoning laws, or the preferences of other members of your family.

You'll also want to consider the fact that successful, practical architectural design requires an ability to juggle several elements in the air at one time. You need to stay aware of what you've already done so that you can measure what you're doing now against it. You probably don't want to discover just before you start construction, for instance, that you've created a dining room twice. You have to keep track of the choices you make and the budget you have available to realize them. At the same time, not too far from the front of your mind, you will be holding your plans and ideas for what comes next—and what comes after that. Do not, in other words, expect a direct, linear process: you will go forward and back throughout the various phases of creating your design: reassessing, refining, and remeasuring.

But there's really no other way to do it. Building and designing a home may be the single largest investment you make in your life, and certainly one of the most important. It's not just a matter of forgetting the baby room or building the entire house before you realize *you forgot the turrets*—the whole reason you wanted the house in the first place! These are annoyances—expensive though they may be. But if you select cheap materials, attempt an engineering marvel beyond your ability, or fail to follow various codes and zoning laws, you can literally find yourself with a disaster on your hands.

In the end, there is little in life more satisfying than a job well done. And like gardening, much of the joy of designing your own home lies in watching it grow and develop over time, building to the day you open the front door and close it behind you, knowing that this home—the product of your imagination and inspiration, your mumbled curses and loud hurrahs, your broken pencils and sleepless nights—will be here for generations to come.

### Flashpoint

In 1978, Francois de Menil of the Houston, Texas, family of art collectors and patrons, commissioned an 11,000-square-foot bachelor pad as a vacation home. The house, created by architects Charles Gwathmey and Robert Siegel and nicknamed Toad Hall, included tennis courts, a screening room, and a Jacuzzi.

De Menil, then a 30-year-old filmmaker, was captivated. Six years later, just as the house was completed, he enrolled himself in architecture school in New York. Shortly after that, having recently wed, he sold the house. As he told *The New York Times* in 1988, it was "a house for a family I didn't have and a life I wasn't leading."

There are two morals to this story: first, design your home with your lifestyle in mind, but with an eye to any anticipated future changes; and second, realize that you, too, could get hooked, return to school, and become a major architect yourself.

## The Least You Need to Know

- The choice to design your own home is made as much for personal and aesthetic reasons as practical or financial ones.
- Prepare accordingly: doing it yourself is not without challenges—it will likely take more time and effort.
- Consider engaging an architect for a part of the process to avoid (costly) errors.
- Have confidence in your own design abilities and enjoy the process.
- The home you create for yourself is a home, sweet home, indeed.

# The Shape of Things to Come

## In This Chapter

- Your dream house, for starters
- Creating an ideas file
- Finding new possibilities
- Brainstorming ideas for the life you live
- Visualizing your new home
- How your marriage can survive the process

Few things better reflect who we are, our place in the world, than the place we make our home. You've decided to design your own home because, ultimately, you want a home that works perfectly for *you*; but it is also a reflection of your self-image, how you see yourself in relation to the world and your community. Your personal home design, in other words, should speak for you—not just of who you are but of all your aspirations.

In this chapter, you'll explore what that means—not only how many bedrooms you need, but what shapes you want them to be and what features you want them to have. Do you want walk-in closets? Bay windows? Fireplaces? Here is where you'll create your program: the portrait of what you want your house to be, what you need your house to be, and what you will later measure against what you can realistically afford in order to make it the house it will eventually become. Think of your program as a letter to Santa: what is *everything* you want?

## Finding Ideas

Architects have systematized the design process into six phases:

- Predesign
- Schematic design
- Design development
- Contract documents
- Bidding and negotiation
- Construction

**Architerms**

The **predesign phase** concerns the fundamentals of planning a home: selecting and documenting your site, gathering ideas, and building a personal "program" for what you want your home to be.

You will need to follow these phases in sequence, as each phase builds on the one before it. The topics covered in this section comprise the *predesign phase*. We will discuss each phase as we encounter it throughout the process.

You probably already have some idea, somewhere in your mind, of what you want: large, small, traditional, modern, minimalist, ornate. Maybe that's as far as you've gotten. Or maybe you already know *exactly* what you want, down to the shapes of the chair rails in the dining room.

Either way, you will come to a point when you'll benefit from a little inspiration—or a lot. And you may be surprised, in searching for ideas, by the things that you discover: how you respond to certain shapes, for instance, or unique storage possibilities you never would have dreamed of on your own.

## Ideas Are Everywhere

Your first assignment is to buy a file folder—the accordion kind—and organize the sections in ways that make sense for you: "Window Ideas," "Bedroom Ideas," "Façade Ideas," "Lighting Ideas," for instance, or find your own system. Include at least one section for "Things I Like But Don't Know Why." You could do this collectively, or all family members could create their own—a good idea, especially if you have children old enough to want to be involved in planning their own rooms.

As you start to train your eye and grow used to the kind of unexpected inspiration that can strike at the most inconvenient moments, you'll also probably want to carry a notebook or notepad with you everywhere, to record observations—for example, while you definitely want bay windows in the living room, you do not want them to be as narrow as the ones on Mrs. Finley's house, and why did you never notice before the airy feeling of the stainless steel that wraps the stairs at the local mall?

Write it all down. You don't even have to like it, but if something strikes you in some way, you may want to come back to it. Even better, if your cell phone has a camera function (or if you have a camera—even a point-and-shoot disposable you can carry with you), use it.

## Books and Magazines

There are countless so-called shelter magazines on the market, publications filled with glossy photographs, usually of very high-end homes whose rooms have been tweaked for the photographers by professional stylists much in the way makeup artists do a model. These are pictures of homes made more perfect than reality could ever bear—but that doesn't mean they can't be helpful. Observe specific components: the way a doorway separates two rooms, wooden beams across a kitchen ceiling, an office under the eaves, a bathtub by a window with a view.

Women's magazines are also useful, providing ideas with articles about "storage solutions for small rooms" or "restyling your child's bedroom."

Another unexpected but rather obvious source is the real-estate insert of your local newspaper or the papers for the area to which you are moving, some of which are even produced in color. Each edition is a "design your own home" idea portfolio in itself.

You will also find similar inspiration in books; in fact, the way that some books are themed can make focusing on your own personal tastes and preferences easier: often they will concentrate on, say, country homes, or contemporary experimental designs. Be sure always to look for the small details and unexpected situations: niches built into a wall will save floor space otherwise used by cabinets, for instance. Walls—or sections of wall—can serve decorative functions, adding shape and shadow to a room or creating private corners.

Also look beyond the obvious titles; just because a magazine or book is about home decorating or celebrity lifestyles or vacation spots, and not architectural design, doesn't mean it won't ignite the kinds of inspiration you are seeking.

## Explore Your Neighborhood

Where do tourists go? What draws them there? What sites do tourist boards promote, and why? Next time you drive to see a friend, try circling her block before you stop in. Start driving the "scenic route" or go running on streets you haven't been on in a while.

## Other Sources

Various aspects of your life can bring inspiration. Consider treasured memories: what did your best friend's house look like when you were 12? Who had the best porch, the biggest bedroom?

What about vacations? What are some of the memorable places you've been? What did you see? Have you ever visited a landmark or historic home? What struck you about it? What have you admired in the architecture of other areas of the country or other countries? Almost every culture has its own unique, indigenous architecture, created of its own particular history, climate, and lifestyle. Think of Georgian mansions, London brownstones, the adobe structures of the Southwest, and the clapboard houses of New England. You can adopt any of these (or elements of them) for your own home.

# The One Good Use for Prefab Designs

Websites and computer programs offering template homes actually *can* be useful when considering your own design. They allow you to experiment with the looks of various shapes and materials. You can, for instance, reface the same home in brick or wood, try different roof styles, and consider a detached or attached garage.

This revisualizing of your home will be one of the most important and helpful explorations you pursue in the early planning phases of your design. How a house looks has a lot to do with what it's made of, while the materials are often in turn governed by your budget. In later chapters, we will look more closely at the various differences (both physical and financial) among various materials. For now, you're just looking for ideas and clarity, testing out the possibilities, training your eye to view things architecturally while stretching your imagination as far as it can reach.

## Creating Your Program

Programs, in fact, stand behind all design ideas, though some more specifically than others. This is what distinguishes the custom object—be it a custom-made suit or a customized home. One client, for instance, came to us requesting a table that would not only add an aesthetic accent to a room, but would be practical for those evenings when he retired to the couch with brandy and cigar, listening to his wife at the piano. The solution: a small walnut table with rotating marble top—discreet, elegant, and exactly suitable for holding an ashtray and a glass.

*The best custom designs begin with knowing what you're looking to achieve.*

*(Photo © Maria Ferrari, New York.)*

## What Is a Program?

Your program is your wish list. We mean this literally. There are no bells and whistles, no fancy formulae, no scaled and measured drawings or annotated margin scrawls (unless you want them there, of course). Forget any formal, complex associations you may have with the word "program." In this case, it's just architect-speak for "list."

But at the same time, it's one of the most important factors of the design process: without it, how can you know what you're doing?

Like many elements of this book, the idea of creating a program is equally useful if you are planning an expansion or renovation of your current home. It's one thing to say, "We need an extra study," but what do you want that study to look like? What features should it have? Is there a garden—or could one be placed—just outside, inviting a picture window? Will you want it insulated against noise? What kind of work will you do here? What mood are you looking to create?

## Interview Yourself

Here is where you start brainstorming, determining your "letter to Santa" based on what you need, what you want, and other things you haven't thought of yet. You will, once you start asking the right questions.

It's a good idea to go back to your ideas and inspirations folders—those magazine pictures and photographs you collected earlier. Looking at these images, ask yourself what specifically appealed to you about each one. Try to separate the interior decoration from the *structure* of the room, and determine clearly what about that room (or house or door or window) attracts you? Is it the light? The color? (That's an interior-design issue, so be careful.) Are the windows high or low? What shape is the ceiling? Are there turrets, towers, dormers, porches, decorative ornaments on the home? Is the 13-foot sunken bathtub really something you can't live without?

Sit down with pencil and paper—really—and ask yourself questions not just about your needs but about the way you live your life. Who lives here? A family with small children may want to have a "mud room" outside the kitchen, for instance. A collector of Meissen figures would be wise to consider built-in vitrines, which are more stable than free-standing ones—and a good idea if those same small children are running around.

Consider, for instance:

- What about your current home do you love?
- How could you make it better?
- What do you miss from previous homes? Childhood homes?
- Are floors important to you? Windows? Views? Natural light?
- Will you use the house full-time, or only in certain seasons?

*The sequence of events in the*
*design process from start to finish.*

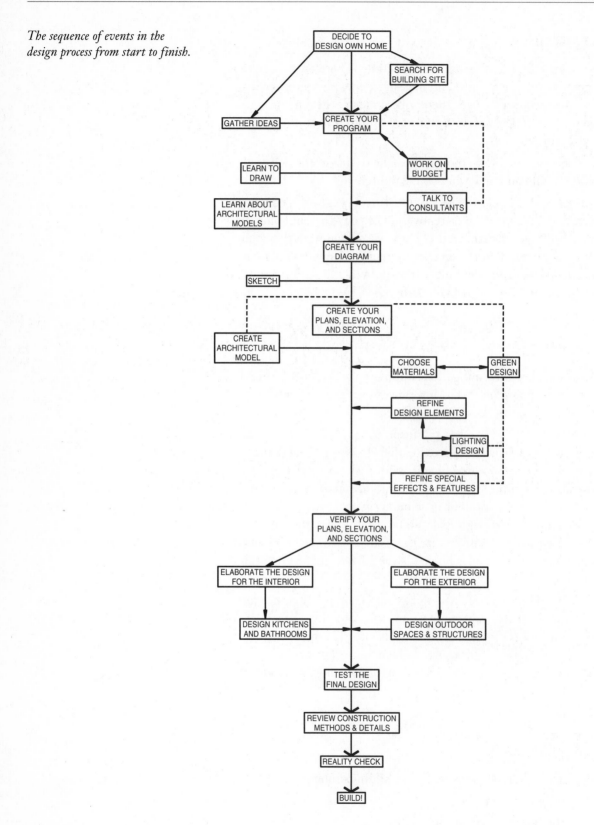

Remember, too, that ideas come from dialogue (ideally with a glass of wine and a close companion). Talk to friends and members of your family. And every artist knows that inspiration never comes on command. It is far more likely to show up in the shower, at a coffee shop, while you're pumping gas, or just before you fall asleep. Be prepared with a notebook and a pen.

## Selecting the Basics

To start, you want to figure out the basic rooms of your home—both private, such as bedrooms, and public, such as living and family rooms. How many bedrooms do you need? How should they be spaced apart? How large do they need to be? How small *can* they be?

What adjustments might you have to make to suit the climate?

Will there be a finished basement? Do you want an attic? No attic? Bedrooms under the roof? These differences can also influence the roofline of your home.

### Flashpoint

Many rooms—especially bedrooms—do not need to be as large as you may initially think. Because you're likely to spend most of your time elsewhere, you may want to reduce the size of (some of) your first bedroom designs in order to enlarge other areas of the house.

Think also in terms of "spaces," not just "rooms": you may not have a dining room but a dining area or breakfast nook—or you may choose to have a formal dining room with a different space used for everyday.

You'll probably live in this house for some time, so try, when organizing your plans, to think long-term. While it may be convenient now to have a door connecting your bedroom and the baby's, it won't be long before you and your child both find that configuration less than ideal. Be sure that if you do insist on this for now, you also provide other, independent doorways which will allow you at a certain point to seal off the adjoining one. Similarly, if an elderly parent might possibly move in with you in the future, consider a downstairs bedroom and wheelchair-access options that will make his or her life easier and more comfortable when the time comes.

### Flashpoint

Don't forget to consider the nature of your site. When Lisa Ramaci transformed two New York apartments into one, she immediately knew the bedroom belonged in the back of the building, overlooking the garden—not the front, where she would be disturbed by sounds (and gawkers) from the street.

## Starting to Sketch

Many people find it handy to try ideas out visually. Start sketching concepts and explore some of the possibilities you come up with. Don't worry about how the drawings look, whether they're to scale, whether anyone but you will even be able to decipher what they are. This is just for you.

As the rooms and form and structure of your house begin to take shape in your mind—and on the page—you'll find yourself thinking more and more about the details and the accents you want to add. Don't be afraid to get distracted— you can always come back to where you were. A fireplace in every bedroom? Why not? Bay windows? French doors? Granite counters in the kitchen? A sauna in the master bath? A closet just for shoes? Sure!

For now, this is your wish list. As you sketch or continue your list, you'll find more and more ideas coming at you.

*Sketching out the ideas you put in your program can help you visualize the way your house will look.*

![Flashpoint]

**Flashpoint**

Design is a process: don't be afraid to blurt ideas out quickly, but be critical. Don't fall in love with a design just because you drew it. Challenge yourself by questioning what your house design does well and what not. Ask yourself if there are other ways to shape a room, place a railing, flow through the space. By clearly understanding the qualities of your design, you can enhance its good features and eliminate or minimize the shortfalls to create your best possible design.

## He-Wants/She-Wants

And about that notebook by the bed—try not to fight over it too much. There are bound to be disagreements—about budget, about taste. We are not marriage counselors. But a great deal of architecture involves finding solutions that do not feel like compromises—so you can consider it a part of your architectural training, if you like, to bring this same approach to reconciling differences between you regarding your design. This is also a technique you will appreciate when you begin measuring your "dream house" against your "real wallet."

It can be useful at such moments to remember some of the areas we often overlook, such as attics and basements, which can be important and useful areas for storage, playrooms, guest rooms, home offices, or a practice indoor driving range for an avid golfer. A laundry room set up in a basement can also free up other space in the main part of the house, or make a larger kitchen possible.

Reconsider, too, the sizes of all the rooms: do all bathrooms need to be full baths, or can some only have a shower—or even just a washbasin and toilet? Savings in space and money here could be applied to more "controversial" subjects, like that shoe closet, marble in the entryway, or fountain in the backyard.

Be as creative in your thinking as you can; allow yourself to be playful and don't rule anything out at this point. You may find you can do much more with your new home than you ever imagined!

## The Least You Need to Know

- ◆ Start an ideas file—for the house as a whole and for each room.
- ◆ Stay clear of prefab designs, though they may be helpful sources of inspiration.
- ◆ Create your program—a general list of what you want and need in your new home.
- ◆ Start with the basics: how many rooms, how big, and so on. From there, continue on to the details and accents.
- ◆ Consider the future needs of your home.
- ◆ Remember that site considerations may determine some aspects of your program.
- ◆ Be willing to think creatively. Get a little crazy. Ideas breed ideas.

**Flashpoint**

Throughout the process, challenge yourself: for every idea, try to think of at least two alternatives: does it have to be a garage, or can it be a driveway or carport? Can one fireplace be kept open to serve both a family and a living room? If not, can an upstairs and downstairs fireplace share a single chimney?

# Selecting Your Site

## In This Chapter

- ◆ Setting the shape by your site
- ◆ Zoning laws and your home design
- ◆ Getting oriented

Where your house is built can be one of the primary factors governing how you build and design it. If you haven't yet selected a site, this chapter will supply you with information that can help in the selection process; if you have, we'll tell you how your site will influence your design, and how to use it to your best advantage.

## Why The Site Comes First

You may have chosen—or be looking for—a site for your home primarily with aesthetics in mind: the lakefront views, the neighboring meadows, the distance from a major roadway. Perhaps lifestyle issues played a role: school zoning, for instance, or proximity to relatives. But there is more to take into account about your site when considering what you will build there, and how. Is it urban, suburban, rural? What is the climate? What are the land conditions? All of these will factor in to determine the final design.

Among the qualities of your site that will determine aspects of your design are…

- ◆ Size.
- ◆ Zoning laws.
- ◆ Physical (aesthetic) features.
- ◆ Access to utilities.
- ◆ Climate.

## Sizes and Spaces

Various aspects of your site—from local zoning regulations to the nature of the ground itself—can have a dramatic impact on the appearance of your home. Zoning laws may, for instance, require that your home be below a certain height, while your living needs demand a certain number of square feet, creating the need to build a home with a larger *footprint* and fewer floors. A small lot space or *easement* regulations might mean, by contrast, that in order to achieve the square footage you need, you'll be building high and narrow—and hoping that you can build all those rooms within the allotted space and height restrictions.

Physical features of your site, however, might allow you to work around such regulations. If you're lucky enough to have selected property with a bit of sloped ground, for instance, you might be able to stretch the height regulation a bit by building on the lower level of the site. (No, it's not cheating.) On the other hand, you may find that, right beneath the spot where you'd planned the living room to be, the earth is solid rock. This doesn't mean that you absolutely must rethink your plans, but it certainly means that if you don't, you're going to have to rethink your budget. A lot.

**Architerms**

A building's **footprint** is the exact space it occupies on the land—literally as if it had left a "footprint" in the soil. **Easements** are defined as the right of a third party to access your land. Usually this applies to utility companies, though it can also relate to a neighbor's home or public access ways.

**Flashpoint**

A site survey of your property as early in the game as possible will head off unpleasant surprises and annoying design do-overs. A survey produced by a professional land surveyor will tell you exactly what is where, defining the utilities and easements, height relative to sea level, and other aspects of your property. Such surveys stand as legal court documents and offer the best option; however, some Google maps will show much of this information if need be. By combining the information in survey documents with your own photographs, and by walking the site yourself, you will produce the most complete index of the property, and therefore, the first and most important defining elements of your design.

# Zoning Laws and Other Considerations

Obviously, the size of your site itself will be the primary determinant of the size of your house: it is impossible to build a 5,000-square-foot home on a 6,000-square-foot lot. But zoning laws will also often dictate a number of the parameters, from buildable area and height restrictions to rear-yard setback. Consequently, if you've not yet purchased your site, consider obtaining information on building zoning requirements and restrictions before making any final decisions. Either way, you will certainly want to familiarize yourself with local laws before you even begin putting pencil to paper for your design.

Among the regulations you'll need to consider are …

**Architerms**

**Setback regulations** stipulate the minimum distance from which you may place your home from the lot line of your property.

- Front, side, and rear-yard setbacks.
- Height restrictions.

◆ Maximum allowable percentage of lot coverage.

◆ Maximum allowed floor-to-area ratios.

Zoning laws also include easement restrictions governing the amount of space that must be maintained unbuilt in order to provide access to a public road or utility. Lot-coverage regulations could make it tricky to include the 20-foot-wide staircase you've been dreaming of from the start. Some of these things are unpredictable at this point, but you should know that they might happen. In addition, the position of your septic tank will be governed by various factors, including its distance to the house, wells, various utilities, neighboring houses, and setback requirements.

These kinds of complicated multiple calculations may seem daunting, but they also help to guide your final plan. Outside engineers, contractors, and architectural consultants can also be of help here, if need be.

# Orienting Your House—Aesthetics

Where is the front of your house? Will it face directly toward the road, or will you build a winding driveway that leads from the road to the front porch? Views, of course, will be a huge part of this decision, as well as access to natural light (and remember that light in the eastern-facing rooms will be different— and appear at different times of day—than the light that reaches rooms facing the south). Also consider elevation: entrances placed on higher ground and framed by trees have majestic impact.

How you orient your home will also make a difference if you have plans to do major landscaping—or even to build a small garden: if your backyard is shady and your front yard opens to the sun, you may later find yourself regretting that your sun worshipping can only be done in public view—and your bed of roses out back is dark and sodden.

Considering the aesthetics of your site doesn't just mean enhancing its beauty, though. Likely there are also house features you will want to downplay, camouflage, obscure. A garage and its doors or a boiler room can be hidden behind a rock formation, a group of trees, a weeping willow, or a small dip in the terrain (though a way-out ramp may be no more than 5–7 percent, and the latter is considered a very steep grade).

When you start actually planning the layout of your house, keep these things in mind as you explore ways in which you can incorporate this effort into the structural form of your design. Again, sketching out a map of your site and taking lots of photographs—preferably at different times of day so you can capture the changes in light—will provide insight and guidance.

On a final note, remember that views are not the only aesthetic consideration: the sound of a nearby brook as you fall asleep at night, the fragrance of jasmine through the living room windows in late afternoon—these and other poetic moments can play a rewarding role in enhancing the pleasures of living in your new home.

*A site plan can show the placement of your property in relation to your neighbors, while a more detailed survey will define the specific features of your land.*

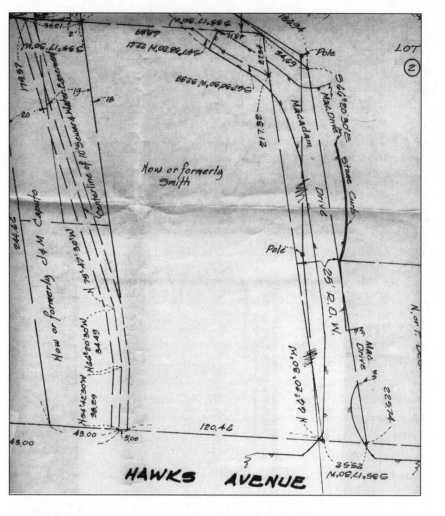

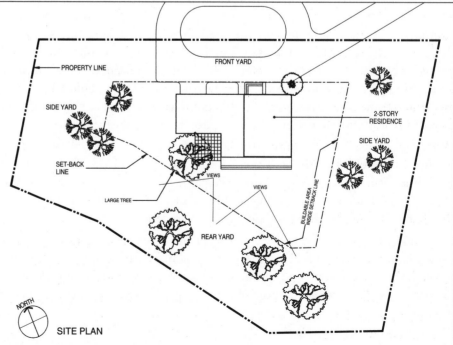

SITE PLAN

# Orienting Your House—Practical Concerns

Practical considerations affecting your design include not only zoning issues and setback and easement regulations, but the physical characteristics of the terrain. This is another reason to commission professional surveys of your land: a geological analysis, especially within the planned footprint of your house, will help you determine how much weight the land can take. If you're building on clay, for instance, you'll end up having to place piles beneath your home to support it. We also would advise against placing your house in a valley (though sometimes there is no choice) as mud, water, and debris can accumulate there.

Watch out, too, for ridges, which can shear in heavy rain. Have you ever seen the images from California showing houses sliding down a hillside?

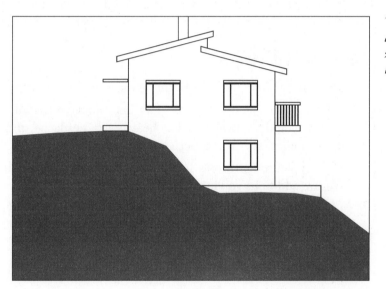

*The natural layout of your site can actually help you to work within zoning laws without changing your house design.*

## Nature

And speaking of sliding terrain: take care that your home plan accounts for nature's fluctuating moods. As Hurricane Katrina showed the world, design considerations based on local weather and careful research of the region can make all the difference between a house that lasts and a home that nature sweeps away. We, therefore, strongly recommend factoring into your plan such forces as wind dominance, snow accumulation, and flood elevations (based on historical heights).

## Energy Considerations

Where is the sun strongest? How can you orient your house to take the fullest advantage of this? Hills and slopes create air movement, as everyone flying a glider knows. In daytime, colder air comes from lower levels up the slope; at night, it's the reverse. This is part of natural ventilation. Similarly, locating the house 20 degrees off the main wind direction will create extra turbulence—and so, better natural ventilation.

## Utilities

The proximity of existing pipes, electrical and phone wires, and similar utility sources to your house can easily influence your budget—shorter connections save money.

That said, you're also not going to want to live too close to high-voltage electrical lines and poles. Bear in mind that not only electrical but also phone wires emit strong electrical fields.

And don't forget water and septic options and regulations. Where will your water come from—town source or private well? Does one area allow you to choose between the two? Septic regulations (and your own preferences) will govern distances between your septic system, if you have one, and other features of your land (trees, streams, and so on). And if you do build a well, remember that the deeper you go, the more costly—but purer—your water will be.

## The Least You Need to Know

- Your site is the most significant factor in determining your design.
- Having a site survey done and familiarizing yourself with zoning laws before you design can save you heartbreak, headache, and money later. A geological survey is especially recommended.
- When planning, think also of future landscaping possibilities and any future additions you may make to your home.
- Allow your home to afford you the best of all the natural gifts your site has to offer.

# Part **2**

# Foundations

What's the first thing that comes to mind when you think of architects? Blueprints and floor plans? They are the essential ingredients for creating a building, not just in terms of formulating your own plans, but in order to communicate those plans to contractors, building departments, banks, and so on.

Now, don't panic because you've never drawn a floor plan before, let alone built a maquette or model in your life. We understand that you may have trouble figuring out where the arms on your stick figures are supposed to go, that your best drawing of a house resembles something like a square with a triangle on top. By the time you finish this section, you won't be Frank Gehry, but you'll have a better clue about what it takes than you probably do right now—and you'll have learned to do a lot more than you think you can!

# Drawing Basics

## In This Chapter

- ◆ Tools of the trade
- ◆ Drawing freehand
- ◆ Hard-line drawings
- ◆ Gaining perspective
- ◆ Working with computers

Architectural drawing is not about landscapes and portraits; it's about sizes and scale, about how big a room is in proportion to another. An expert architect knows how to draw these in such careful proportion that if you look at his drawings and then measure them, you'll find they're very close to being accurate. Your drawings, whatever method or methods you choose, are not only points of reference supporting future steps in the design process; in effect, they comprise the very essence of what your home will be.

## Tools You Will Need

You can have architectural drawings done in several ways, and it's good to familiarize yourself with all of them. You will need, first of all, plain white, graph, and tracing paper—and lots of it. You should purchase an architect's scale—a rather odd-looking, three-sided ruler with markings on each side.

In addition to the architect's scale, you'll still need a straightedge, preferably a solid ruler, a parallel ruler, and an adjustable triangle; in addition, depending on the specific design of your home, a protractor or compass could also be handy.

Of course, you will need a good supply of pens and pencils. Though your first instinct may be to say "a pencil is a pencil," when you're actually doing the drawings, the right one can make all the difference. We recommend that you try several first, testing different levels of hardness: a nine- or ten-gauge pencil can be sharp enough to scratch glass, which isn't going to be much good. We find that ideas come more easily with a soft pencil, which moves faster and creates less resistance (though some people prefer felt-tip or roller-ball pens, instead). Try a number 2B or even 3B pencil to get a feel for what works best for you.

### Flashpoint

While an architect's scale may at first appear confusing, you will master it quite quickly. On one side of the zero mark of the scale, wide divisions run for most of the length of the scale to denote size in feet; inches and their divisions run opposite, in smaller increments.

*Tools you need include an architect's scale.*

# Learning Freehand Drawing

Freehand sketches make the transition from abstract concept to the higher plane of actual design. The sketch implies a search for shape—spaces and volumes—which is what a house is made of; and so the sketch as a search for shape is the first step toward actually building a house. It is here that your house transforms from an idea in your mind to a tangible object on the page, and gains a life and permanence for the first time.

*Freehand sketches turn your ideas into a house, situated on your site—the first real image of your home.*

*(Photo © Nick Buccalo of the Drawing Studio for Michael Davis Architects, PC.)*

### Flashpoint

Creating your sketch marks a significant change in the planes of operation. At the moment when the pencil searches for shapes on the paper, it becomes an extension of the mind that imagines those spaces. The hand merely translates, by means of these symbols (the shapes), a real-life house for discussion: here is the living room, here is the hall, here is the coat closet. The mind imagines, but the mind forgets. That's why your hand commits the ideas to paper.

When drawing, even freehand, you should keep an architect's scale with you. A drawing without scale is essentially a *bubble diagram*, whereas here, you will start to assess the sizes, the needs, of your home: do I want a living room that is 18×20 feet, or one that is 40×80?

Pick up your pencil and doodle a bit. Relax—this is like what you did in grade school. You might start with a rectangle that represents a living room proportioned to, say, an 18×30 foot rectangle, and off that is a dining room, which is about as big in proportion to the living room, and after that is the kitchen which is maybe 12×16 feet, and so on.

In the beginning, size is relative: the size of a room that is drawn on paper at the initial stage is merely a proportion, so that given a room of 20×30 feet, the room in your drawing would have the same ratio of two to three (2:3). (Remember that doing this without proportion makes no sense—it simply brings you back to the bubble diagram.)

**Architerms**

A **bubble diagram** is a schematic map of the spaces of your home and how they intersect. You will create the bubble diagram for your home design in Chapter 8.

**Flashpoint**

Architects and other designers work according to the "golden ratio" or "golden section"—a formula said to be the most pleasing to the human eye and based on the principle that "the whole is to the larger part as the larger part is to the smaller part." It is said that women are built in such proportions: the length from head to navel and navel to feet in proportion to her entire height equals the ideal ratio.

When drawing, look not just for sizes and shapes, but for *comfortable* sizes and *pleasing* shapes. You can even try measuring your current home and your body in various spaces to determine what is a comfortable size for you: some have suggested, for instance, that one reason Frank Lloyd Wright designed buildings with low ceilings was that he himself was only five feet tall.

At the same time, look for practical solutions and be open to new ideas. Perhaps you need a corridor somewhere, but you want it to be short because you don't want to spend your money on a corridor—you want to spend it on finishes, or designer wallpaper, or a chef's stove in the kitchen. And yet, as you sketch, it occurs to you to use the corridor as a gallery for family photos—and so you try this arrangement as well. The more you do this, the more you'll sense—and appreciate—the synergy of the design process.

Usually, professionals will also sketch a few people in their freehand drawings to further indicate scale, creating a sense of the actual size of the rooms, doorways, windows, and so on in relation to the people actually living there. A house with low ceilings can feel cramped and claustrophobic (which is why some people find it so awful to go to New York's Penn Station), while by contrast, you can nearly feel your spirit literally soar on entering a Gothic cathedral.

# Learning About Hard-Line Drawings

Hard-line drawings are the measured, drafted renditions of your design that bring the vague shapelessness of a sketch to what is basically a working two-dimensional model of your home. These drawings are made with the help of a straight-edge (triangle, T-square), compass, templates, or stencils—or with the aid of a computer. They are, in essence, a two-dimensional representation of your home.

The raison d'être of hard-line drawing is accuracy. Working in hard-line allows you to examine your project for alignment, actual size, and placement. It has long been favored by architects for its capacity to create as precise an image of the building as possible (although the Parthenon wasn't built using a T square, and it's lasted a pretty long time!). It is also the method you will likely use later on (unless you use a computer) as you develop your drawings for use by your contractors. Moreover, hard-line drawing, once you understand the concept, is actually faster than sketching.

You will need a drafting board, pencils, paper or Mylar film (not graph paper), an adjustable triangle, and a parallel ruler or T square (we prefer the parallel ruler). The process is not much different from freehand sketching, except, of course, that you will be measuring and aligning as you go, creating straight (not rough) lines, and definition. You can draw a simple, basic floor plan quite quickly, as well as an elevation and site plan (we will get to these in Chapter 10) so that you can actually see the house on the site—how it is situated on the land, the setbacks, and so on.

# Computer-Assisted Drawing (CAD)

Computers bring the process to a whole new level. Computer-assisted drawing, or CAD, may feel like a computer game, but it is an amazing tool that can provide accuracy within two decimal points of a millimeter—that is, four one-thousandths of an inch. Using CAD, you can edit a project without constant redrawing, and create multiple replications of an object: choose a countertop, a fireplace, a sink, and you can make a thousand copies of it in two seconds. You can compare shapes, sizes, even colors. A computer program, after all, is a repository of all the data you give it: it knows where everything is, can find it in a flash, and shows you what you want to know. (To an extent, anyway.) It can, if you supply the geographical location, or the sun's coordinates of your location, show where the sun comes from, which openings it enters—which skylights, which *clerestory windows*—and where its rays fall in the afternoon.

The other extraordinary advantage of working in CAD (besides the fact that you don't have to be able to draw to use it) becomes evident in the editing process. Although inputting the data is enormously time-consuming, once done, you can make changes in the blink of an eye (or the push of a button): mirror, rotate, mirror and rotate at the same time, locate—you name it. This can, however, lead to obsessive-compulsive types getting totally out of control.

**Architerms**

Clerestory windows are windows (usually relatively small) set high in the wall, near the ceiling, to bring additional light deep into a room.

The downside? CAD programs are, like all programs, dumb. They can't do anything without the proper dimensional input. If you miscalculate the direction of the sun, you'll get a result that does not correspond to reality. You can't fudge things the way you can with a sketch: put the wrong information in, and the wrong information will come out. It is also, for the same reason, limited: you can't necessarily see the house that's in your dreams, because the computer only offers so many options. It has specific colors available, but they may not be yours. Materials are not as well rendered as they should be: you can't expect that it will replace seeing, feeling, and touching the material in person. The result is that, for all its facility, working with a computer program may still leave you hungry for the dream.

# Creating Perspective Sketches

For us to explain to you how to draw without being there to show the process makes it all sound much more difficult and complicated than it really is. Our best suggestion, if you find yourself growing confused, is to pick up a pencil and follow along. Trying to visualize too much can be overwhelming.

*Perspective*, literally, means "point of view" and refers to how you see things (literally or figuratively). Perspective drawing, then, is about drawing objects so that they appear the way they would in real life—in 3-D. In this case, perspective refers to the drawing representing a house, as it would appear in three dimensions, or in a photograph taken with a normal lens from normal eye level.

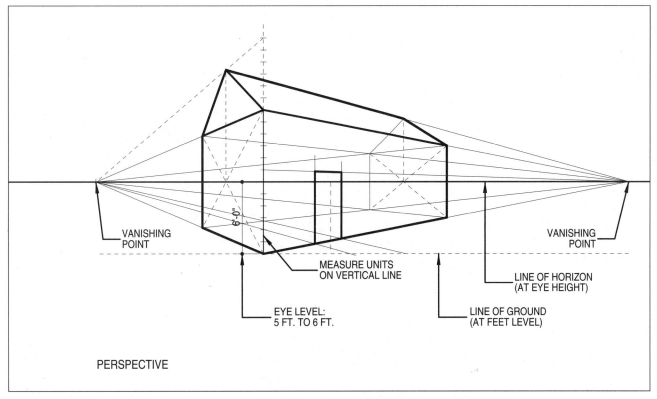

*Perspective drawing is based on the idea of parallel lines intersecting at a point located in the infinite distance.*

It's not a terribly intuitive representation; as children, we do not draw that way instinctively. The basic rules of perspective drawing didn't appear until the fifteenth century, in Florence, Italy. However, once understood, these rules are fairly simple to follow and the result is quite satisfying.

In perspective drawing, parallel lines are represented as if they intersect at a point in the infinite distance which is located on the line of the horizon. Imagine looking down a long, straight road: its sides seem to meet somewhere very far away, toward the horizon. (We can debate why the horizon equals "infinity" on another occasion.) Since a simple house shape could be approximated as being a rectangular prism, the first rule would dictate that the parallel lines (edges) of the prism appear to converge with the distance, that is, they appear to be closer to each other the farther they are from our vantage point. (An example of this is what happens when you look from the base of a very tall tower up toward its top: the sides seem closer at the top than at the base. This is the perspective effect on the z-axis.)

Conversely, on paper, we start by drawing a horizontal line representing the horizon. Then we draw a vertical line at 90 degrees to the horizon—the edge of the prism closer to us. Then we connect the top and bottom of this vertical line to one point far to its left, and another to its right. We now have the famous converging parallel lines, intersecting in pairs in two points, called *vanishing* points. All other horizontal parallel lines will meet in the same two points— and not just the edges of the prism, but other horizontal lines contained in its faces. Meanwhile, the verticals remain at 90 degrees to the horizon and do not appear to converge anywhere. In this exercise, we discuss two-point perspective; in a three-point perspective, the verticals are also tilted toward the sky or down into the earth. For our purposes, two-point is sufficient.

There are ways to measure in perspective, to a certain degree of accuracy. For instance, the closer vertical can be made 12 feet high at a scale of $\frac{1}{8}$ inch to the foot. The divisions can be carried farther back by way of horizontal line. At the base of the first vertical we can place a line parallel to the horizon, which carries the same units as the vertical. This can become quite elaborate, and, again, isn't needed for the moment.

Perspective drawing is an astonishing device in that it makes a flat drawing appear to have sculptural qualities, allowing us to "see" an image of a house that hasn't even been built.

## The Least You Need to Know

- Start bringing your home from vague idea to tangible reality by making freehand sketches.
- Always use an architect's scale when you draw, even for freehand sketching.
- Sketching your home is a part of the creative process; allow your imagination and your hand to work together.

◆ Use hard-line drawings for accuracy, working with architect's tools.

◆ Give computer-assisted drawing a try if you are unsure of your drawing skills, want to work quickly, or have a penchant for computer graphics.

◆ Always make sure the information you use for your drawings, whatever style you use, is accurate.

# Chapter 5

# Making Architectural Models

## In This Chapter

- ◆ Why do you need a model, anyway?
- ◆ Basics of model-building
- ◆ Models in paper
- ◆ Other model types

Models allow you to visualize the entire ensemble—the house on its site. Because they offer a full 3-D experience of your design, you are able to review the full volumetric composition of your house, and acquire a sense of how it fits (or doesn't fit) on your specific site. By the time you're ready to build your model, you'll be eager to see what your drawings have actually created and gain a sense of what this entire thing will actually turn into when it's done.

## Why You Need Them (And Why You Don't)

Your model is as close as you will come to a true vision of what your house, according to the plans you've created, will be. It allows you to see exactly how the porch moves along the façade of the building, ensure that alignments are proper, and fully understand the ratios and feelings of the space. Moreover, if there are any problems with your design, you will be much happier fixing them in paper than in stone. For this, your contractor will also thank you; some contractors don't always read architectural drawings very well, so your model could become invaluable in the building process.

Granted, some trained architects who have years of experience conceptualizing three-dimensional space will occasionally work without a model, but it's generally not advisable for nonprofessionals. If you skip the model, you'll certainly save yourself time and trouble now, but you may well make up for it later. However, if you are confident about how things look in space as three-dimensional objects, if you've had experience working with two-dimensional–to–three-dimensional space, then it may not be entirely necessary.

# Tools for Model-Building

You will need the following for this process:

- Fine-blade knife
- X-Acto knives and blades
- Larger knife or cutter
- Set square and triangle, metal, minimum eight inches
- Straightedge ruler, metal, minimum 12 inches
- Dedicated cutting mat, plastic, minimum 12×18 inches (you can find these in most art-supply stores)
- Attaching pins, metal, minimum 0.75 (¾) inches
- Glue, for paper
- Paper, cardboard, or foam-core board (⅛ to ¼ inches thick)
- Masking tape

> **Flashpoint**
>
> While making your models, make sure you have a complete first-aid kit nearby. You will be using extremely sharp knives and cutters and accidents *do* happen. In all events, keep these items far from the reach of children.

Other possible materials: polystyrene, wood, plaster, metal. However, for our purposes, we will assume that you are working with paper, cardboard, foam-core, or another easy-to-handle material.

## Building the Model

Start by deciding the material you will use—cardboard, paper, etc.—and the scale, maybe ⅛ inch to the foot. When you're actually ready to build your model, you will already have created plans and elevations of your house, which you can copy to make your task easier. Cut the copies on the lines, glue onto model boards, and cut the boards to shape. Assemble using glue, pins, or other materials.

Though it is possible to build a house model without also building a model of the site, architects rarely do this. Site models are excellent tools for helping you to visualize and understand the actual configuration of your site, its ridges, valleys, mounds, boulders, and crevices, and how they relate to your house *in situ*.

> **Architerms**
>
> **Floor plans,** previously called blueprints, are scaled drawings, like a map, of your home. Elevations are almost the vertical equivalent: they show the vertical interior and exterior walls, without suggesting three-dimensionality, as if you had drawn a line around the house after it had been built.

The site model is usually built like a layer cake—each contour line stacked over the previous, usually every vertical foot.

To build, make copies of your survey map (more on this in Chapter 7), glue to ¹⁄₁₆-inch thick chipboard (the thickness is in keeping with the rest of your proportions), cut along the contours and assemble in a stack, like a terrain map. Allow a few possible spots for placing the house on the site model.

*Customarily, architects build the house model to fit right on a model of the site.*

*(Photo © Michael Davis Architects, PC)*

## Small-Scale Models

You'll now build a model of the house, to be inserted or placed on the site model. It will look like a small box (hopefully a bit more complex!), with the roof as a lid. It helps if you can remove the lid to expose some of the interior of the house for viewing.

The scale for this exercise should be 1:96 or ⅛ inch = one foot, meaning an eighth of an inch on paper would be one foot in reality. Even at this small scale, though, the play of volumes will be quite visible.

## Large-Scale Models

Your large-scale models provide a three-dimensional study of an element of the house, such as a room, a room with a special ceiling (or that ceiling itself), a dormer, a fireplace, a room with its fireplace and built-in bookcase—you get the idea. For these models, work at a scale of 1:24 (½ inch to the foot) or 1:16 (¾ inch to the foot). Here, the geometry will be unforgiving: every shape intersects another, and the intersections must be resolved.

# 3-D Computer-Assisted Drawing (Modeling)

A model can be built in a CAD program that incorporates 3-D features (some do, some don't). Hollywood uses these programs all the time, though their tools are more sophisticated than what you'll probably use. However, there are some extraordinary programs written with the general public in mind that, though far from Hollywood requirements, are quite adequate.

The idea behind accessible 3-D CAD is that the software has built-in shortcuts that allow you to choose a project type from a menu with options such as two-story home, large living room, a deck, a gazebo.

By clicking on menus and interactive dialog boxes, you can input the desired information into the program, which then builds a mathematical interpretation

**Flashpoint**

Don't get caught on the roof! Roofs can be especially challenging, as they require familiarity with spatial geometry (unless it is a flat roof, where your challenge will be to keep it from leaking).

of walls, floors, ceilings, roofs, columns, light fixtures, trees, persons, etc. For instance, the software asks you the height of the walls—type 8'6", or 8.5 ft, or 102", depending on the software's instructions. It will ask you to choose from a list of available doors and windows (36-inch door for entry, 28-inch door for bathroom, 96-inch-wide window at living room, and so on), probably from a list of models from real-world manufacturers. It will prompt you for the location of those—at this point you could try to give exact coordinates, or click a point nearby.

*A rendered CAD model shows lighting or solar effects.*

*(Photo © Michael Davis Architects, PC)*

The program will give you a choice of ceiling configurations and placement of light fixtures. It will also give you a choice of roofs—with dormers, even—that match the contour of the house.

On top of all these elements, you will choose materials and colors, all available at the menu level—it's really just a click away! The choices may not all be exactly what you want, but they'll be close enough to the concept of, say, wood shingles for outside walls, asphalt shingles for the roof, green granite for the kitchen counter, mahogany for the living-room bookcases.

It is important to remember that these programs, such as FloorPlan 3D (www. broderbund.com) or Punch! Super Home Suite (www.punchsoftware.com), have built their popular accessibility on two core assumptions: you do not need the extensive features similar to Hollywood productions, car manufacturers, or professional architects; and you will use as much as possible from the available choices. From these you derive the excellent price for the software and ease of usage for the novice. The drawback is the limited choices—it's too easy to choose a preprogrammed arched window than to invent one, or choose something ready-made and forget your own unique vision.

## The Least You Need to Know

◆ After mastering the drawing of your home, create a 3-D miniature version of your house: a model.

◆ Use floor plans and elevation drawings to simplify (and clarify) the model-building process.

◆ Take extreme care when handling knives and other tools for this process!

◆ If you are computer savvy, give some of the CAD programs a whirl instead of or in addition to building a physical model.

# Part 3

## Your Money

You know we had to get to the reality part eventually. In this part, you'll start coming a bit out of the clouds and take a look at your budget and the very real costs of home building, from calculating costs per square foot to estimating the expense of building a septic tank. And because there are aspects of home design that go beyond the basics of architecture, we will familiarize you with various affiliated services for which you might consider hiring a consultant, be it a site surveyor or structural engineer, or something a tad more indulgent, like a light designer, computer expert, or someone to design your landscaping and gardens.

Do you need all these things? Some, yes; others, no. Again, because this is your house and your budget, you will have to make those decisions on your own. But we will be there to steer you toward making the very best decision for *you*.

# Chapter 6

# Watching Your Budget

## In This Chapter

- ◆ Do you need a budget?
- ◆ Figuring out your costs
- ◆ Saving energy to save the planet—and your money

Everything costs. Checking soil conditions, digging a hole in the ground, laying the foundation—it all costs money. Roof shingles and windowsills, bookcases and hardwood floors, fireplaces and kitchen sinks, they all come out of your budget.

To a certain extent, you are in control: if the fireplace you can't possibly live without costs three times what you'd planned to spend, you and you alone (and your family) can decide what changes you're prepared to make in your initial program to have it. The way to do that, of course, is to develop a reasonable estimate of what you can expect to spend on all the rest.

## Creating A Budget

The first thing you need to know about budgets and home design is: the design comes first. While you will obviously need a certain amount of cash available to build any house, the money you can spend is simply all there is. What you do with it, how you apportion it, is entirely up to you. This means that if the 250-square-foot marble bath is non-negotiable, but doesn't leave much to spend on a roof, you'll need to think about building a roof of straw. If you've planned a bigger house than you can afford, you'll either have to rethink the total space or change some of the materials you plan to use.

And most likely, you will. In fact, this is a process you can expect to perform repeatedly as you create your design. There is no way to know in advance what a house will cost before you send it to bid, and there are no real hard-and-fast rules, except to design a structure that is safe to inhabit. If your design skimps on safety, you won't get a building permit anyway. But ultimately, it's all your decision, your choice. And isn't that the whole point of designing a custom home?

**Flashpoint**

Could you perhaps combine two functions in a single room? The home-office/den/guest-room combo has become increasingly common of late. One man we know keeps his library in the wine cellar—a true haven of spiritual pleasures. We also encourage you to think in terms of spaces, not just rooms. Is a breakfast room really necessary, or will a breakfast alcove do?

That said, a few pointers.

♦ Local contracting costs will vary. Check the construction costs per square foot in the region where you plan to live.

♦ Expect your builder to include in his price:

Site Prep (which may mean creating road to get construction equipment to the building, removing rocks and trees, and removal of any radioactive or toxic materials)

Digging the foundation

Building foundation walls

Construction of roof and framing

Interior carpentry

Exterior finishes

Interior finishes

Roof finishes

Doors and window

Pipes, utilities, wires

Bringing utilities to the house

Kitchen and bath finishes

Heat, air conditioning, and ventilation systems

♦ We advise you to have a soil test performed by a structural engineer who will check the integrity of the site. Include this in your projected costs.

Remember that where the house is located will also largely affect cost. It's easier to change the granite counters in the kitchen than it is to re-orient the house; make sure you know where you want it!

# A Word on Building Green

Environmentally conscious approaches to the design and construction of your home are becoming increasingly popular but can affect your budget considerably. That said, more and more local governments are requiring builders to incorporate ecologically sound methods and materials into their projects. As a result, demand for such materials will inevitably increase, causing prices to drop. If you are looking to incorporate sustainable living concepts into your home, we've included a whole chapter on the subject in Part 4.

# Figuring Out Costs per Square Foot

Don't make yourself crazy with this. Put down the calculator, put down your pen, and pick up the telephone. Realtors in the area where you plan to build are a fount of information, and this is one of the things you can rely on them to tell you. Another option is to check real-estate ads, some of which will include prices per square foot (for others you'll need that calculator back). Either way, you should get a solid impression of what you can expect to spend.

Remember, though, that an "impression" is by no means a guarantee: the house built of stucco and vinyl will cost less than the same house built of fieldstone and marble tile. There's just no getting around that. Ditto for simple versus elaborate wiring systems, measures that encourage energy efficiency, and any work you'll have performed on the site itself: leveling terrain, removing existing foundations, and so on. These last are necessary costs unique to your own situation, so you'll want to be conscious of this while looking at local averages.

## Materials

And so it should come as no surprise that another crucial means of determining a more specific estimate of your costs—or deciding how you want to apportion them—is to study the materials you plan to use in your home and explore options for each. We will discuss individual materials and their properties, their pros and cons and similarities, in Chapter 12; that information will also help you make decisions and refine your financial plans. (You will also find cost-range estimates for many of these materials by checking the resources mentioned in Appendix B.)

Be aware, however, that the materials you select for the exterior and structure of your house are likely to influence the costs of living in it. (Energy use, maintenance, and even insurance rates can vary significantly depending on your choice of building materials.)

As you become more familiar with various options, though, you will be inspired to find new ways of using materials you might not have previously considered. One architect, for instance, chose to use stainless-steel siding on the exterior of his house, with slate floors and wooden beams within. Or you might extend a stone foundation above the foundation line, create another low stone wall nearby, and fill the area with plants to create a luxurious garden terrace.

Also keep an eye on spending when designing kitchens and baths, which will consume a huge portion of your budget a lot faster than you think. Keep an eye out and plan accordingly.

But because money isn't everything, make certain that you select *quality* materials that suit your taste and fit into the vision you have of your future home. This is one of those places where it doesn't pay—literally and figuratively—to

**Flashpoint**

Surprise! Foundations and roofs on a ranch house can actually cost you *more* than those on a two- or three-story home of the same total size, as they will necessarily be larger. (5,000 square feet situated horizontally requires a larger roof and foundation than does 5,000 square feet divided among two or more levels.)

**Design Tip**

The trick is really to concentrate durable materials in certain areas, and accept simpler ones elsewhere. This gives delight while still maintaining affordability.

compromise: you can always build the playroom, guest room, pool house, or second wine cellar later. You cannot easily rebuild a vinyl-sided house with granite.

> ### Flashpoint
> This is one phase of the process where you can expect to do a lot of the back-and-forth we mentioned earlier. As you find a size and shape for each room and then the material with which to build it, you will have to come back to your budget plans to be certain that it all works. If not you'll need to change the choice of material, change the size of the room, increase your budget, or reapportion the amount you plan to spend on this section of the house. Then you go back and do it all again.

# Using Low-Maintenance Materials

Using materials that require minimal maintenance can also help you save dollars (and headaches) over the long term. Where appropriate, consider utilizing some of the following:

- Concrete (if carefully poured. Otherwise, less reliable. Note: Painted concrete is vulnerable to chipping.)
- Stainless steel
- Stone
- Brick
- Ceramic
- Adobe
- Teak
- Cedar

Other possibilities to consider if you're feeling crunched: ask yourself if you really need all the embellishments you included in your original program. Coco Chanel is renowned for her statement: "Get completely dressed. Then take one thing off." Or in the words of the great 20th-century architect, Mies van der Rohe, "Less is more."

Finally, do not, do not, do not order materials on the basis of an image on the Internet or in a catalog, or even on the recommendation of a designer or friend. One couple we know recently added a wing to their vacation home, including a new brick fireplace. When they arrived at the site, they discovered that their designer had chosen—and installed—bricks in a color they never imagined bricks were even made in. Promptly, the couple drove to a brickyard, surveyed options, loaded their car with bricks of every imaginable hue and drove back, the car's belly barely skimming the surface of the highway. They tested each and every brick, holding each one to the fireplace as you would a paint chip to a wall, until making a final selection. Had they spent more time and paid more attention in the beginning, they'd have saved themselves money, time, and headache later on. (Yes, we used economically tinged verbs here. We know.)

# HVAC and Other Energy Considerations

If there is one time to hire a consultant in this home-design project, it is when you're designing and developing the energy systems that will virtually rule your every waking—and sleeping—moment. How will the house be heated? Cooled? Is the house intended for year-round or seasonal use? What kinds of ventilation systems will you have, and where?

How much electricity do you use? Are you a multiple-TV, high-tech-stereo-system, remote-control, six-computer, wireless-everything kind of family with a double refrigerator/freezer and a bottomless pile of laundry to wash and dry each day? Or are you more the eat-out, order-in, computers-make-me-nervous type who isn't home all that often anyway?

Much of the design of these systems will also be affected by the kind of fuel used (water, air, gas), the number of ducts, the distance between the house and wiring sources, and so on. Some of these determinants you will know already from your site survey. Others, a local electrical or HVAC engineer can help you with. Generally speaking, you can expect central air conditioning and heating to run in the area of $50,000, depending on the number of zones you create; making each room a separate zone will easily run you hundreds of thousands of dollars.

**Architerms**

HVAC is a standard term referring to heat, ventilation, and air-conditioning systems.

# Energy Efficiency

One way of saving on long-term energy costs is to use energy-efficient materials, techniques, and products wherever possible. There are, in fact, two ways of considering "low energy"—the first involving materials that require little energy to produce or transport, and the second involving materials that, by nature of their construction, allow you to reduce your energy costs.

Of the latter, much of the way a house can be made energy efficient has to do with technical design. However, the following materials do make a difference:

♦ Concrete transmits energy well unless extremely thick.

♦ Thick logs combined with adobe provide excellent insulation in any environment.

♦ Autoclaved concrete—a Swedish invention less well-known in the states—is very lightweight and yet can hold two stories and is highly effective.

♦ Concrete with high ash content is usually used on ground floors.

♦ Polystyrene insulation is more efficient than mineral wool or fiberglass wool.

Some items cost more in the beginning but can save you over the life of your home. Double-glazed windows, for instance, are more expensive than regular ones, but—especially in cold climates—will provide substantial reductions on your heating (or, depending on your geographic location, air-conditioning) bills.

Similarly, running insulation continually between wall studs will increase the thickness of the walls—but it also increases energy efficiency by 40 percent or more.

**Flashpoint**

As you work on your budget and make necessary adjustments, go back to your early-ideas files and notebooks to see whether anything jogs your creativity. What alternative room arrangements, materials, or details would help resolve any budget crushes and conflicts you may be facing?

Walls can also be made using staggered studs and gypsum wallboard to create sound insulation. This, too, will result in thicker walls (and so, greater square footage) but increases privacy between various zones of the house.

# Utilities

Here, too, proximity to pipes and power grids will have a decided influence on your costs. If you need to build a roadway, drill through rock, or otherwise alter your site to obtain access to main power lines, you can expect this to take a considerable chunk out of your piggy bank—another reason why site selection should preferably precede actual home design. Building such a roadway (and applying for permits, variances, and the like) could add to your basic costs, for instance.

# Property Improvements

Like taxes, septic tanks and wells are there because you cannot get around them. In fact, connecting to city sewers and water sources is much easier; while you do pay for access, maintaining them is no longer your problem.

**Design Tip**

Generally speaking, the depth of your well and septic systems and the conditions of the soil on your site will determine your construction costs.

Should you, however, find yourself with a private system for your home, take care to check regulations regarding maintenance and distances between well and septic tank, and take care with various detergents and other agents that can interfere with the proper functioning of your pipes. When planning your well, check regulations of sizes, and depth necessary to ensure clean water (which will be tested for purity).

How much will this cost? How far will you have to dig? That will be the major determinant, though soil formations and natural gradations of your site also play a role. Clay soil will require fortification of well walls, for instance, and you will want especially to avoid having to blast rock if possible.

### The Least You Need to Know

- Put time into careful planning of your home. It will save you money in the long run.
- Determine rough costs per square foot by checking local real estate ads and talking to local brokers or contractors.
- Remember that both materials and site conditions will influence your final costs.
- Rethink your design as necessary to adjust overall expenses.
- Invest wisely now to save (in energy and other expenses) over the long term.

# Working with the Pros

## In This Chapter

- ◆ Working with architects and draftsmen
- ◆ Consulting with engineers
- ◆ Getting help from building and site consultants
- ◆ Consultants for the "extras"
- ◆ Partnerships: do you need them? The pros and cons

Consulting with professionals can be not only helpful but potentially lifesaving—though some are certainly more vital than others; your structural engineer will do more to secure the inherent safety of your home, for instance, than your lighting or computer consultant.

You'll also find that in many cases, hiring a consultant will *save* you money in the long run: consultants are experts in their field, trained by schooling and experience to determine methods of getting the most out of your home as well as to spot potential problems before they start and you have to rip half the house down to correct them. In many cases, they'll also know of lower cost, more effective, or better quality options (in method or materials, say) than the ones you might currently have planned, further improving the quality of your life in your new home.

## Finding and Hiring Consultants

As with most things, the best way to find a good professional is through the recommendations of people you know and trust. Barring that, if you'll be moving to a rural or even suburban community, try local home-supply shops, even home-decorating stores, for names.

And again, hire carefully. Check backgrounds. If possible and where relevant, try to see some of their previous work—live and in person. Call references. Ask about their approach to their work, their ability to troubleshoot when faced with the unusual circumstances that inevitably come with a custom home—and their ability to do so without breaking the bank. You've got a lot of money and a lot of future riding on these decisions. Yours is not a standard, cookie-cutter home, and you don't want cookie cutters building it.

# Working with Architects

The purpose of an *architect*, ultimately, is to design a space in which you'll feel at peace with the world. It makes perfect sense, therefore, that the best architect for *your* home is *you*. But that doesn't mean you necessarily have to go it alone: there can be significant advantages to hiring an architect to create a house based on your basic ideas, or to working in partnership with an architect who can help guide you along the way.

### Architerms

An **architect** does more than just design a home. He (or she) oversees the construction process, integrating and coordinating everything from the first site survey through the laying of electrical systems to assuring that the kitchen floor doesn't land in the master bedroom. Even if you plan to do all the design aspects of your home yourself, an architect can still provide services you may need.

### Design Tip

Since for most people, time spent planning and building a new home is time spent also paying the costs of the old one, having an architect on board to speed up the process is a prime example of the time-is-money equation in action.

Experienced, licensed architects, for instance, are able to ...

◆ Arrange special analyses of your home or site and integrate the results into a design change—quickly.

◆ Coordinate the expertise of others.

◆ Coordinate the schedules and activities of workers on the site.

◆ Work within various regulations.

◆ Handle bidding processes.

◆ Make quick decisions regarding (and resolving) complications during construction.

◆ Incorporate various hard-learned, cost-saving tricks of the trade into your design you might not have considered. (We give you a few in Chapter 9.)

They also inevitably speed up the process, simply because anyone who has experience is faster and more efficient than someone who doesn't. If time is a factor for you, you may want to consider involving an architect at least as an advisor to the project.

Without an architect on board, you'll have nobody but yourself to blame when things go wrong. It's also good to have someone who can interpret and coordinate the advice of others, read architectural drawings, and understand the design and building process.

Essentially, your success in going solo depends largely on your ability to coordinate and integrate people, tasks, and the various elements involved in designing and building a home (and it is important to recognize that architects are almost always involved in the actual building phase).

# Draftsmen

A draftsman knows the various details of architectural drawing. You can hand him your sketch and miraculously he will return in days with a heap of hard-line drawings for the contractor to use. If you're unsure about your own ability to create these drawings yourself, it could be worthwhile to hire a draftsman to do some or all of them for you, or to review your work and make appropriate revisions and corrections. Your drawings are essentially the instruction manual for your home: you want to be sure they are as clear and as accurate as possible.

# Engineers

You will also need to consult with engineers of various sorts. Simply defined, an engineer is someone who is schooled or practiced in a subject—an expert of sorts—which is exactly what you want when thinking about the structural integrity of your home, and the best possible investment of your budget. Because yours is a custom home, your needs will be specific and unique. Engineers will work with you to ensure that you make the best decisions based on what suits *your* needs and desires.

## Structural Engineers

To put it simply, your structural engineer makes sure that things stand up and don't fall down. His role is to confirm that all aspects of the structure are safe—or to alert you to anything that might be dangerous. He will know and advise you about anything you might need to change in the plans to avoid any disasters during (or after) construction.

We recommended that you hire a structural engineer early in the process—even, if possible, before actually purchasing your site. His expertise will help determine, for instance, any premiums you might have to pay for changing the actual land to build a sound foundation, whether you'll need to blast rock or can build around it, whether you can use block concrete or poured.

During the design process, your structural consultant will also be able to …

- ◆ Advise you on any elements of the house that won't align themselves properly—and help you find a workable solution.
- ◆ Guide you on any design tricks (such as cantilevering) that will help increase views from your home.
- ◆ Inform you about various materials, their safety, and their performance in local weather.
- ◆ Analyze the conditions of your site before you buy it (assuming you hire him in time!).

Again, we advise you to explain your project with any structural engineers before you hire them to be certain they are willing to work on a non-cookie-cutter home. While most of us are inclined to try to focus our spending

**Flashpoint**

Be sure, when hiring a draftsman, that he does what he should do. Simply copying your sketch is useless. He should put it into hard-line form, with dimensions indicated, and check that spaces flow appropriately.

**Design Tip**

Your structural engineers are trained to think first of safety; they tend, therefore, to be particularly cautious, but often will allow more than they initially indicate. Ask repeatedly for what you want, and suggest alternatives; they tend to have their standard ways of working and are unlikely to think outside the box without being prodded.

on what *shows* in our homes (the finishes, the details, the materials), the soundness of the structure is, in the end, what is really worth investing in.

# Mechanical Engineers, Electrical Engineers, Plumbing Engineers (MEP)

Mechanical, electrical, and plumbing engineers are usually packaged together either in a single firm or with strong connections between their respective enterprises. Generally, they are referred to as systems engineers.

## Mechanical Engineers

Your mechanical engineer is concerned with issues regarding air movement. He calculates the size of air-conditioning systems, for instance, based on the size and orientation of the house (a particularly important aspect of building "green"), or with an eye to protecting the environment. In fact, a mechanical engineer can also help advise on other "green building" issues like solar energy. He calculates various loads of air conditioning needed if a centralized AC system is used. On the other hand, if you buy a window-model AC at your local Home Depot, you've just dismissed your mechanical engineer. Just be sure to have fans in your kitchen and baths for appropriate ventilation and circulation of air.

## Electrical Engineer

An electrical engineer examines your electrical loads from a mathematical and scientific perspective, advising on minimum requirements for electrical loads and what they should be based on. He looks at your unique living situation: how many people live in the house, how they spend their time there. Consulting with an electrical engineer at the early phases of the process is strongly recommended because adding electrical wiring to the house *after* construction can be very costly, even requiring excavating through the walls. In general, a good rule of thumb is to allow for twice as much energy use and activity as you think you'll need.

## Plumbing Engineer

Based on the number of people using the house and the number of baths you plan to include in it, your plumbing engineer calculates the plumbing load of the house, which can influence the drainage of the site, and the size and placement of the septic system. He also ensures that all design elements are up to local code (remember, there will be an inspection!).

# Building and Site Consultants

After the engineers, the other experts get their say. These include the people who can advise you on such things as the legal and physical parameters of your site—what you can build there, and what you can't.

## Zoning and Code

Zoning and code inspectors and consultants get regular updates on all local changes in regulations. They can be invaluable in terms of telling you whether your house complies with various ordinances—*before* you build it. Obviously, the cost of redoing any aspect of your construction to accommodate laws you didn't know about will be substantial; it is probably more than worth the expense of hiring experts. However, you should verify with an architect any suggestions the zoning experts give you in terms of revisions to your building plans. These people know legal issues; they may not know everything you'd like them to know about energy use, structural stability, and aesthetics.

If you choose not to hire a zoning consultant, though, we do recommend that you contact the local building department to review your drawings and plans and advise you accordingly.

## Surveyor

When your surveyor shows up, he will develop drawings of the physical characteristics of your land, indicating land heights, locations of water bodies, major trees, easements, and utilities and wires—information he calculates by measuring the geographic coordinates and actual lengths between them. The document can become a part of the deed to your land, defining your property's legal boundaries (and therefore what you may and may not build where). In essence, your survey report tells you where the fence goes: it makes good neighbors. In addition, a survey report constitutes a legal document that you will provide to your bank; make copies and keep the original in a safe place.

## Buildings-Department Expeditor

No surprises here: a buildings-department expeditor expedites the process of obtaining your building permit. He files the necessary documents, keeps track of the process, and handles (and keeps you informed of) any possible objections from the buildings department.

# Consultants for the Extras

Depending on your own skills and expertise and on the elaborateness of your plans, you may also want to seek professional advice on the little things, the special touches you plan—or hope—to include in your new home.

## Lighting Consultant

Lighting creates sculptural space: we live in a world defined by light and shadow—with no light, there is no space. Much of our sense of balance and well-being comes from our responses to shapes and shadows, light and dark.

Lighting consultants calculate mathematically the amount of light available in your house (both solar and artificial) and recommend what light levels are best for the function of spaces and for the requirements of the owner. Someone who spends a great deal of time reading is going to want appropriately bright and focused lights (or lamps) in certain rooms, while those same lights would be too stark for a dining area.

## Acoustic Engineer

If you prefer privacy in some areas of your house, play an instrument, or have a teenager, an acoustic engineer could save you thousands on Excedrin. In fact, you might be surprised by how sound can be altered and magnified by the shape or size of a room, or the materials with which it's built. Drop a penny on the marble floors of the library, and you will hear it all the way to the kitchen. Interior acoustic engineers can explain to you what sound does in a room, recommend sound insulation materials and techniques, help avoid disconcerting and disorienting echoes—in short, control the behavior of sound in your house.

## Audio-Video Consultants

Audio-video people are the experts on sound wiring and integrating sound systems throughout your house. In addition, some companies are now creating integrated remote controls that can raise and lower your shades, turn lights on and off, and so on (though of course, they don't control the kids!). If you're going to have this stuff at all, you may as well go all the way. Even so, it's pretty much a personal thing: don't expect it to increase the actual value of the house.

## Computer and Data Systems

Even if you don't plan on having complex computer (or computerized) network systems installed, you may want to have a computer/voice-data expert review (or install) any wiring systems you put in place, including phone wires. (An electrician can also do the phones, though not the computer stuff. However, in a typical example of how all things fit together in building a house, it's the electrician who installs the conduits the computer guy runs his wires through.) Again, you should weigh any cost benefits in doing these kinds of jobs yourself against the time expenditure and any safety concerns. Wiring is not a part of this project where you'll want to take any risks.

## Security Advisors

If you are considering installing a security system in your home, a security advisor helps design or recommend one appropriate for you and coordinate with the electricians so that systems perform properly together.

## Landscape Architects

Landscape architects do not just trim hedges in the shapes of poodles and plant rose gardens. To a certain extent, yes, employing a landscape architect involves a certain amount of luxury, a higher level of design. However, experts in landscape management also can advise you on drainage for your site and how to locate your house so it functions best with the earth floor that surrounds it. They can also help you use your existing land to its advantage, rather than having to excavate and move earth from one end of your property to the other—an expensive, not to mention physically exhausting, enterprise you may well want to forgo.

# Partnerships: How Do You Approach Designing *Your* Own Home?

Obviously, only you can decide what your individual needs are and what your budget will allow. In some (rare) cases, it's possible to do (almost) everything yourself. In most instances, however, you'll want to work with others in various measures. Do not assume that working with professionals is an all-or-nothing proposition. There are countless options, and again, only you can know what's right for *you*.

## Working with an Architect

Architects' fees vary greatly, but are usually based on a percentage of the overall budget. Obviously, this can set you back several thousands of dollars—money you could have spent on your home itself. At first glance, that would suggest that you're better off doing it yourself, at least from an economic standpoint.

But not always. Architects can do all of the work for you (in which case, you wouldn't need this book!)—or just some of it. In the process, they may be able to alert you to potential problems with your site or your plan before it's too late, or recommend cost-cutting measures only experts would know, such as how you can exchange one very expensive material for another, more affordable option, for instance, without losing your desired effect. And because they work fast (since you probably have another job to keep you busy all day), this could save you from carrying the costs of your old home for the extended period that you're working on your second one.

Other tasks an architect can perform, either as a partial consultant or if taking over the project completely, include …

 ♦ Overseeing the plans.

 ♦ Drafting more complicated elaborations of the plans.

 ♦ Supervising the construction.

 ♦ Coordinating various consultants and contractors.

 ♦ Advising on site conditions and other elements external to the actual house itself.

> **Design Tip**
> An advanced architecture student may be qualified to handle some of the tasks, such as drafting plans or reviewing your drawings, at substantially lower rates.

Consequently, it may be worthwhile to speak with an architect (make sure he is licensed by the American Institute of Architecture) about ways that he might assist you, not in designing your home itself (we already know you're handling that job), but in advising you and facilitating the process. See what kinds of fee arrangements you can work out based on the specific work that you hire him to do.

## Going Solo with Selective Consultants

Everyone is an expert at something, but no one is an expert at everything, so gathering a group of experts together to advise and supervise your work (as we've suggested doing with an architect) can be an effective way to ensure the best quality for your project for your dollar.

It is not, for instance, vital to the safety of your home that you enlist the aid of lighting or A/V consultants; but your MEP team and site surveyor can make a significant difference in the structural integrity and some of the most basic quality-of-life aspects you'll encounter there. After all, it's not a bargain to build a home you end up not wanting to live in, and correcting a problem is always more expensive (and annoying!) than getting it right the first time.

**Design Tip**

Always discuss fee arrangements with potential candidates. Ask what you can do to reduce the costs: can you take on part of the job for them? Do they have junior assistants who are capable of handling the task at a lower rate?

# Your Solo Show

If you've stretched your budget as far as you can to design (and build) your new home, it can be tempting to try to do as much yourself as humanly possible. A word of advice: don't. While this may seem like the most cost-effective option, it will likely cost you far more in the long run, both in time and money, than you anticipate or possibly can even afford. Besides the more obvious costs like finding out your entire plumbing system doesn't work or springs a geyser in the middle of the lawn, the tricks of the trade your experts have picked up along the way will in many cases pay for themselves—and then some.

## The Least You Need to Know

- ◆ Hiring engineers and other consultants can greatly facilitate the designing (and building) process.
- ◆ Consolidate fees where possible: some consultants' areas of expertise may overlap with one another's, allowing you to reduce the fees you'll have to pay for these services.
- ◆ If you can do it, consult with surveyors, architects, and zoning engineers *before* purchasing your site to avoid any unpleasant surprises later.

# Part 4

## Getting to Work

Remember all that talk about dream homes and floor plans? This is where paper and pencils come out and creative thinking becomes the act of creating. You will learn about bubble diagrams that help you plan the overall layout of your home, gradually increasing the detail to develop general floor plans, elevations, sections, and finally, 3-D models—the actual drawings that will serve as the how-to manual for your builder. Along the way, we'll also alert you to some helpful tips and whisper a few professional secrets in your ear.

Then we'll go on and introduce you to the materials you will use in your house. Understanding the materials goes hand-in-hand with creating your drawings and models, as you juggle between keeping the extra room or covering the living room and entryway floors in marble. These considerations are especially important if you are looking to build an environmentally sound home—one that protects the world around you while it shelters you and your family within.

# Chapter 8

# Using Bubble Diagrams

### In This Chapter

- ◆ Understanding bubble diagrams
- ◆ Deciding what goes where
- ◆ Finding the right fit
- ◆ Thinking creatively as you work

Here is where the real drawing and designing begins, the part you've been waiting for all along. You've made your lists, you've built your files, you know—sort of—what you want your house to look like. Now you will take your plans from words and lists to diagrams and images.

## What Is a Bubble Diagram, Anyway?

A bubble diagram, very simply, is a bunch of circles with arrows connecting them, each circle representing a room in your future home. It is meant primarily to explore the circulation of traffic throughout the house: what room leads to what, and how.

If you think of your bubble diagram as a preliminary sketch, you can start to see the progression: you've determined your site, completed a site survey and research into zoning regulations, created your program, and gained a sense of your budget. The bubble diagram is now your intermediary step between these abstract, conceptual parts of the process and the creation of an actual architectural design in the form of floor plans and elevations. For many architects, it's where visualization of the final project begins.

The first thing you need to know about bubble diagrams is that they have nothing to do with bubbles. They're called this because they are customarily drawn with circles: but the truth is, if you happen to prefer squares or triangles or trapezoids, you can use them and it won't make any difference. (Our description, however, will take the traditional route and go with circles.)

*A bubble diagram is a way to see how spaces and their respective functions are linked.*

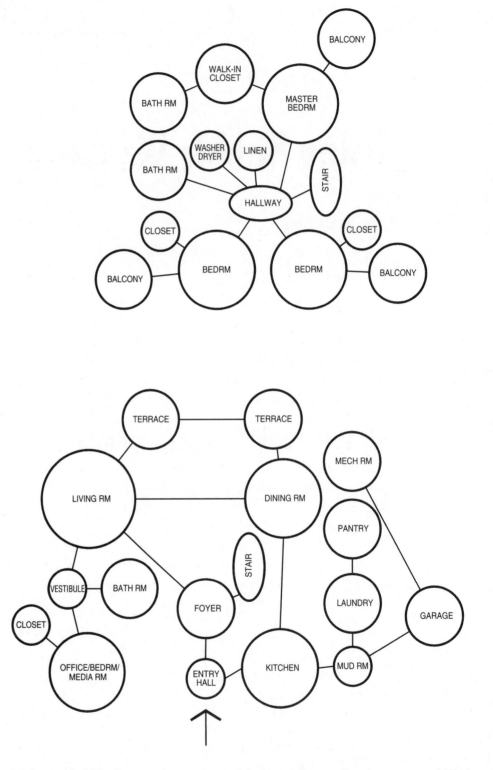

Making a bubble diagram is pretty straightforward, even for the most unskilled artist: for every room, draw a circle and label it with the name (or purpose) of that room. Place arrows between conjoining rooms. It is useful, but not necessary, to create a rough sense of scale as you do this by making circles bigger or smaller, according to the planned size of each room.

### Flashpoint

In 1935, Edgar J. Kaufmann, owner of the Kaufmann stores in Pittsburgh, commissioned Frank Lloyd Wright to design a family home near a waterfall at Bear Run, Pennsylvania. That home, now called Fallingwater, stands as one of the paramount examples of twentieth-century architecture. In 1991, members of the American Institute of Architects declared it "the best all-time work of American architecture."

According to legend (and to the conservancy that oversees Fallingwater), Wright went for weeks after receiving the commission without drawing a single line. And yet whenever the client called to ask how things were going, Wright replied, "All is fine."

Eventually, of course, Kaufmann wanted to see what Wright had come up with and made an appointment to visit. The architect went into his drafting room, sat down at his table, and began to draw. Shortly after, he emerged with the final drawings complete. The whole design had been shaping itself in his mind, and all he had to do was put it down to paper.

Not everyone, however, has Wright's talent. For most of us, drawing is how we find ideas and making mistakes is how we find solutions. In other words, we suggest you not try this at home.

The bubble diagram shows what goes where, what rooms connect to what, to ensure that you can get easily from one room to the logical next (kitchen to dining room, for instance, or bedroom to bath). Traffic and circulation are critical elements in home planning. The living room should be easily accessed from the front door. If you entertain often, consider a larger room and wider entranceway. Is there a stairway? Where is it? Can it be easily reached from the public areas of the house without invading bedrooms or studies? And do not forget the practicality of hallways: especially in the bedroom area, you'll want private entrances to each room, and some distance for the sake of privacy.

### Architerms

You are now entering the second phase, **schematic design (SD)**. In this phase, through floor plans, elevations, and budget calculations, your house—its shape, its size, its structure—begins to take form.

# Placing Rooms

Bubble diagrams also help determine room placement. You probably don't want your home office next to the kids' playroom, for instance. Playing with circles at this stage allows you to work this stuff out *before* you get to the more difficult, demanding, and exacting phase of drawing floor plans and elevations.

This kind of schematic planning is why bubble diagrams are used not only for building architecture, but also for the architecture of websites, landscapes and gardens, even video games.

## Solving the Circulation

You'll need a separate bubble diagram for each floor of your new home. As you start, think about the functions of rooms and how they are ordinarily grouped: public living area, cooking and eating, private quarters. Different is good, but you'll probably want to stick to similar groupings when considering traffic flow

**Architerms**

Solving the circulation is a term architects use to describe finding solutions for connecting spaces efficiently and elegantly (including between inside and outside).

through the house, noise and accessibility, and the economics of things like plumbing systems. Two bathrooms, for instance, could share a common wall; a laundry area or downstairs bath could be placed against or directly below the kitchen, and so on. Certain basic configurations—dining room on one side of the kitchen and garage on the other side, for example—may seem boring and routine, but they've become standardized for a reason: they make sense. Even if you choose not to follow these patterns, you should consider why they were initially put in place (ease of bringing groceries into the kitchen and prepared food into the dining area) and make allowances accordingly.

When architects speak of the circulation or traffic of your home, they're not just talking about ferrying people from place to place. There are technical requirements to consider, like making sure everyone can get to an exit easily in case of fire.

## Processions

There's something else to consider as you picture the entrances and traffic patterns in your home. This is a concept based on Greek architectural ideals that turned away from the Roman, "head-on" interaction with space. Think of the actual experience of entering the house: what do you see when you first open the door? What do you see after that?

Your "procession" through your home can make a huge difference in your experience living there. Imagine, for instance, the steps you take coming home from a long work day after a hot, crowded commute. You step out of your car, and you see a lane, and then a tree, and then you turn and see your front porch and perhaps your family waving, probably in slow motion, your spouse and well-behaved children waiting eagerly for your arrival. Your devoted Golden Retriever leaps to your side. Continuing into the house, you enter the vestibule, follow a corridor with its gallery of family photographs, to the drawing room. As you enter the drawing room you see the awaiting martini, and the picture window with views of your gardens and the valley beyond …

This is, of course, a highly dramatized example, but an important point: while creating your bubble diagram, try to experience the actual movement through your home and how it can very literally affect your psyche and your spirit.

In the process, however, as you plan the situation of rooms, don't forget to take advantage of the unique and specific characteristics of your site: which rooms will have what views? Bubble diagrams aren't generally intended to consider room placement in such detail, but it's a useful time to begin thinking about what you have and what you want, and exploring the possibilities for creating agreement between them. Where will morning sunlight fall? Are there elevated areas that might mandate the shape or size of a room you'd planned to place there? Some of your initial planning may need adjusting: for the study to be comfortably distant from the family room, it may need to go where you thought the guest room would be; if you want a picture window looking out onto the valley while you work, perhaps the guest room should go upstairs, instead. Try it!

# Exploring Shapes and Sizes

Although it's still an abstract, schematic set of what is essentially (to paraphrase the immortal words of folksinger Arlo Guthrie) a collection of circles and arrows with a paragraph next to each one, your bubble diagram will gradually develop into the first raw sketch of your home.

We've sometimes found it useful to explore room sizes and shapes by cutting paper rectangles and arranging them in various patterns, using the bubble diagram for reference. This helps visualize the spatial and proportional relationships between rooms and the ways in which they may fit to one another before you get to the more complex and detailed floor-plan stage. While doing so, keep in mind the paramount principle of scale in architecture—the relation between the space itself and the human body. Ask yourself: how big is this room, in relation to the house? How big is it in relation to me? One way to test this is to see how you feel in the rooms of your current home.

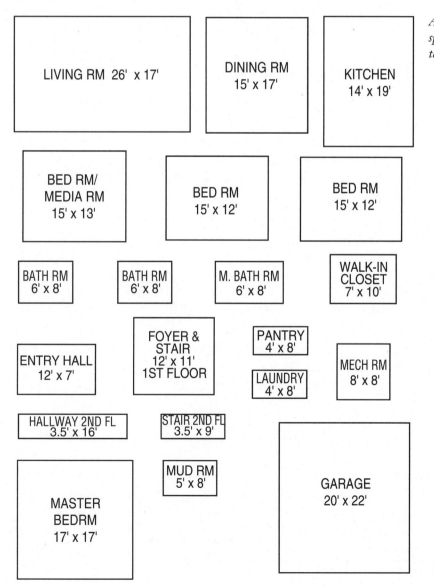

*A "kit" of forms that represent the spaces in the house helps to design the layout.*

As you sketch (and revise) your bubble diagram, remember that these are all experiments. You will not get it absolutely right the first time. You don't *want* to get it right the first time. Think creatively, and give yourself the freedom of new options and better ideas. Remember: ideas breed ideas. Keep experimenting. You might even try out things you know aren't going to work, especially if you get blocked; sometimes these are exactly what you need to prompt the "Aha!" solution you've been struggling over. If it's easier for you, trace over the parts you want to keep while you do battle with the rooms you just can't figure out: that's why you bought all that tracing paper!

### Flashpoint

The relationship between your own body and the size of the space you inhabit is at the core of architectural theory. Think of the effects of Gothic cathedrals, for instance, and their soaring ceilings, or the overwhelming power of a temple, or the majesty of a royal palace. A huge structure has enormous impact, imposing in its presence; a smaller one is more intimate, human, approachable. Which do you want? What is the mood of each room? How does it fit *you*?

## The Least You Need to Know

◆ Establish connections and interactions between spaces of your home by drawing a "bubble diagram."

◆ Think of your bubble diagrams as the transitional step between the planning and designing phases of your project.

◆ Use your bubble diagram throughout the process as you continue to elaborate on your design.

# Creating Floor Plans

## In This Chapter

- Creating your first plans
- Modifying your design
- Insider tips

Congratulations! Having gotten this far, you will now do what you thought you were going to do at the start: draw the floor plans of your home-to-be. This is where you really get to "see" your house for the first time, moving from the general to the specific, with increasing detail as you progress.

## Making Plans

First things first: keep reminding yourself that nothing you put to paper at this stage is permanent. You can expect to make continual changes and refinements in your plans as you go: what's "good enough" on paper may not feel "good enough" when you're actually living with it. If you find that an aspect of your design isn't quite working out the way you expected, play with it until you find something that does.

You will make most or all of the following plan drawings:

**General plans:**
Site
Cellar
Ground floor
Each additional floor
Attic and partial roof, if applicable
Roof

**Partial plans:**
Kitchen
Bathrooms
Living room showing built-ins, fireplace, etc.

Any other relevant rooms (family, media, closets if elaborate or special storage
configurations)

Staircase(s)

Others as needed

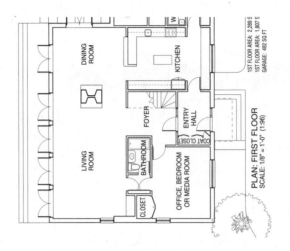

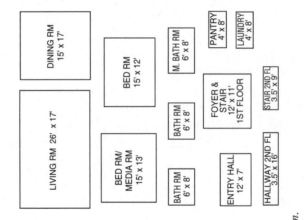

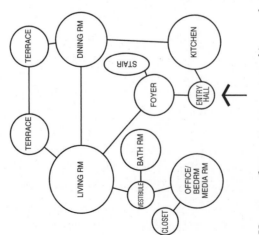

*How to get from a concept to an architectural plan.*

## Order and Your Design

Although you are not usually conscious of it, the rooms and spaces of most buildings—and certainly most homes—play off one another, creating a sense of order and rhythm. Think about the layout of your current home, for instance, or examine the floor plan of a museum. These offer excellent examples of what a floor plan can and should do, and of how rooms can be arranged to work together both efficiently and aesthetically.

The tendency toward order in architecture is not accidental. Humans are instinctively drawn to a well-ordered environment. Predictability helps us to understand our surroundings and our place in a larger universe. This is why, for instance, societies create train schedules, ordinances, conduct codes; it is why we tend to follow habits, like taking the same route to work each day. Rhythm, pattern, and harmony are part of what allows us to feel at peace—to feel, ultimately, at home.

There are also, however, practical reasons for doing this. For example, by law (based on the Americans with Disabilities Act) certain parts of the kitchen require a 2.5-foot module, to allow enough space in front of a sink to accommodate a wheelchair; but 2×10 lumber typically is sold in two-foot lengths (a standard that predates the Americans with Disabilities Act). This suggests two options: You could design the entire house by the 30-inch (2.5 foot) module— hence, with cabinet measurements at 30 inches and room sizes at 10, 12.5, 15, and 17.5 feet. Or you could design the kitchen on the 2.5-foot module, but base the rest of the home on the two-foot lumber length, thereby saving substantially on the cost (and headache) of cutting and incorporating the additional six-inch lengths. (For reasons both technical and aesthetic, we do not recommend combining a 2-foot and 2.5-foot module in one room—in this case, the kitchen.)

Similarly, you may want to base ceiling heights on the eight-foot gypsum wall standard. An 8'2" ceiling will cost you almost as much to build as 9' ceiling; either way, you'll have to have additional gypsum wallboard cut and added to the standard board anyway.

## Break Out of Your Bubble

Your first plans are meant to define the placement and properties of the basic elements of your home: walls, windows, doors, built-ins, fireplaces. Later, you will trace over these drawings and add further details: wall thickness, materials, finishes on floors, window types, door types—even down to the product name for stock items.

After that, you will begin focusing on individual rooms, enlarging each to a scale that allows you to see the finer details and to ensure that all connections are solved and there are no misalignments. These plans will also note the placements of electrical outlets and switches, wiring throughout the home, and so on.

The purpose of your hard-line drawings is to establish scale, which shows true sizes and the order and alignment of architectural elements (walls, staircases, and so on). Each of these plan drawings will help you resolve the various and

**Flashpoint**

Remember that for any of these plan drawings, should you get stuck, feel overwhelmed, or just plain not have the time, professional draftsmen can be a big help. Don't give up on designing your own home just because you (think you) can't draw.

often complex details of your home design and assist in clarifying particulars throughout, including …

- ◆ Exact sizes of rooms.
- ◆ Thicknesses of each wall.
- ◆ Location(s) and size(s) of staircases(s).
- ◆ Locations and sizes of doors and windows.
- ◆ Locations and sizes of appliances.
- ◆ Locations and sizes of furniture.
- ◆ Locations and sizes of built-ins.
- ◆ Furniture and its layout.

Pencils ready? Begin.

Your first drawings will be on graph paper. Professional architects commonly work with a ¼–1.0 scale, or one-quarter inch to the foot.

Basing your drawing on your bubble diagram, program, and any previous sketches, begin drawing the outlines of your rooms. You may choose to do this freehand or using tools such as a straight edge, T square, set square, protractors, and rulers (hard-line drawing). This helps ensure accuracy and order in the composition. Do not forget to include the thickness of the walls!

Once again (we can't say it enough), before you start, check your bubble diagram and programs to remind yourself of the main and secondary spaces (private, semiprivate, public), storage, and—again—circulation. A key tip: circulation should represent between 15 and 25 percent of the total surface area of your home.

## You Have the Floor

There are no rules for how to draw a floor plan, but we'll suggest two methods you might try, at least to get started.

The first option is to think of circulation as a spine, or a main artery feeding the main spaces. At the main entrance, for instance, you could place a small vestibule from which you run a straight corridor, about five feet wide, to the back of the house where a second entry would be. Place rooms on each side of the corridor (see the analogy to a spine?) including the staircase, if there is one. You might also leave spaces *between* rooms, which could become outside spaces—areas for small, semiprivate gardens.

Alternatively, you can begin by deciding the general shape of the footprint of your house on the ground floor, drawing it on your graph paper, and then inserting rooms into the space. With this method as with the other, begin with the entrance, vestibule, and corridor, and arrange the remaining rooms to fit. Expect to make adjustments here and there to the general shapes of rooms, and to the number and placement of closets and vestibules where necessary.

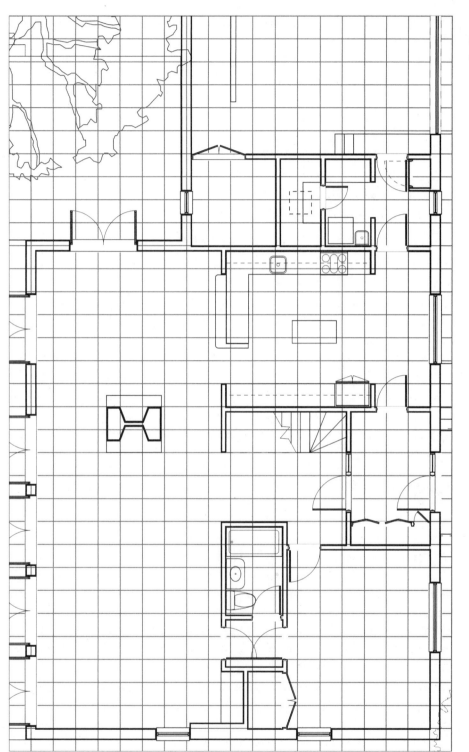

*Using graph paper helps you work at scale quickly and easily at an early stage of the process.*

**Design Tip**

Several Internet sites offer tips and ideas on drawing plans:

www.sanford-artedventures.com/create/try_this_floorplan.htm.

www.rentaldecorating.com/Floorplan.htm

www.about-building-in-canada.com/drawings.html

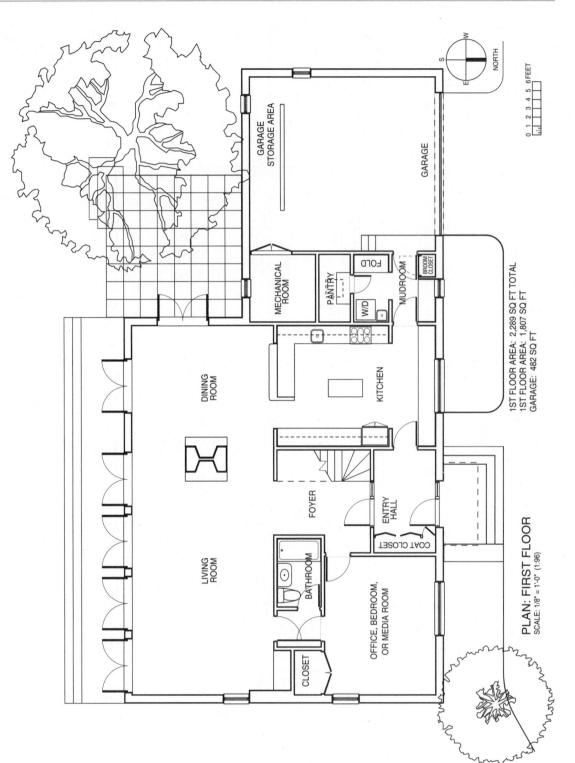

GARAGE
STORAGE AREA

GARAGE

MECHANICAL
ROOM

PANTRY

FOLD

W/D

MUDROOM

BROOM
CLOSET

DINING
ROOM

KITCHEN

LIVING
ROOM

FOYER

ENTRY
HALL

COAT CLOSET

BATHROOM

CLOSET

OFFICE, BEDROOM,
OR MEDIA ROOM

1ST FLOOR AREA: 2,289 SQ FT TOTAL
1ST FLOOR AREA: 1,807 SQ FT
GARAGE: 482 SQ FT

0 1 2 3 4 5 6 FEET

S          W
E          N
NORTH

**PLAN: FIRST FLOOR**
SCALE: 1/8" = 1'-0" (1:96)

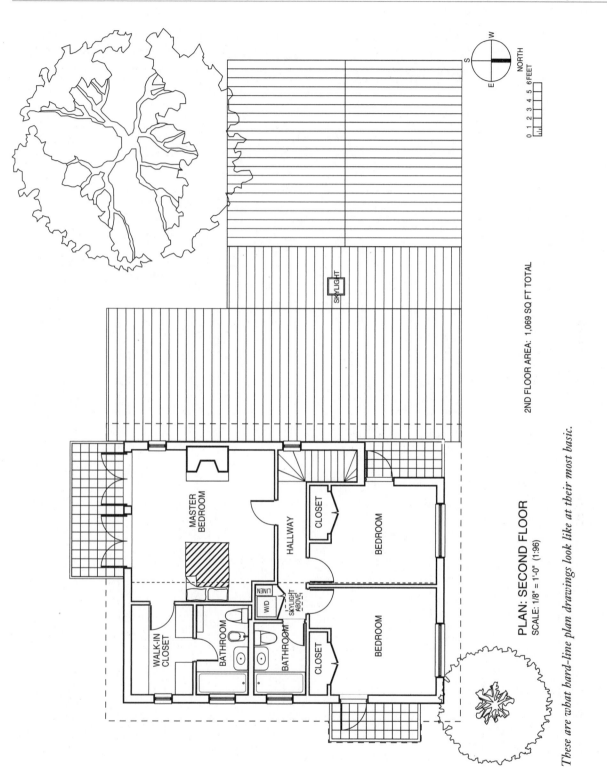

2ND FLOOR AREA: 1,069 SQ FT TOTAL

PLAN: SECOND FLOOR
SCALE: 1/8" = 1'-0" (1:96)

*These are what hard-line plan drawings look like at their most basic.*

Professional architects create ceiling plans as well, indicating lighting arrangements, fans, diffusers, vents, and the like. You may also wish to draw roof plans, especially if your home will have a particularly complicated roof.

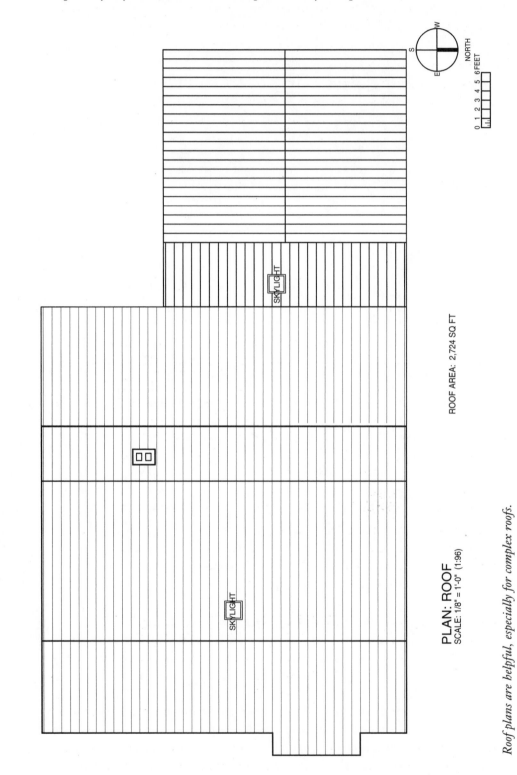

PLAN: ROOF
SCALE: 1/8" = 1'-0" (1:96)

ROOF AREA: 2,724 SQ FT

*Roof plans are helpful, especially for complex roofs.*

## Watch Those Walls!

A wall is thicker than a line! Be sure to account for the thickness of your walls, or you will find yourself with a larger house, smaller rooms, or both—resulting in a house (and expenses) quite different than what you'd planned.

A standard measurement is to construct inside walls of one stud 2×4 (3.5 inches deep) and two layers of gypsum wall board (2×⅝ inches, or 1¼ inches), for a total of 4¾ inches; and outside walls with one stud 2×6 (5½ inches deep); one layer of gypsum wall board (⅝ inch); one layer plywood (¾ inch); plus one layer siding (¾ inch), totaling 7⅝ inches. Outside walls, however, can reach as much as 10½ inches or more.

# Tracing and Modifying Your Design

After you complete your first overall sketch, you will begin adding more and more details and measurements, indicating positions of appliances, built-ins, and the like. Here again you will reach for that ream of tracing paper: trace over your current plan and begin filling in the missing information.

Your second-stage drawing might include windows and doors for each room and their dimensions, as well as fireplaces, staircases, and major closets. Remember your feedback loop: keep going back through all the phases, making certain they continue to coordinate with one another as you go, ensuring that you kept track of special features (wine cellar, sauna, sunken bathtub … ) and followed general rules about room groupings and circulation.

As your drawings become increasingly detailed, you may find yourself stuck in decision traps: if you put that built-in vitrine where you'd thought you would, the door won't open all the way. Be sure to check circulation throughout, noting all links (or lack of them) between entryway, rooms, vestibules, stairs, etc.—the "spine" of your project. Don't forget, too, to check your drawings against any preliminary sketches you may have made of your façade, to be sure that all lines (floor to wall, plan to footprint) match.

Nothing is set in stone until it is, well, set in stone. Should there be more windows? A dormer here? A skylight there? This first rendition (or these first renditions) of your floor plan aim to establish the locations and shapes and sizes of these elements.

## Flashpoint

Doors, windows, and even ovens require special attention. Verify that all doors can open to 90–105 degrees (to be sure furniture can be moved in and out) and windows open according to manufacturers' specifications. Oven doors must open fully, allowing a minimum of 36 inches beyond the fully open position.

# Design Shortcuts and Professional Tips

Traditionally, the best way to utilize space and minimize construction costs is to group certain areas of your home together, as when two bedrooms share a bath between them—often a good option for young children. A similar idea is to place two separate baths against one another; the shared wall reduces plumbing costs. In fact, you could, for instance, build the two rooms early on, but install fixtures only in one of them, using the other as a playroom or for storage. (That is, you can install the electrical wiring and roughing—or plumbing pipes, capped—as if it were a bathroom, without installing the plumbing fixtures.)

As the children grow older and are ready for separate baths, the playroom can be broken out and the pipes made active. This saves you the cost of installing the fixtures at an early phase, when you are already overwhelmed with other expenses, while allowing you options later on.

Another option, generally more for the grown-ups in the family, is to create a vestibule between the master bedroom and master bath, which can be utilized as a walk-in closet. This allows privacy (let's face it, we'd all prefer a little bit of distance between bedroom and toilet), while providing a touch of luxury (the walk-in closet), convenience, and an effective consolidation of space. Imagine it: you wake, stumble through the closet to your shower, eyeing an outfit or two along the way. You assemble the ensemble in your mind while bathing, step out, dress, and reenter the bedroom ready to start the day.

## The Least You Need to Know

◆ Drawing floor plans gives you your first *real* look at your home.

◆ Use a standardized scale for your plan drawings to ensure accuracy, both in your own planning and in the construction phase.

◆ Create a sense of rhythm by establishing a basic proportions module; the most cost-effective option is to work on the basis of 2-foot measures.

◆ Keep refining your drawings, growing increasingly detailed as you go along.

◆ Have fun with this! There are no mistakes here—only adventures and solutions.

# Chapter 10

# Elevations and Sections

## In This Chapter

- ◆ Getting the composition
- ◆ Exterior and interior elevation drawings
- ◆ Plane views and intersections

For your floor plan, you developed a bird's-eye view of your home with its roof removed. The elevation drawings are in principle what that same bird would see flying alongside the façade of your house: windows, doors, roof, porches, and other details.

Now imagine you've sliced the façade off the rest of the house. What you see now is what you will record in your section drawings. These reveal the core of your home—its structure; the heights and shapes of ceilings; configurations of stairs; shapes and locations of balconies, dormers, and skylights; and the special relationships among all of these elements. They are critical tools for your contractor when you are ready to start building.

The purpose of drawing elevations is to help visualize the heights of various elements of the house: door header, windowsill and header, ceiling, beams, roofs, dormers, chimneys, light fixtures, and so on. Your elevation drawings depict the house as if photographed head-on, with as few perspective effects as possible, looking perpendicular to the main wall. It is basically the view of a house as a child would draw it: most elements such as doors, windows, eaves, roof, dormer, overhangs, pergolas, and so on will be visible—and measurable— in the drawings. In addition, your elevations will reveal and articulate the materials you are using for your home, their textures, their colors—all of which will have a role in the general composition of the whole.

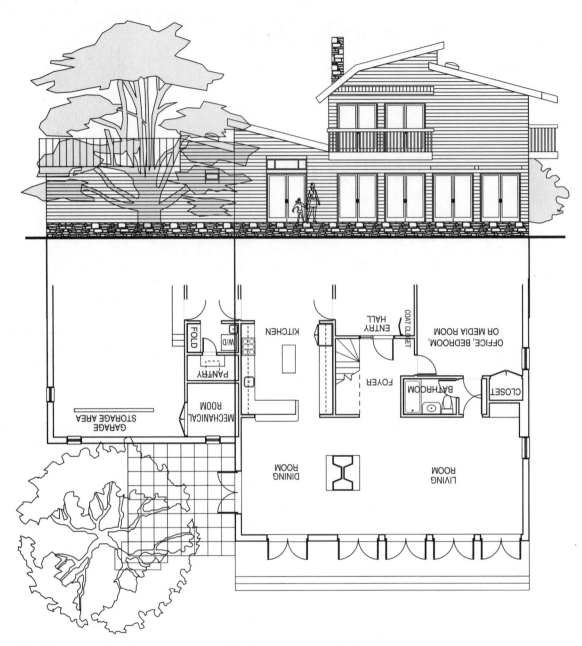

*This illustration shows the correspondence of the elements between the drawings.*

All told, you will make the following elevation and section drawings, in this order:

- Site
- Cellar
- Ground floor
- Additional floors
- Attic/mansard

- Roof
- Exterior elevation 1, 2, 3, 4, etc.
- Sections 1 and 2
- Additional sections as needed

# Drawing the Outside of Your Home

Façade drawings reveal the proportions—the ratios of different dimensions—of various elements of your home. These include ...

♦ Height and width of windows, walls, and roof.

♦ Ratios of window area to wall area.

♦ Distance to and from wall corner to door (or to window).

♦ Distances (and ratios) between windows and doors.

Ideally, you will want these proportions and their relationships to one another to be visually pleasing, creating rhythm, harmony, and balance. This may mean some adjusting (again) of the design here and there: if you've planned a large window in the living room and initially expected to place a single small window in the bedroom directly above it, you might find the overall appearance somewhat askew. Play with it—and remember that windows do not always have to be rectangular or square! Expect that you will spend time arranging and rearranging these elements until you find a design and composition you're happy with.

It is generally a good idea to start with the façade (face of the house) that contains the entrance—the main façade. Though typically a house has four façades, there are exceptions—and your house may be among them. Each façade will require an elevation drawing. Make certain as you go that all dimensions of your plans and elevations coordinate fully—that the width of the front façade (the one with the entrance) lines up with the width of the floor plan at that wall.

Start by drawing a horizontal line where the ground is—elevation zero—at about an inch or two from the bottom of the page, and adding lines to denote various levels:

♦ The level where foundation walls stop above the ground

♦ First level

♦ Windowsills and headers

♦ Door headers

♦ Eaves

♦ Dormers

♦ Rooflines

♦ Chimneys

♦ Others, as appropriate to your personal design

These construction lines, which you will draw in faint lines, help with placing these various elements. Only then will you begin drawing the elements themselves (doors, windows, and so on).

Using the ruler, draw one façade of the house. Do not attempt to make it appear three-dimensional; you want the image to be flat and if portions protrude (balconies, windowsills), indicate them only by defining their forms, as if they'd

**Design Tip**

Imagine this as a house of cards, or even as if you were building a box: all vertical walls must match the horizontal floors. This may seem obvious, but it can be easy to overlook!

been drawn onto the house. By the same token, there is no definition for the porch from the front view—only from a side view. Basically, you only want a flat, line drawing.

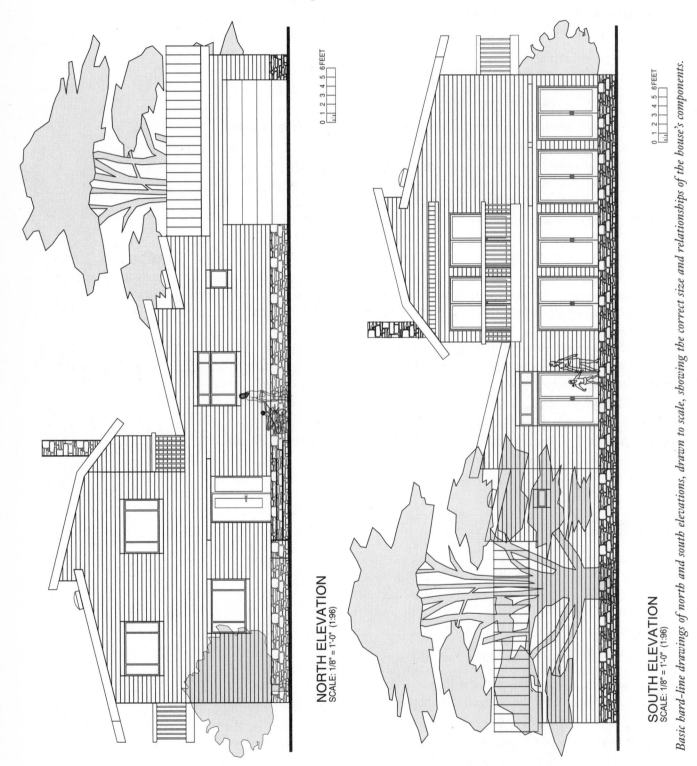

**NORTH ELEVATION**
SCALE: 1/8" = 1'-0" (1:96)

0 1 2 3 4 5 6FEET

**SOUTH ELEVATION**
SCALE: 1/8" = 1'-0" (1:96)

0 1 2 3 4 5 6FEET

*Basic hard-line drawings of north and south elevations, drawn to scale, showing the correct size and relationships of the house's components.*

Use the adjustable triangle to get the correct angles for corners, the roof, and such. It's better to use something that tells you the actual angle than just to guess using a ruler and what looks right.

Add windows and doors where you would want them placed on the actual house, making sure to use the scale correctly.

This is also the moment to draw your terrace, porches, balconies, dormers, and similar elements and ensure that they form a compositional whole with the rest of the house and that any relationships you'd intended to have between them (bedroom window overlooking terrace garden, for instance) line up accordingly. Again, work and rework these parts until you are pleased with both the aesthetics and the practicality of the design.

Be sure in your drawings to verify that ceiling heights, although not visible from outside, do not interfere with door and window heights. For ceilings in the main rooms, we recommend a height of 8'6" or more. Others decrease in proportion to their importance—a basement could be 7 feet high, while an attic with dormers might be 7'6".

As you go, you'll need to account as well for the depth of the structure—beams, stairs, and so on—of the house, so that the floor-to-floor height and total height of the house are correctly determined. This is especially important for a habitable attic, which usually has dormers. An experienced builder could determine the depth of the structure, although even they usually prefer to confirm with an architect or a structural engineer. For simplicity, you can approximate to a (relative) standard of 12 to 14 inches, to which we add ceiling and floor construction (1½ inches each).

The floor structure is made of beams and subflooring, (the most common of which is plywood); the ceiling is extra. The total (typical) sandwich, from parquet down to the ceiling below is …

parquet (0.75") + plywood (0.75") + joists (9.50" or more) + ceiling (0.625/0.75/1.5") = 12 to 14 inches.

> **Flashpoint**
> One more time: as you work on your elevation drawings, continue to refer to your program, bubble diagrams, and idea files, and bear any budgetary restrictions or potential extras that you have in mind.

# Drawing Interior Elevations

After the outside, you do the inside. Interior elevations follow the same principle as the exterior, showing the walls and any features such as built-ins, archways, countertops (and splashes), appliances, fireplaces, the interiors of windows, moldings, and so on: if it's on your wall, it belongs in your drawing. (We'll review these special features in more detail in Chapter 18.)

As with your exterior elevations, you will create a series of drawings, tracing over your basic template and adding various notes and details accordingly, indicating materials to be used, dimensions, finishes, and so on. Remember to keep the drawings flat and to scale. A complete set of interior elevation drawings will include all views of the walls to each room (or the main rooms) including closets (so that builders can estimate shelving, and so on.).

# Drawing Cross-Sections of Your Home

With floor plans and elevations in place, your next step will be to verify these by creating section drawings. Here again, you will find yourself moving hither and yon among your drawings, matching plans to elevations, elevations to *sections*, sections to plans, and back again, until you are thoroughly satisfied with the plans, and the house they represent appears structurally sound.

Traditionally, sections in architectural drawings reveal the discrete components of structure: walls, floors, ceilings, roofs, and other important elements, such as foundations, retaining walls, and fireplaces. Sections are also a means of designing, verifying, and controlling the three-dimensional quality of the spaces and their technical requirements: size, clearance, and accessibility. By combining information from the plan—sizes and locations of building elements—with the distance from ground to those elements, they serve as repositories of building data and especially of dimensions on the z-axis.

Section drawings, like floor plans, begin with the basics and become more intricate as you progress. Because many of these drawings will require a certain amount of technical know-how (knowledge of insulating materials or electrical systems, for instance), we do advise consulting with a professional.

The result—and purpose—of drawing a section is the view behind the plane of the cut. This sounds a lot more complicated than it really is, though, so visualize it this way: say you've placed an orange on a table and are slicing it in two, using a large knife. The knife forms a plane perpendicular to the tabletop. The "view behind the plane" is the exposed orange half—what you will see after the knife comes down: the orange seeds, the sections, the membranes, and pith. Those are, in essence, like your interior elevation drawings—views of walls in your rooms. These drawings play an important role in determining the interior design: layout of walls, doors, windows, and their decorative accessories.

At this point, by combining information from the section line with the interior view, it also becomes possible (and advisable) to look carefully at the natural and artificial lighting throughout your home. You should now be able to plot the sun's path over the living room or master bedroom or breakfast area, and decide about the quantity and quality of light throughout your house: where, for how long, for which part of the day or of the season.

> **Architerms**
>
> **Sections** are drawings of a building (or a section of the building) rendered as if the building (or section) had been cut vertically to show the interior.

> **Design Tip**
>
> Another way to think of your section drawings is as if you were cutting a fish in two, first for a fillet and then for a steak. Each cut is distinct: the filet reveals the inside of the fish along the length of the spine, while in the steak, we've cut across the spine. Both sections make visible things we could not see before cutting, but that are crucial for the function of the fish. In the same way, the section drawing reveals important aspects—structure, components—that comprise the whole of the object.

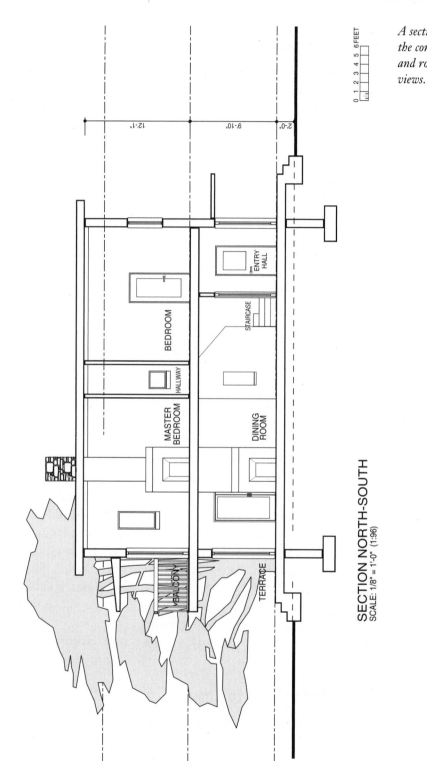

*A section drawing, at scale, shows the configuration of terrain, walls, and roofs, as well as the interior views.*

0 1 2 3 4 5 6FEET

12'-1"    9'-10"    2'-0"

ENTRY HALL

BEDROOM

STAIRCASE

HALLWAY

MASTER BEDROOM

DINING ROOM

BALCONY

TERRACE

SECTION NORTH-SOUTH
SCALE: 1/8" = 1'-0"  (1:96)

You will need to make a minimum of two section drawings of your house, rendered at right angles to one another and including the main entrance—one going east-west, for instance, the other north-south. One of these will be required by your local building department in order for them to issue a permit to build. The sections almost always traverse doors and windows as much as possible, so that the relationships among door and window headers, window sills, steps, beams, ceilings, dormers, roofs, and so on are all documented. It is useful to draw a person's outline in the sections, so that the proportions of space to humans can be judged. A 7'6"-high family room will be too low for most people, but it can be fine for a powder room.

While drawings in addition to these basic sections are useful and desirable (especially for kitchens and other rooms with fireplaces, tiling, built-ins, or other weight-bearing features), they are not necessary. However, your builder will need to measure and know as much about as possible about any walls that will be (or need to be) thicker than typical sheet rock. Similarly, if you have niches in your walls, even sheet rock walls, you will need to draw these as well.

In addition, if the plan view is of (or through) an attic, it will include a bit of the roof as well—like a skirt—because the plan is like a horizontal section taken at 3'4" above floor level.

The dimensions for the sections—widths and lengths of building elements—are taken from your plans and elevations for the x-, y-, and z-axes, respectively. Anticipate more to-ing and fro-ing: sections may reveal that some dimensions do not actually work on the z-axis (height), for instance. Let's say you suddenly discover you can smack your head on the underside of the stairway while going to the kitchen—a rude awakening before a midnight snack. Well, now you'll need to move the staircase (or the kitchen), adjusting the plans and elevations accordingly. Expect this, by the way, and expect it to happen and more than once: stairs, joists, and flooring are likely to demand some attention and reconfigurations at this stage.

What you're doing with all this, from a geometrical/technical point of view, is describing the separation between the outside and inside—the contour—of your house. If you have ever seen the engineering drawings of a gearbox of a car, you know how useful it is in conveying a relatively clear idea of the shapes of the components and their relationship to one another. The same applies to a house: in order to build properly, we need to know the components—studs, joists, wall boards, plywood sheets, floors, doors, windows, ceilings, skylights, roofs, dormers, chimneys, trees, fireplaces, flues, built-in furniture, ceiling fans, HVAC ducts, other fans, recessed lighting fixtures, and so on—their sizes, their required clearances, their relative position to each other and to the earth.

**Flashpoint**

Plans are the everyday tool for placing rooms and functions in a desired sequence, but sections are the professional's main tool for designing a structure that can be actually built from the ground up.

## The Least You Need to Know

- Draw elevations of the exterior and interior walls of your home to determine placement of windows, built-ins, porches, etc.
- Define the inner structure and components of your house with section drawings.
- Section drawings are difficult even for beginning architecture students; don't hesitate to call for help or hire a professional for this task if needed.

# Chapter 11

# A Few Words on Stairs

## In This Chapter

- ◆ How stairs function in your home
- ◆ Technical requirements
- ◆ Using the space beneath your stairway

Staircases have long been associated with aesthetic and psychological values, with a sense of greatness: think of the stepped pyramids of the Aztecs. Think of Rocky running the stairs of the Philadelphia Museum of Art.

## Stairs Step by Step

Staircases have fairly clear technical requirements, set historically by experience and then codified into legislation because of their importance in emergency evacuation and as a potential source of accidents. Consequently, you will need to observe some basic rules and formulas while attending to stair design:

- ◆ In the United States, a stair's riser (the vertical part of a step) and tread (the horizontal part) must comply with the following formula:

  2 risers + 1 tread = 24–25 inches (nosing excluded)

- ◆ Maximum height between platforms should be generally 12 feet.

- ◆ Stairs must be kept free of all protrusions, such as doors and windows opening into its path. However, niches with some of your statuary collection or a vase of flowers could be placed strategically along the stairway wall(s) as long as nothing interferes with the stairway itself.

- ◆ Railings around landings should be made childproof, with the vertical bars at about four inches from one another.

- ◆ Lighting is important for a good stair, both to illuminate where to put one's foot and to reveal the splendor of the different materials and shapes. It is a good idea to accentuate the landings, niches, handrails, and the *newel* posts.

*This building block of stair design is important to safety and comfort while climbing.*

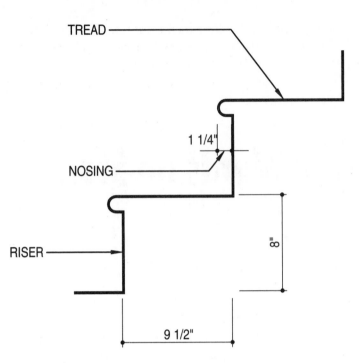

**Architerms**

**Newels** support and beautify stairway railings (banisters) at the top and bottom of the stair.

*The shortest distance between two points on different levels is the one-run stair.*

♦ In residential codes, widths of 30 or 33 inches are sometimes the minimum dimensions. Actually, this size works well just to get from floor to floor, but hardly suffices as a generous main stairway. Rather, we suggest allowing a minimum of 36 inches, to enable you to get your furniture upstairs. From an aesthetic standpoint, any width from 36 inches on up appears fairly generous. Do not be tempted to build narrow toward the basement: at some point, a large object may have to travel that way.

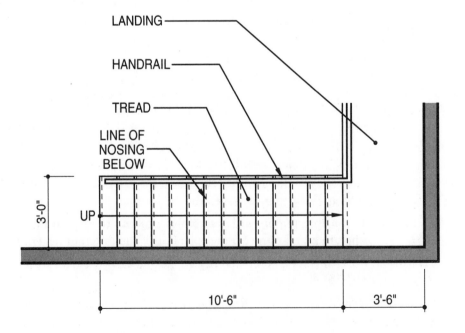

Landings are also important, both for functional and aesthetic reasons. They allow the climber to pause between flights, to rest any heavy items he or she may be carrying, or to step aside to allow someone to pass. They serve as the "front door" to each level of the house, an entryway into that (usually private or semiprivate) section of your home.

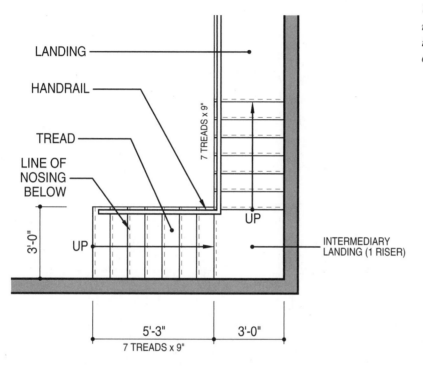

*Under certain conditions, the stair requires an intermediate landing, and could be a practical use of space.*

# See the Possibilities

If possible, you should incorporate natural light; a ray of sunlight guides the eye upward from the lower level, perhaps highlighting a remarkable piece of wood work in the banister or a beloved object set into a niche. And because people do use a landing as a place to take a momentary pause, a well-placed window could also reveal a landscape detail that would be unnoticeable from the ground level: imagine seeing a patch of grass with hyacinths visible behind a rock, and beyond that a pond with lilies, swans, and slow-moving tall grasses that rustle in the wind at dusk, as Johnson brings the Sauternes at proper temperature. It is time to descend your stair and retire to the patio.

All this in mind, the actual design of a stairway is, again, somewhat formulaic (though best left to those with arithmetic talent).

- ◆ Establish the floor-to-floor height: add ceiling height, ceiling construction, structure, flooring construction.
- ◆ Calculate the number of risers needed to get to the next floor by dividing the above-mentioned height to 8 inches; it will result in a number close to 14, 15, or 16.

♦ Establish the length of the stair: subtract 1 from the number above and multiply the result by 9 inches or more.

♦ Establish the size of the landing: at minimum, the same as the width of the stair (square), but not less than 36 inches deep.

♦ Remember that 2 risers + 1 tread = 24–25 inches; verify.

**Example:**

Ceiling height = 8'9"

Ceiling/structure/flooring sandwich = ⅝" + ¾" + 9½" + 2¼" = 13⅛"

Floor-to-floor height = 8'9" + 13⅛" = 9'10⅛" = 118⅛"

Riser = 118⅛" divided by 15 = 7⅞"

Riser/tread formula: 2×7⅞" + 9" = 24¾" within range

Length of stair: (15–1)×9" = 14×9" = 126" = 10'6"

With two landings: 10'6" + 2×3'6" = 17'6"

In this example, we would need 3'×17'6" of available space to install the stair. The first landing is actually just clear, unoccupied space at the foot of the stair, which is essential to the correct, unimpeded flow of circulation between floors, preferably within a distance from the front door. (This may become a very important detail in the event it becomes necessary to exit the house rapidly.)

*By turning the corner, this stair offers an efficient use of space and attractive design.*

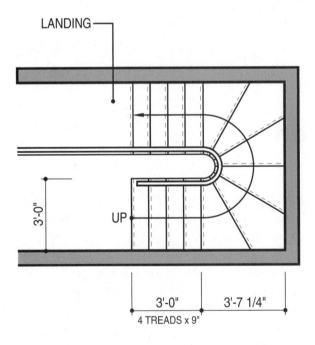

Though usually rectangular, curved stairs emanate a certain elegance and drama: old Hollywood loved circular stairways, making them feature figures in films from *A Day at the Races* to *Gone with the Wind*. In practical terms, however, curved stairs present a peculiar problem—how to adjust dimensions so that the steps (more technically referred as treads) near the small radius do not become too small and dangerous, and the ones on the large radius not become too large and tiresome to negotiate. Much back-and-forth adjusting may be necessary before arriving at a technically sound solution that is also aesthetically pleasing. At its best, a curved stairway will appear as collection of 3-D spirals crisscrossing in front of the audience.

Don't forget the space beneath a staircase, which may lend itself to various efficient uses: you could place another stair immediately under the main one for access to the basement, for instance, or use the space as a storage closet. Some have also been known to install a powder room, a tiny home office, or a hobby room—which, while perhaps noisy on occasion, can embrace a certain intimacy and charm.

## The Least You Need to Know

♦ Allow your staircase to be more than a place for getting from here to there—make it an architectural highlight of your house.

♦ Provide at least 36 inches width in your main stairway.

♦ The formula for stair height: 2 risers + one tread = 24–25 inches.

♦ Be sure railings are childproof.

♦ Provide adequate lighting.

♦ Use the space beneath the stairs for a powder room, office, or closet.

# Chapter 12

# Using the Three-Dimensional Model

## In This Chapter

- ◆ Exploring small-scale models
- ◆ Moving to larger scale
- ◆ Walking through your model

Some areas of your home will be easier to see in certain sizes than will others. Consequently, models are made in different scales (and so, different sizes): for instance, to see the whole house, you would use a small-scale model, so called because its ratio to the original full-size object, is reduced.

By contrast, when deciding to study discrete elements of the house—a well-sculpted fireplace, a pergola, a part of the roof with a special dormer and balcony, perhaps near a special chimney—you would use a large-scale model.

## Small-Scale Models—Your Whole House

For an average house, the recommended reduction ratio would be about 1 to 96 or 1 to 192—that is, the real-world dimensions are divided by 96 or 192, resulting in a small model that can be held in your hand. These numbers correspond to a rational division of the feet and inches, a difficult and laborious vestige of Imperial Rome and the British Empire. (Try to divide $2 \times 7^5/_{16}$" by 2 and compare this to the ease of dividing 79.60 centimeters by 2.) In any case, 1:96 means that one eighth of an inch on paper or on the model would represent one foot in reality.

By using a small scale for your model, you can show the whole house and possibly part of the adjoining land in a manageable size. This scale is adequate for reviewing the roof configuration—with dormers, skylights, chimneys, and so on. We assume the roof is sloped—the most common configuration in the United States. Even if not, it is still advisable to review the roof in model form.

*Small-scale models can include all the smallest features of your house. Allow elements to be temporary, so you can continue revising your design.*

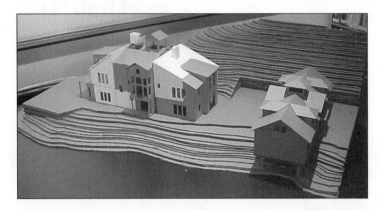

You are ready to start building a model. You have decided on its footprint and its placement on your land. Take advantage of the small scale and study the various external elements of the house—porches, decks, pergolas, large trees. When constructing your model, make room (as always) for changes, revisions, and new ideas by building those elements so that they can be removed and replaced by better or different designs. These elements, although secondary, have a significant influence on how the house is perceived and experienced. They make the building feel at home in its own place, at peace in the world.

Address the roof and its accessories—dormers and chimneys—in the same way: make all of them detachable and replaceable. You should expect to do quite a bit of work on this model of the roof. Moreover, if the roof itself is detachable, we gain the ability—via even more work—to see a simple version of the interior walls and therefore the rooms of the house. This could be quite valuable: an early view of the design, and so an early assessment.

## Large-Scale Models—Individual Spaces

Large scale is used for the discrete parts of the house you want to show in greater detail. Suppose you wish to design a beautiful fireplace, something a bit more elaborate than a box the size of an armoire with an opening in it. In this case, a model would be helpful in revealing the overall volume, the proportions of various trims and moldings relative to the ensemble, and the proportions of the individual shapes that make the whole. You could build a model of a room, with a removable ceiling, to show the fireplace as it stands in that space. The appropriate scale for this exercise is ½ inch = 1 foot (corresponding ratio is 1:24).

Sometimes a corner of a house can also be complicated enough to warrant its own model, from foundation to roof. Since families and their guests spend a lot of time in the kitchen/breakfast area, for instance, it is not a bad idea to model the space and the counter. If possible, obtain small figures in appropriate scale (available at art supply stores) and place them in the model. The figures will impart the sense of proportion and scale to the model, rendering design judgments easier. These figures (as well as cars, trees, and buses) are available for small scales as well.

# Making It Real

As a valuable tool, consider taking photographs of the model, including some from eye level at scale, close to the model's ground. This will help considerably in imagining how the house or the room or discrete element will appear when built as you approach it on foot or by car.

These principles are generally applicable to computer-generated 3-D models as well (with the exception that the modeling programs do not use the concept of scale until you need to print an image) as one computer-generated 3-D model could, in effect, contain all the relevant information regarding design.

However, the person building a computer-generated model faces a different quandary: how much time to devote to which part of the model. In theory, everything could be created in the modeling program: the foundations, the studs, the wallboards, the nails, doorknobs—everything. But that would take many months to finish, possibly as long as it would take to build the house itself. Don't make yourself crazy. This approach is really more relevant to the automotive and aerospace industries, where enormous development and unit costs are defrayed over many identical products over many years. (Boeing 777 seems to have been the first airplane designed fully in computer modeling.)

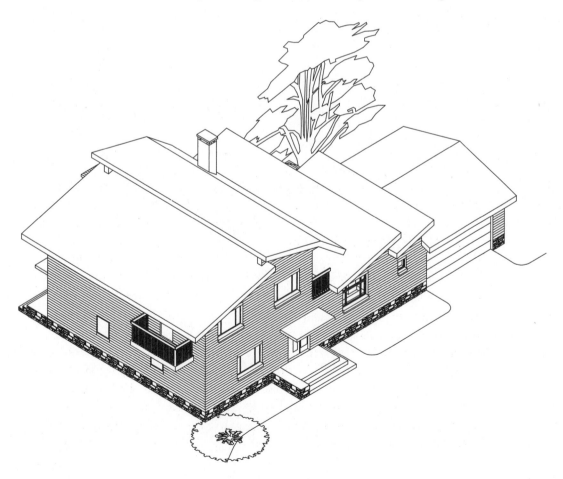

*A 3-D computer model shows views from various angles of the house.*

The computer-generated 3-D model further differs in that the output in this case is a print on paper—a two-dimensional interpretation of a three-dimensional world. Through proper lighting effects, however, it can become quite realistic, the way a vaguely doctored photograph often does; the limits are in how many and which snapshots you have the patience or experience to choose and to print.

Despite this limitation, the computer-generated model is invaluable as a repository of all the shapes, their relative position to each other, and dimensions of everything in and around the house and has an unparalleled ease to edit all this.

You can choose to see the whole model at once, or any part of it, rotate it, zoom in or out, change colors, play with materials, adjust textures, design lighting and indeed, mess with all the building elements ad infinitum until finally you are either thoroughly exhausted or, hopefully, satisfied with the design.

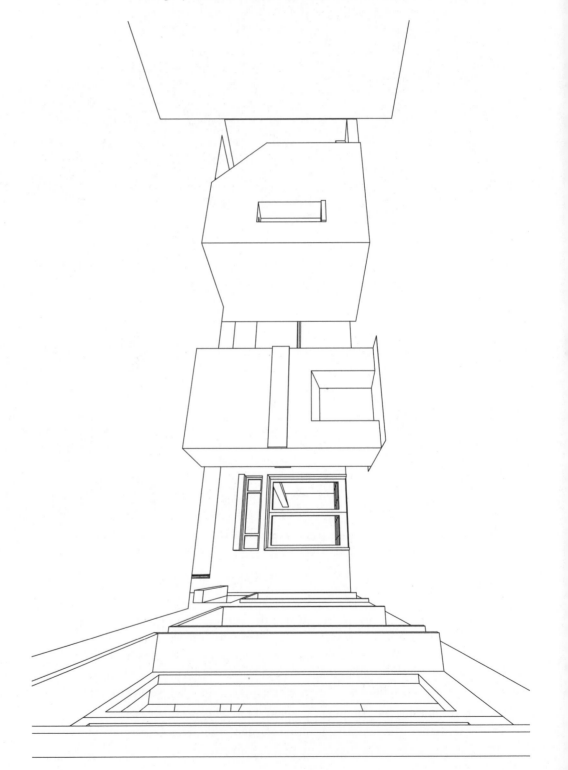

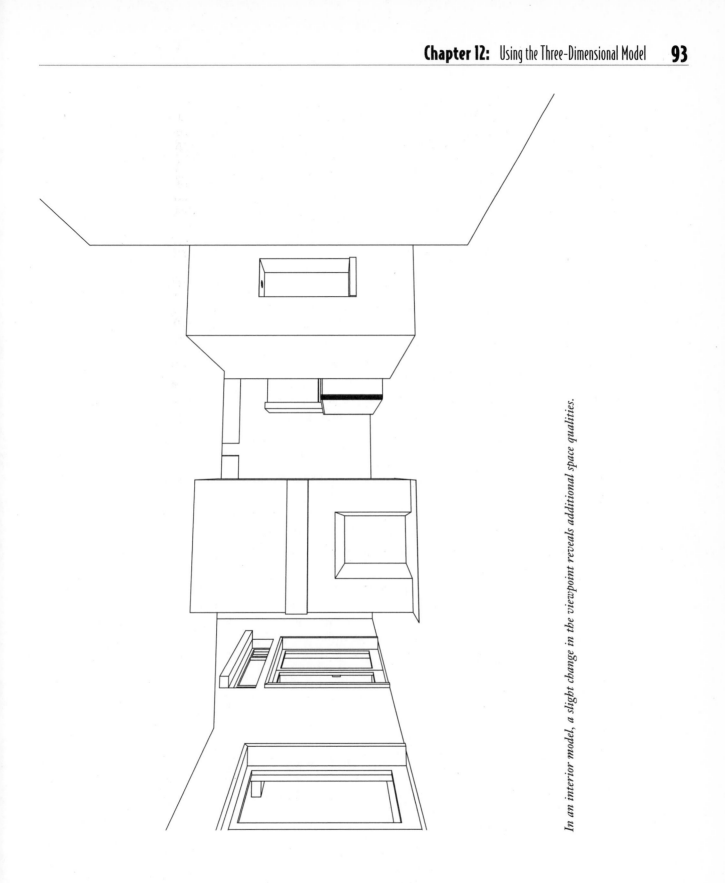

*In an interior model, a slight change in the viewpoint reveals additional space qualities.*

# Animating Your World

CAD 3-D models allow animation, a simulation of a film or video camera being walked around or inside the model. This opens up a lot of viewing opportunities. It is also hazardously addictive: so many parameters to change, so many ways to play!

Once you choose a design and the walls, floors, and ceilings seem to be in the right place, you can build a model. Then comes the enormity of the other two tasks: placing the textures for materials on those walls and setting lighting scenes—both natural and artificial. These tasks can become all consuming, as there are infinite possibilities to chose from.

Once you settle the above, you can decide on the itinerary of your camera—in cyberspace, as it were. From where would you like to view the house—as you approach by car or foot or both? What would you look at? (Usually it would be the front door.) You could choose to simulate taking a walk around the house, maybe walking toward it from two opposite directions. Think about what comes to mind when you see it—pleasant thoughts? Does it *feel* like coming home? Then you're on the right track.

The same mechanism works for the interiors, with the same caution: it can become all-consuming.

Imagine you are about to open the front door—start the animation at that point. Have the software open that door (if this feature is available), and then move the camera into the entrance vestibule. Make the camera point to at least one wall of the vestibule, and then the corridor, if any. Continue on, stopping where you would if you were actually walking through a home—statistically, most people would stop in the kitchen or family room. Program the camera to look around those spaces, possibly pausing in front of the fireplace, the library, a window (that is, actually staying and looking at one place for a few seconds). Wander through the living room toward the garden to see how the inside relates to the outside, something you will want to think about throughout the design process.

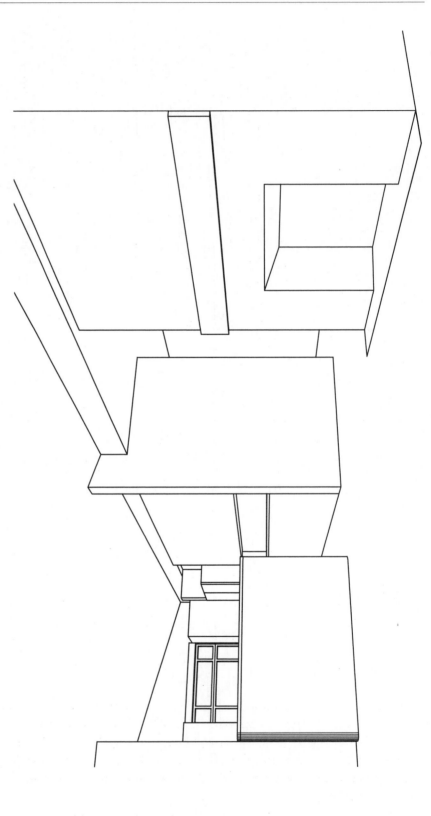

*Take a walk through your house. Does it feel like your home?*

If mastering these programs proves too time consuming or distracting, there is always professional help: specialists in this field (often also called upon by architects, real-estate developers, and city agencies) can render a specific project in 3-D. Don't be put off by the idea that most of their work seems to be larger and more complex; they are perfectly equipped to model your house quickly and fairly inexpensively.

It will help if you use vector-based CAD software such as DXF files (Autodesk Drawing Interchange/Exchange Format). Because these files will then become the basis of a professional digital 3-D model, be careful that the information is absolutely correct. The 3-D specialist will then build his model of your house using the contours from your files and add the rest.

Generally, you will receive photos of various parts of the model or a computer file of a movie—the walk-through—that can be viewed on any personal computer (using Windows Media Player or QuickTime). You could visit the specialist in person and be present at the screen for the walk-through, and ask to view various parts of the house. It can become quite exhilarating and, again, a consuming activity. Remember, these captivating tools and images are a minuscule part of the whole endeavor. There is still much work ahead.

## The Least You Need to Know

- Because you can't make a life-size "practice" version of your home, build scale models to get a feel for how it looks in 3-D.
- Create models of the entire house in small scale and use larger scale for individual spaces and features.
- Add model figures and take photographs to further establish a sense of your home in real space.
- Try working with computer programs that let you walk through your home before it's even built.

# Chapter 13

# Can I Blow Your House Down?

## In This Chapter

- ◆ Wood, paper, rock: choosing your materials
- ◆ Roofs and foundations
- ◆ Making materials fit your design (and vice-versa)

Everyone remembers the story of the three little pigs and the wolf that huffed and puffed until he blew all their houses down but one …

In fact, nothing about your house is more important than what it's made of. This will define the way it looks, how much it costs to build and maintain, how well it stands up to time and the elements, how it interacts with the land on which it stands, and how it feels to live in. Inside and out, the materials you select for your house will be a major determining feature in its design.

## Understanding Different Materials

The more you know and understand about the various materials available in building your home, the more intelligently—and confidently—you will select them. We encourage you to look beyond your initial inclinations, investigate the possibilities, and discover what works best for *you*.

### Wood

Wood burns. Wood dries, bends, warps, rots, splits. Consequently, all wood used in a building must be treated to withstand the elements and ensure the safety and security of your structure, particularly (but not only) when used on the exterior.

The wood most commonly used for construction, of course, is called lumber, which is cut in beams and, ideally, combines strength with elasticity. The wood needs to have some give in it, as this allows you, among other things, to notice changes if it begins to fail over the years. Douglas fir is especially good for this, as it is for exteriors; it is a strong, hardy wood that, because of its wide availability, is also affordable. (Scraps from Douglas fir are made into plywood, which is usually used for the sheathing in walls.)

**Design Tip**

A wood's grain has the greatest influence on its appearance: a slight grain, like poplar, is best painted, while intriguing woods like cherry or walnut take well to oils or staining. We advise you to visit suppliers and see for yourself, though these samples will usually be coated in polyurethane, which can affect appearance. Ask for samples of about 12"×12" and ⅜" thickness. This is true for any wood veneers you plan to use for your interior. How a veneer is cut (along the grain or against the grain) will affect its look, and you want to see as many as possible before making a selection.

**Architerms**

**Joinery** options concern the various ways in which boards in the siding of a house are joined together. They can overlap, for instance, or be held together via tongue-and-groove, or can be built either horizontally or vertically.

Wood siding, often found in New England and the upper Midwest, makes for a traditional look, though is easily combined with a modern (or postmodern) design. Cedar withstands weather like no other wood, and requires no painting or sealing, though both, of course, are possible: remember that stain penetrates and enhances the wood; paint covers it. Cedar is golden when cut, and ages into a fine, ashen gray-black. Different *joinery* options allow for varying visual effects as well. You could, for instance, apply shingles, in which small pieces overlap one another; or use siding, placing boards vertically or horizontally against the exterior wall. Horizontal siding, called "clapboard," offers further options—either overlapping or flush. (A note regarding vertical siding: usually this is made of boards and battens, which prevent water from creeping in.)

*Three examples of joinery used in wood siding construction.*

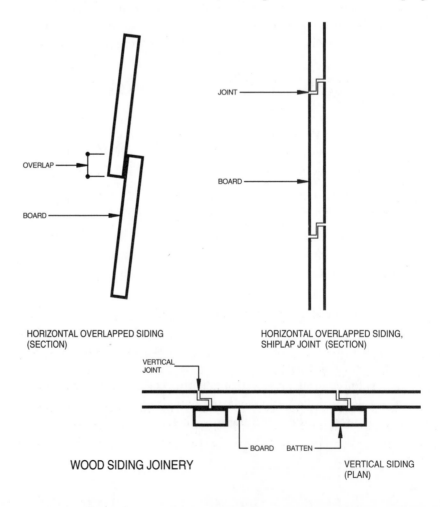

A new interest in log houses has inspired production of log-house kits, which use timber, a thicker wood than lumber, constructed with a post-and-beam technique. It's a specific look, and one you should consider only if that's a look that feels like "home" to you.

### Flashpoint

"Warm, dry, and noble" is how Samuel Mockbee described his goals for the homes he and his students at Auburn University's Rural Studio have designed for poverty-stricken regions in rural Alabama. Mockbee, who founded the program, inspired his students to follow a "scavenging" approach to architecture, using any materials available to build his "warm, dry, and noble" homes: tiles, hay bales, old steel and plastic signs, glass bottles, and other unlikely items. "Everybody wants the same thing," he believed, "not only a warm, dry room, but a shelter for the soul."

Mockbee passed away in 2002, but his project continues. You might find yourself inspired! Check the Rural Studios website at www.ruralstudio.com for more information.

Most often, people paint or stain the wood on the interiors of their homes, which makes poplar and pine particularly suitable. Look for dried wood; if it's too moist, it will bend. Moldings, baseboards, chair rails, windowsills, doorframes—all can be produced well in poplar and painted or stained to suit. (Again, you are probably best off painting a less-interesting grain.) The lowly knotted pine is actually en vogue and fetches premium prices for floors and furniture.

A finer veneer, called furniture-grade, comes nicely mounted on plywood sheets, which keeps it from warping as much as it might as solid wood. Most showrooms will offer five basic finishes, but there are several more available; check with a cabinetmaker.

### Design Tip

Insider's secret: when building a porch or deck, always build "bark-side up". (You can determine this by noting the width of the rings: they get wider as you get closer to the outside—bark— of the tree.) This keeps the planks from cupping when they eventually warp; instead, it they will bend in the other direction so water drains off.

## Stone

Much that is said of wood is also true of stone, although it is, of course, far more durable, less flexible, and more expensive to work with. Like wood, though, stone has been used for architectural exteriors, interiors, and structural framework—even as beams (as in the Parthenon)—since time immemorial. Like wood, the many varieties and colors and patterns make for countless inspiring possibilities. And like wood, the ways in which those colors and patterns appear—the deep green, white, or ruddy tint and translucent veins of marble; the gray or black of granite; the cool gray-blue of New England fieldstone or slate—are often a result of the way the stone was.

Different stone requires different kinds of finish, though most do require one finish or another. Remember that the higher the polish, the more impermeability the stone will have: think of the difference between the slickness of polished marble when it is wet, versus the rough texture of a raw boulder in a landscape.

> **Flashpoint**
>
> Granite, limestone, and marble are the most commonly used stones in architecture, though some people use "marble" as a generic term to include other, similar-looking stones like quartzite, which in fact has more crystals than true marble. You can look up most stones on the Internet to get a sense of how they will look either rough or polished, and according to the directions of their cuts.

Stones that do not take well to polishing include flagstone, slate, bluestone, or sandstone, which are better choices when considering terraces, walkways (if recommended by manufacturer for exterior traffic application), and (depending on the look that you prefer and your susceptibility to slipping) interior floors. Even marble, which takes magnificently to high polish, is usually best "honed" when used on floors. A fall on marble can, to put it mildly, hurt—a lot. At the same time, to some degree, polishing protects the stone from moisture, which can, over time, cause cracks.

In practical terms, while certain celebrities have been known to decorate their entire home—even the ceilings—in stone, most of you will not be inclined to go that route. Generally speaking, stone is used as tile for floors or in 1¼-inch slabs for countertops.

Still, now is an exciting time to work with stone, thanks to recent developments in stonecutting, like laser-jet and water-jet, which have made it possible to create virtually anything. Talk to local stonecutters, even sculptors or artisans who work in this material, to get more of an idea of the kinds of detailed touches available.

Although stone is decidedly expensive, small accents here and there can add a luxurious, elegant, and calming feel to your home. Visit local quarries or stone fabricators, if you can; some people like to go and select the actual stone that will be used for their kitchen countertops, for instance, and the fabricators can actually trace the outline of your counter as you watch, so you are able to select the precise section of the stone.

## Brick

Brick comes in almost as many finishes as stone, and abundant choices in color. A brick wall ensures a warm house, especially when used as it is in Europe, 1½ inches thick. In the United States, brick is most frequently used as facing. Thermal brick, with holes of about ⅝", has also been developed that further improves the thermal rating of the walls (though if you were to use this material, you would still want to install an additional form of insulation).

Some tend to forget, however, that brick is really just baked clay and basically porous. Consequently, any brick used on the exterior (and this includes steps and pathways) should be covered with sealer, glaze, or stucco. (Though if you're going to pay for brick, why cover it with stucco?) Above all, you want to keep moisture from getting into the brick (or mortar); the greater the density of its surface, the better it will withstand moisture.

Similarly, when using brick for walkways or steps, watch that the joints are tight. Even so, be prepared for expensive repairs at some point: whenever you have mortar looking at the sky, you can expect rain and moisture to wash the mortar away or to infiltrate the brick, eventually causing it to expand and split. When water gets into the surface and freezes, it expands; this breaks the mortar. If it also gets into the brick, say, through a hairline crack, it does the same to the brick.

By contrast, highly glazed brick is almost as impermeable as glass, and the effects of using highly glazed, colored brick on the exterior of your home can be remarkable. Inside, too, glazed brick can add a touch of warmth (especially if left its natural color) or whimsy (particularly if *not* left in its natural state, but glazed in a brilliant or rich, deep hue). For aesthetic purposes, it is best to use smaller-sized brick in the interiors, or the effect can be overpowering. And in all cases, take care (or ensure that your contractors take care) that mortar is evenly and neatly applied, with the thinnest joints you can get. A sloppy brick-laying job shows.

None of which is to say that brick is a material to stay away from. It affords some of the best insulation; it can be laid in decorative patterns of one or many colors (allowing you to design unique ornaments literally into the exterior walls of your house); and, as the seventeenth-century brick homes that have lined the canals of Amsterdam since Rembrandt's day attest, brick endures.

## Aluminum

Like vinyl, aluminum is an easy-to-handle material with virtually no maintenance requirements. It's easy to cut and comes prefinished: you apply it, you're done. It is not the preferred material in terms of the investment value of your home, however, as its popularity pretty much peaked in the 1960s and has never quite risen to that level since. That said, it's harmless enough, extremely easy to care for, and cost-efficient. (Although there are some quite fancy cast aluminum panels available, like the polished aluminum used by Audi).

## Metals

It is not impossible to build a house of metal: metal-paneled warehouses, storage facilities, and (occasionally) shopping outlets are increasingly a part of the industrial landscape. But the materials are rarely found in residential buildings, largely because the cost savings come with volume—and a single-family house just doesn't use enough to make it worth while. And even if you were to use it, metal without proper insulation would be horrendous: you would bake in the sun and freeze in winter.

There are exceptions, however. A friend built a house not long ago in Sagaponack, New York, entirely of stainless steel. Or, that is, the exterior was steel; in counterbalance to the high-tech, industrial façade, golden cedar glows throughout the interior of the home. The materials were chosen in part to protect against the dampness of sea air, which tends to cause mildew, but also, of course, for their aesthetic effect: sunlight on the steel echoes the richness of the yellow wood within. Carefully selected insulation and an open floor plan keep the house warm without becoming stifling (as one might expect in a steel house), while traditional references to old American farmhouses, large windows, and skylights imbue it with an elegance that is as timeless as it is welcoming.

Renowned architect Richard Meier uses square metal panels on many of his structures, each panel covered with a ceramic finish, but the price for such a house would exceed anything except, perhaps, a house built entirely of glass or stone; you could expect to pay somewhere around $150 per square foot for such a façade.

On the interior, however, metal finds a host of uses, including room dividers, railings, stairs, banisters, and details like hinges or door handles.

Where metal can be put to particularly good use is in roofing materials, especially copper, zinc, or galvanized sheet metal. Some zinc roofing has a particular coating that allows it to weather as it ages, acquiring a green patina. For gutters and leaders, your first choice would be heavy-gauge copper. Alternatively, look to galvanized steel or painted steel. Aluminum and plastic (PVC) are satisfactory, but probably your least desirable choices; aluminum bends easily, and PVC is not the most attractive option.

Because metal loses energy immediately, it is less effective for window frames than vinyl. If you do choose to use metal frames, ask for "thermally broken" ones. Alternatively, wood *cladding* over metal frames (for windows as well as for doors) will protect you from feeling the cold when you touch them.

## Stucco and Plaster

Few building materials are as timeless as stucco and plaster, which for centuries have lined the inner and outer walls of homes throughout the world. Composed of Portland cement, sand, and water, both are usually applied over a hard backing, usually a metal *lath*.

Because the cement, sand, and water composition absorbs moisture from the air, it remains flexible and takes paint well. Textures can be designed from smooth to rough, so that the surface takes light in different ways, absorbing and refracting color across its surface. (Imagine the sun setting over red-orange stucco. You could think you were strolling along the cobblestone streets of Rome on a luminous August afternoon ….)

Interior architects and designers have also developed innovative ways of applying, coloring, and shaping plaster over the years, such as the medieval Venetian plastering technique, a way of creating texture through depth of color coated with a reflective finish. Venetian plastering adds an elegant, romantic atmosphere to a room, making it an ideal substitute for more expensive materials

**Design Don't**

Although hollow sheet metal is often used for many of these elements, it does not hold together well over the long term. Try to use the heaviest gauge you can afford.

**Architerms**

**Cladding** is a protective or insulating coating fixed to metal, usually under high pressure. Cladding can also mean siding, or covering, as in "glass-clad façade."

A **lath** is a metal mesh or wood strip, usually installed in rows as a support for tiles or plaster.

(such as marble or exotic woods); a fireplace wrapped in Venetian plaster lends a unique, welcoming, and exquisite touch to a standard living room. Painted stucco also bestows an inviting depth; it has the effect of looking more solid, so you feel truly anchored—at home in your home.

## Vinyl

Though cost-effective and quite popular in some areas, vinyl is not our first choice of material; it can look and feel cheap, and, as a petroleum product, it is counter to the growing trend of creating environmentally friendly buildings. It is not particularly safe in the face of fire hazards, it produces fumes, and because it is vulnerable to UV light, it can become brittle over time.

That said, you can't beat the price! The ease with which it can be worked makes it possible for many nonprofessionals to install it themselves—and to do so quickly and easily, as opposed to, say, putting up individual shingles, which have to be done one by slow and tedious one.

## Hardiplank Cement Board

A combination of cement powder and silica mixed with glues and water and cut into ½-inch thick boards, Hardiplank has become one of the most popular building materials in America (though it was first invented over 100 years ago by the Australian James Hardie Company). The material can be made to simulate wood siding (either painted or with imitation wood grain, though the latter isn't all that convincing), stucco, or stone.

Unlike its vinyl counterpart, Hardiplank (and other cement-board products) is fireproof and does not grow brittle, crack, or rot, which, along with its termite-resistance and affordable pricing, accounts for much of its popularity. It is, however, not without its downsides: Hardiplank is in fact so durable that, like uranium, it never goes away, making it an ecologically questionable material. The silica content makes it dangerous to work with, as inhaling silica dust can lead to lung disease. And though less expensive to use than wood, it is still more costly than vinyl.

## "Alternative" Materials

Eco-friendly materials are becoming more popular as the damage we have done to the earth becomes more of a concern, especially for parents of young children. While we take up this subject more specifically in Chapter 14, some materials are worth noting here:

◆ **Linoleum**—Linoleum is making a strong comeback with the interest in recyclables, as it is not PVC-based, but made, rather, from linseed oil and ground cork. Its poor stain-resistance, however, probably makes it best for laundry rooms, closets, and kids' playrooms (where the floor will get dirty and need to be replaced no matter what you do).

- **Cork**—Wine growers are starting to put plastic in their bottles. Home owners are putting cork along their walls and across their floors. Cork, obviously a renewable resource, provides excellent soundproofing (a plus with teenagers at home) and, if painted or sealed, lends a velvety, special feel and appearance to a wall.

- **Adobe**—An excellent material where rain is not a factor, adobe imparts the same finish as stucco, refracting and absorbing color beautifully. Made of sun-dried clay mixed with straw, the material is commonly used in the American Southwest (it has almost become a symbol of New Mexico); it would not work, unfortunately, in Portland, Seattle, or San Francisco.

- **Zinc**—Now being used for siding (it requires an expert to install), zinc gains heat much faster than wood, and so must be combined with other materials (wood, copper, or a combination).

# A Word on Roofs

Asphalt shingles are, hands down, the material of preference when it comes to roofing, as they offer the most durability and ease. And while zinc and copper can be exquisite, the prices are shocking. Round or half-round tiles are another option, but require extensive work: because American tiles lack the thickness of the European ones they need to be nailed over one another, one by one. For a fun effect, consider corrugated metals—the kind used on chicken coops. Laugh, if you will, but it has an unexpectedly pleasant effect.

# Foundation Materials

Anything built below ground level is subject to high physical pressure and to water infiltration, and, if above the frost line, but still underground, there will be additional pressure exerted by freezing water.

The house walls are anchored into foundations, which in turn are built securely into the ground. This connection to the ground is critical to the stability of the house; obviously, a secure connection to a weak ground is useless, as the house can slide atop (or with) a large piece of earth, as happens in typical severe mudslides.

> **Architerms**
>
> The bottom of the foundation is called the **footing**, while the vertical part is called the **foundation wall**.

To respond to these main concerns, as a basic principle, *footings* are made of concrete and the *foundation walls* are made of either concrete or concrete masonry units.

Foundations are generally built to size. The footings are made of "cast-in-place concrete," resting on undisturbed soil, and the foundation walls are built over them. The footings are continuous, carrying all along the perimeter of the house, while the foundation walls above them, while are mostly continuous, with occasional openings such as access doors and windows to the basement. All footings should be built on ground that is below the frost line.

Foundation walls of any materials require thermal insulation, protection from water infiltration, and a moisture barrier. It is also a good idea to drain the water from near the foundations and footings; the usual method is to install perforated drains close to the footing, in a gravel bed.

If you plan to have a basement in your home, you will probably use a concrete slab floor. In cases where there is no basement, a concrete floor slab is poured on the ground, over a gravel bed, with no space (basement or crawl space) beneath. This slab, known colloquially as a rat slab (due to its resistance to rodents), is in fact a requirement in some locales. Check any local regulations.

Depending on site conditions, it is also possible to build foundation walls of specially treated wood (*not* deck-type variety, but specifically grade-stamped for foundations), so long as it rests on concrete foundations. The detailing is more complex than typical wood framing, due to the extra pressure exerted by the earth. Though generally a cheaper material to use, treated wood is not, however, a totally inert material, and it requires timely inspections and repairs from water and termite damage. It also needs specific drainage solutions, different than other foundation materials.

> **Design Tip**
>
> Most homes have concrete footings with concrete masonry units above them. It is a more durable and practical solution ensuring the most strength for the expenditure of energy and money—considering that most homes have a usable basement, and most homeowners prefer to avoid having to deal with damaged wood.

# Making Sure Construction and Materials Work Together

Designing your own home gives you tremendous control, of course, but with that control come overwhelming options, choices, decisions, possibilities, and, as you toss them around, ideas. And then there's your budget.

Think of this as the "You Can't Always Get What You Want" section. Not everything is going to fit together the way you might wish it to: structural systems will inform the way you design your house, as will the environment in which you live. Is it usually very cold? Very wet? Ceramic and stone floors are lovely to look at, but in climates like Portland, Oregon, make for very cold bare feet for most of the year—unless you install radiant floor heating, in which case they are absolutely wonderful.

Think about the natural properties of the materials you wish to use, and the effects you hope to achieve, both on the inside and outside of your home. Brick isn't flexible like wood or steel; consequently, a steel archway will look quite different than a brick one, or even a wooden one. Flexibility is also crucial for the structure of your house: beams must be flexible or they could snap like icicles, suddenly and catastrophically, without warning. (Wood, by contrast, deforms before it collapses.)

Here again is where structural engineers, architects, and other professionals can give invaluable advice. Of course you want your home to be beautiful. But you also want it to last. Explore your options, and your reward will be having both.

## The Least You Need to Know

◆ Explore different materials to make the best choices for your home and lifestyle.

◆ Research the various properties, both physical and aesthetic, of wood, stone, vinyl, plaster, and other possible options before making your final decisions—you may find some surprises!

◆ Consider using renewable materials to help preserve the earth (and the health of your family).

◆ Talk to experts, who can guide you to achieving the results you're aiming for.

# Chapter 14

# Sustainable Living

## In This Chapter

◆ Going for the green

◆ Design, materials, and ideas

◆ Saving money, saving nature

◆ Other sources and information

With growing concern for the environment, more and more people are looking for ways to combine living well with preserving and protecting the earth— a trend increasingly noticeable in home building and design. Biodegradable and recyclable products such as paper and aluminum replace such chemicals as acrylic and formaldehyde, and, for reasons both ecological and economic (and often, in accordance with the law), people are looking to make their homes more energy efficient, situating them as much as possible in the best position to the sun and wind. Although not everyone can or will build an entirely "green" house, we do encourage you to take whatever environmentally friendly measures you can.

## Why Thinking Green Matters

Poisons lurk in the corners of your home. Formaldehyde-filled carpets, plywood, and insulation; chemical-laden air fresheners; and volatile paints rich in organic compounds create toxic fumes that penetrate the very air you breathe all day—not out in the polluted city streets, but in your family and living rooms. Political concerns aside, U.S. reliance on foreign oil is crippling many of us as energy prices skyrocket, and drilling for oil wells endangers many of our natural resources. Landfills threaten the future integrity of our planet and some of our most precious and delicate ecosystems.

Is there a cure? Well, no, not really. But we can all help lessen the damage by recycling, conserving energy, and using fewer chemically tainted products. And building "green" *sustainable architecture* as much as possible can make a huge contribution, while lowering energy use (and cost) over the long term. In many instances, it can also help stimulate local economies and small businesses—a nice way to start off in a new neighborhood.

### Architerms

Sustainable architecture seeks to have minimum impact on the environment through the use of minimally polluting or recycled materials and moderated energy expenditure. A fair amount of information about sustainable architecture (and helpful links to other resources) can be found at en.wikipedia.org/wiki/Sustainable_architecture.

# Considerations for Environmentally Friendly Design

To a large extent, environmentally friendly design begins with the cardinal rule of real estate: "location, location, location!" Where and how you situate your house can heavily influence its energy needs, from solar-generated heat to garden-generated shade—and then some. A very rural house, for instance, will possibly require more extensive (and un-green) transport of materials than will a centrally located one. On the other hand, you may be able to use local materials, such as stone and wood from your own or other nearby lots (green). However, when using materials from your own or a neighbor's land, take care not to strip the area of shrubs and trees that maintain the earth integrity (un-green). Cut too many, and the land could slide!

How strong are the winds where you live? How cold are the winters, how hot the summers, how heavy the snow in mid-December? Orient your house accordingly: away from cold winds in cold climates, toward them in hotter ones. In the Midwest, for instance, you can lose a lot of heat with Northern exposure; whereas in the South, you'll want as much as possible to help keep your house (and yourself) cool, and to lighten the air-conditioning load. Again, double-glazed windows are helpful here, as well.

Also give some thought to the outside of your house: your garden landscape can also influence the climate of your home. Trees and trellises bedecked with climbing plants will shade in summer and allow sunlight (warmth) to pass between their branches in the winter. We're also particularly fond of using *light shelves* above the windows, about a foot deep, which reflect light upward and then, in turn, refract the light from the ceiling. Light shelves have been shown to increase the depth of daylight in a room enough that in many cases, indoor lighting becomes unnecessary during daylight hours. Paradoxically, these same shelves work to shade a room when the sun is higher during the summer season.

### Flashpoint

Proper layout + thought-out orientation + environmentally friendly materials + assembly = efficient, eco-friendly home design.

## Architerms

**Light shelves** are installed either on the interior or exterior of a window shortly below the top portion. These shelves shade the lower window while manipulating sunlight up and into the room toward the ceiling, from where it bounces back to the walls and floor. Depending on the season (and the position of the sun), they can add both cooling and heating to a room in addition to enhancing the depth and quality of light.

According to a study conducted by the Florida Solar Energy Center in the late 1990s, energy savings can increase as much as 50 percent by using light shelves in place of horizontal blinds.

## Design Tip

When situating your house on your site (also see Chapter 3), note the directions of light and wind, as well as snow load, where relevant. To obtain the best and most efficient energy savings, you will need to take these factors into account when planning your layout.

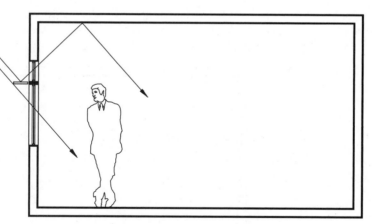

LIGHT SHELF

ONE LIGHT SHELF OUTSIDE THE SPACE

ALLOWS LESS DIRECT LIGHT NEAR THE WINDOW
AND PROJECTS LIGHT INTO THE SPACE, CLOSER TO WINDOW.

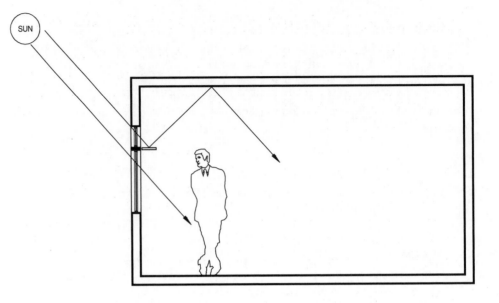

**LIGHT SHELF**

ONE LIGHT SHELF INSIDE THE SPACE

ALLOWS MORE DIRECT LIGHT NEAR THE WINDOW
AND PROJECTS LIGHT INTO THE SPACE.

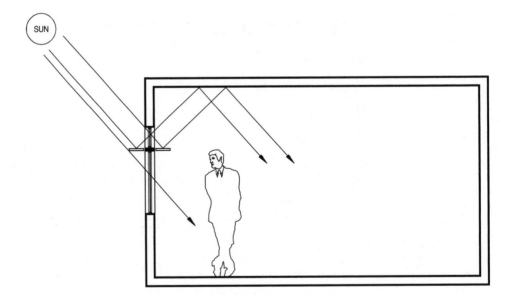

**LIGHT SHELVES**

TWO LIGHT SHELVES - 1 INSIDE & 1 OUTSIDE THE SPACE

ALLOWS LESS DIRECT LIGHT NEAR THE WINDOW
AND PROJECTS MORE LIGHT DEEPER INTO THE SPACE.

*Light shelves.*

# Considering Environmentally Friendly Materials

These days, new, eco-friendly materials seem to pop up on the market every week, with the added benefit that, as such materials grow more available and more popular, prices tend to become more competitive. Some of New York's most coveted apartment buildings are "green," and developers plan to continue the trend, *The New York Times* reported in August 2006.

There is an undeniable financial premium attached to building green (though the big-picture premium is arguably significantly higher if you don't), but increasing demand for renewable and biodegradable products are helping to bring those costs down, as is legislation in several states that actually requires builders to take "green" measures in their constructions. Hopefully you soon won't have to make a choice between building for the environment and building for your budget.

As a general rule, when it comes to materials, you will want to focus on ...

◆ Destroying as few trees as possible.

◆ Recycling.

◆ Reducing the amount of transport required for the use of certain materials; "Made in China" usually means "lower priced," but it also means "traveled a long way on fossil fuels."

◆ Supporting local industries.

◆ Protecting local land.

> **Design Tip**
> Also see Chapter 13 for additional information about the pros and cons of various materials and their effect on the environment.

## Wood

One option for those who particularly like wood is to use products from organizations like the Rainforest Alliance, which plant trees faster than they cut them. Again, these certified woods, as they're called, cost more, but think of it as money invested in the future. Alternatively, look for reclaimed wood products: beams, floors, and even siding is often available. By searching eBay, we've found enough antique floorboards (salvaged from other renovations or—sadly—demolitions) to cover several rooms. And when possible, if using new wood on outside installations, select cedar.

Any wood you use will have been (or will need to be) weatherproofed. Previously, this was done using CCA (chromated copper arsenate). These days, it is possible to buy CCA-free lumber, and we recommend it. These products cannot be used everywhere, but information describing their use and limitations is generally available wherever they are sold. Plywood is also now available without formaldehyde, which is replaced with a soy-based adhesive.

> **Design Don't**
> Steer away from formaldehyde-treated products any chance you get. Studies show that the chemical is even more damaging to humans than it is to the earth. Formaldehyde appears in your home in such common items as carpet, curtains, plywood, and home fresheners.

## Aluminum and Other Materials

It may surprise you to discover that aluminum is actually considered "acceptable" by environmentalists. In fact, it's extremely amenable to recycling—although it requires enormous amounts of energy to manufacture and therefore needs to be recycled several times to compensate. Still, it far surpasses most plastic and plastic-based materials, many of which emit toxic fumes. Here, too, though, progress is being made as manufacturers seek out alternatives to plastic, especially for flooring. If you do use plastic, however, try to make sure it is labeled for environmental preservation.

More attention is also now being paid to concrete, particularly with high-ash content, or mixed with other materials like recycled glass. High-ash concrete compares favorably with regular concrete for use as slabs for structural elements like underfloors. Glass and concrete mixtures can, depending on your own taste, also be incorporated into outdoor structures, from garden paths to terraces and garden walls.

Other recycled materials such as steel and recovered wood are, of course, equally desirable, and we encourage using them. Crushed stone can also be obtained from demolitions for use in both interior and exterior parts of the house, as well as in your landscaping designs.

## Exotic Options

For those who take the environmental impact of home construction seriously, some less-common but highly effective and attractive options include adobe, straw bales, and even grass.

### Design Tip

Visit the website of the extraordinary Rural Studios at Auburn University (www. ruralstudio.com/) or have a look at the books documenting their work and projects for some real inspiration!

*Rural Studio: Samuel Mockbee and an Architecture of Decency*, Andrea Oppenheimer Dean and Timothy Hursley, Princeton Architectural Press, February 2002.

*Proceed and Be Bold: Rural Studio After Samuel Mockbee*, Andrea Oppenheimer Dean and Timothy Hursley, Princeton Architectural Press, 2005.

*Samuel Mockbee and the Rural Studio: Community Architecture*, Samuel Mockbee, David Moos (Editor), Gail Trechsel (Editor), Birmingham Museum of Art, October 2003.

Adobe is, of course, especially well-known in the Southwest, where it has become an architectural trademark. Walls in adobe homes are essentially made of mud, formed, and dried into bricks, with straw added for extra binding strength. These are then laid using additional mud and covered with plaster or stucco for added insulation, protection, and strength.

And insulated they are: adobe houses retain warmth and cool extremely well, even without mechanical help.

Straw bales also provide surprisingly efficient insulation at unbelievably affordable cost. The University of New Mexico's Albuquerque Teacher's Institute website offers substantial information on straw-bale homes, including descriptions of their environmental benefits and fire resistance (reportedly superior to conventional building materials!) at www.unm.edu/~abqteach/ArchiCUs/99-02-08.htm.

Perhaps less practical (especially for suburban homes), but no less worth mentioning, are grass roofs. Done properly, these, too, provide excellent insulation and do not get as hot as common asphalt shingles.

## Watching Your Accents

It's increasingly possible to create a fully ecologically sound home (or close to it). Most stores now stock paints free of volatile oils or compounds (the stuff that smells). Generally, aim for water-based paints (latex), using no drying agents or formaldehyde. Maggie Wood (www.Maggiewood.com) offers consulting on an assortment of ecologically friendly lime-based and milk-based paints.

For lighting, we (and the experts) recommend using compact fluorescents as much as possible. A 23-watt compact fluorescent, for instance, easily stands in for a 100-watt regular bulb.

In addition, they'll work a lot harder for a lot less energy: though compact fluorescents cost more per piece, that price difference is made up within a few hundred hours of use—a mere pittance when you think that they last some 5,000–10,000 hours. (A normal incandescent bulb is usually good for 500 to 800 hours.) Though less efficient than compact fluorescents, halogen lights also surpass the life span of incandescents, at an energy savings of some 15 percent.

> **Architerms**
> Rather than looking at **wattage**, which essentially only tells you what the bulb will use, look for information about the **lumens**, which, put simply, measure how much light actually falls on a given area.

The Department of Building for Seattle, Washington, developed a program for sustainable building in 2000—the country's first. Informative brochures, educational materials, and a comprehensive website combine consumer tips, information, and advice with inspiring ideas. They can advise you via e-mail or phone, or you can write to them at this address:

**Sustainable Building Program**
700 Fifth Avenue, Suite 4900
Seattle, WA 98104-5004
www.seattle.gov/sustainablebuilding
(206) 684-8600

> **Flashpoint**
> Various additional websites serve as centers for manufacturers of green building products. Two we recommend:
> oikos.com/green_products/index.php
> build.recycle.net/exchange/index.html

Ultimately, of course, going the environmental route is a personal choice, and one that can be taken to varying degrees. It is, however, a choice we strongly support.

## The Least You Need To Know

- Building "green" is better for your health—and for the future of the earth.
- Substantially reduce your own energy consumption—and, consequently, costs—by focusing on energy-efficient construction methods and materials.
- As demand for eco-friendly construction increases, materials and methods are becoming more and more affordable—good news for everyone.

# Part 5

# Decisions, Decisions

In this part, we will look at your house almost as if it were a living being: its veins, its arteries, are its electrical, plumbing, and HVAC (heating, ventilation, and air conditioning) systems. And its heart? The kitchen, of course, which is the heart of any home, and along with that, the baths.

While much of this work, especially the plumbing and wiring, is best done in concert with an expert, you should have an overall understanding not only of how these systems operate in your home, but how they influence (and are influenced by) the design.

And here, too, we'll give you a couple of extra tips to inspire you and bring a touch of luxury to life in your future home.

# Setting Up the Center

## In This Chapter

- ◆ Water, water everywhere
- ◆ Getting wired
- ◆ HVAC basics

There was a time when designing—and building—a house involved little more than determining walls, doors, windows, and a roof. None of us would be likely to want to return to those times: the miracles of indoor plumbing and the technological marvel of electricity can practically be categorized as "survival needs" in our culture. Which would you pick—the smaller house with light and running water, or the 45-room mansion on a 75-acre plot…without?

Inside the center core of your house—within the walls, out of view—the main arterial system is at work, controlling and providing water, electricity, heat, cool air, and the power to do your laundry and watch *Friends* and *Seinfeld* reruns at the same time. If these systems function well—if you get what you need when and where you need it—the old adage "out of sight, out of mind" will certainly apply. If not, you'll find yourself glaring at the walls, wondering whether you shouldn't rip them down and redo all the systems until you get it right.

Here's how to make it go smoothly the first time.

## Plumbing: What To Have and Where

Your whole house needs pipes, and not just for kitchen and bath. You may decide to build a wet bar in the living or family room, or a laundry room separate from the kitchen. If you plan to use your backyard, you'll want an outdoor faucet (especially if you have kids), and for gardeners, a sprinkler system is handy and efficient. And depending on your choice of heating systems, you may need water for this as well—especially if you're planning on having heated floors (a delicious detail that, if you live in a colder climate, you will appreciate every winter morning for the rest of your life).

Where does your water go?

- Baths
- Garage
- Laundry
- Wet bar
- Kitchen
- Outdoor faucet or watering system
- Basement
- Heating systems
- Sauna

And don't forget drains! You'll need them especially in the garage, baths, and cellar!

Consider, too, suggestions noted earlier in Chapter 8 for setting up a room now that can become a bathroom later by affixing a fixture and uncapping a cap.

However, what you choose and how you use it will be determined in part by the water-supply system you have in place. Those who draw water from a private well will want to be especially conscious of conserving water (though we all should)—another way that sprinkler systems for your lawn and garden can be beneficial. Irrigation hoses feed water directly to the roots.

Other handy options you might consider include these:

- Elevated cisterns for rainwater are expensive, but save water in the long run.

- Drains and pipes can be built to manipulate the flow of water over your land. (Consult a plumber, landscape architect or engineer for this.)

- Use the conditions of your site to manage the flow of water to and around your home.

**Design Tip**

The best plumber is the one who ...

- Doesn't cross the lines (so that you get hot water out of the cold water tap)
- Insulates all the pipes.
- Organizes the pipes so there are no cuts in the structure.

If you find a plumber who has done work like this anywhere, hire him!

# Electrical and Wiring Systems

Rule one: You can never, ever, have enough electrical outlets.

Addendum to rule one: The number of outlets needed in a standard home is increasing with the use of battery-operated gadgets that require recharging and the number of cool things people keep inventing.

Think for a moment about what you've got plugged in, right now, in the home you live in. It's not just the TV, the toaster, the fridge, the microwave, and all your lamps anymore. There's the computer, the printer, the scanner, the battery charger for the cell phone, the remote phone, the stereo, the VCR, the DVD player, and the battery chargers for the mp3 players and the digital camera.

There's the electric grill, the food processor, the electric blanket, the electric fan. Even the bathroom is on overload: the blow dryer, electric toothbrush, electric razor, heated curlers. And don't forget the coffee grinder, espresso maker, bread machine, answering machine, fax machine, security alarm, and digital clock-radio your little brother gave you just before you left for college.

And outlets. You need outlets. Take an inventory of what you need in each room. Don't forget bedside lamps, the bedside phone, and all TVs and appliances. Where will you keep your cell phone to recharge it—on the kitchen counter? On your dresser? By the door? Is your washing machine in the kitchen, or somewhere else? (Kitchens, by the way, require an outlet about every eight feet at the counter, minimum.)

Along with your electric system you'll want to organize your cable needs. TV only? TV and data? What rooms? How many? Generally, we prefer cable or DSL to wireless. True, the latter is convenient—but be careful with your data; data encryption is only so secure. Glass-fiber optic cable, already being laid down in some European cities, is likely to be in your telecom technology future: it's faster, by far, than any system currently in place.

# HVAC

Frankly, we think air conditioning is best suited only to families (or couples) who can agree on a bedroom temperature. Reality, however, not always being ideal, and bedroom temperatures rarely a reason to wed, we'll assume you can work out any differences between (or among) you on your own.

## Understanding HVAC

HVAC (heating, ventilation, and air conditioning) simply involves the climate of your home: how hot or cool it is, and how fresh the air is. Properly designed, it can also have strong bearing on your energy use and costs.

Central heating, by far the most popular choice, works by heating air, water, or steam and distributing the heat (or cold) via a series of pipes and ducts positioned in the walls throughout the house. The warmth (or cooler air) then passes through vents, usually positioned either beneath a window or in the floor.

Selecting the optimal method—air, steam, or water—is best done in consultation with a plumbing or HVAC consultant (also known as a mechanical, electrical, and plumbing engineer, or MEP engineer). An MEP engineer can review your personal needs, preferences, and budget and give you personalized advice. Often, combining various systems provides the best solution.

**Design Tip**

Keep ducts as short and straight as possible. Air prefers smooth travel, and wherever it finds a corner, it will create turbulence until it finds its way. That turbulence inhibits the efficiency of your HVAC system.

It's easy to forget about ventilation when planning your home, though you will regret it if you do. Ventilation not only provides an exchange of air and keeps the air in the house from growing stale (or toxic), but helps to remove odors and humidity in kitchens and baths. Proper ventilation also protects against mold spores, especially in winter. These can cause rotting both inside and outside your home (and in some people, serious allergic reactions can develop). Attics and basements are particularly vulnerable, especially in wet climates or in homes with vinyl siding, which doesn't allow the exterior walls to "breathe." Also, be careful not to contradict the exhaust fan in a bath or kitchen window with a ceiling fan above.

Ventilation possibilities range from simple fans and windows to stack vents, fans with ducts, and fan systems set to timers, sensors, and other controllers. Another good option is an exhaust air heat pump, an integrated HVAC system that combines water heating and ventilation, or (particularly for colder climates), air-to-air heat exchangers (AAHX).

> ### Flashpoint
>
> The goal of any ventilation system is simple—out with the old and in with the new: you could say that your ventilation system is the lungs of your home.

## Duct and Cover

A few cautionary notes regarding ducts: They can attract or trap rodents. When a captured mouse dies in the system, the fumes of the carcass can infiltrate your ventilating systems. Ducts also get dirty and harbor mildew. They must be cleaned out regularly for effectiveness and health. They are, however, the most affordable and among the most frequently used options available.

Alternatively, you might look into ductless so-called "mini-split" systems—an ideal alternative that functions something like a cross between window-installed air conditioning and a central air system. Mini-splits allow you to regulate temperature by zone, but without unsightly window appliances.

These systems utilize an outdoor "compressor" unit, which sends a refrigerant to *evaporators* installed inside each room, usually near the ceiling. (Though it is possible to use mini-splits for heating, they are most commonly used as cooling systems.) Refrigerant- and suction-tubing link the indoor units with the outdoor compressor through a small opening in the wall.

Mini-splits have received high ratings from energy conservation groups, saving as much as 30 percent of the energy consumption of central (duct) systems, according to the U.S. Department of Energy. However, they cost more to operate than do duct systems, installation is complicated, and they are more obtrusive, aesthetically speaking, than are central air systems. The Department of Energy offers substantial information on ductless systems at www.eere.energy.gov/consumer/ a useful source of information regarding energy efficiency throughout your home.

## Passive Assistance

But even with all these technological possibilities (originating, actually, in ancient Rome), and assuming that you and your loved ones have by now come to an agreement on blankets and room temperatures, you'll still probably want to reduce your heating and air conditioning needs as much as possible to conserve energy and costs. We strongly recommend taking passive measures that will keep the house from overheating, like a white roof to reflect heat, especially in hot climes. Fortunately, nature lends a helping hand: trees and shrubs around your home provide shade in the hotter months, but lose their leaves in winter, allowing sunlight and warmth into your home.

Ceiling fans also help to control temperature—especially if you plan to have high ceilings—and not only in summer or in warmer regions. When heat gets trapped above—as it tends to do, especially in winter—fans circulate the warmth back down into the living levels of the house. (And of course, we assume you have already made arrangements for double-glazed windows, adequate insulation, an appropriate exterior material—or skin—for your particular climate, and so on.

If you live in an especially hot zone, keeping a cross breeze through the house can make a world of difference in comfort: go back and check your design to ensure that you've situated enough windows on opposing sides of the house, and on as many walls of each room as possible. Or add a calming and poetic touch by placing reflecting pools around the house or in the atrium to cool the air.

# Designing Your HVAC Systems

Once you've incorporated energy-efficient ideas into your plan, those who squabble over hot and cold will appreciate the idea of *zoning*—that is, controlling temperatures in different rooms independently of the others. Hotels work this way, for instance: the guy in room 208 could have his air conditioner blowing while he performs his push-ups in the morning, while the one down the hall in 205 is snug beneath his goose-down comforter with the heat cranked up to 70.

Ideally, your home would work on the same principle, but the costs are substantial, and unless you're renting out the various rooms to others, probably more of an investment than you'll want to make. (It is, however, an investment, as the savings in energy costs over time could be significant: why heat the whole house when you're only using three rooms?)

How you choose to split the HVAC zones is entirely up to you (and your budget), of course, but a typical option would be to divide the private and public sections of the house, or upstairs and downstairs. While this still won't allow for individualized temperature settings, it will conserve considerable energy, since as a general rule, the public and private areas are only used simultaneously for limited periods during the course of a day.

However, if you've created an open, flowing design for your interior, with few doorways and a more loft-like feel, splitting zones will be virtually impossible. If you're willing to compromise on the airiness of the space, glass walls or doorways will allow you to keep most of the sense of openness and interaction while still closing off the individual spaces. Heavy curtains, removed in summer months, perhaps, also help delineate space while providing extra warmth and insulation in the winter.

**Design Tip**

Create zones for air conditioning and heating use—as many as you can afford. You will not only save money on energy costs down the line, but find day-to-day living much more comfortable.

**Flashpoint**

Once again—go back through all your stages: have you added or subtracted anything to accommodate plumbing, electric, or HVAC?

First check that all changes do not conflict with your "ideal house" program, and that you are still on budget. Then if necessary, resolve any conflicts before proceeding, revising your floor plans, elevations, sections, and models accordingly.

## The Least You Need To Know

♦ Plan your water pipes and electrical systems carefully before you begin construction.

♦ Install more outlets than you think you need. Chances are, you'll need them.

♦ Develop the best HVAC system for your needs an MEP engineer.

♦ Consider creating "climate zones" throughout your house for optimal, more personalized distribution of warm and cool air. (This system, however, works only if doors separate the zones.)

# Chapter 16

# Kitchens and Baths

## In This Chapter

- ◆ Getting your kitchen in place
- ◆ Appliances and equipment
- ◆ Plumbing—do it once, do it right
- ◆ Your bath is your castle?

They are the two rooms no home can do without, the two essentials to which most of us pay the least attention. Or at least, we used to; in the past couple of decades, kitchens, once reserved for servants and, later, for heat-and-eat TV dinners, have taken on an increasingly large role as the "heart of the house." And according to *The New York Times*, bathrooms are now beginning to follow suit (trend-watchers, pay attention).

In an era of working couples where one or both inevitably will be working late at least one night a week, morning rituals have, apparently, become "couples time." Of course, his and hers baths will always be popular, but the idea of bathroom as an actual *room* is catching on. Still, however simple or elaborate you choose to be, be sure that the designs that you come up with are the ones that will work best for *you*.

## Kitchens

Kitchens have—or should have—a certain rhythm, a rhyme and reason to the way they work and the way you work in them. Ideally you will create a sequence of spaces from the work areas, where foods are prepared and put together, to service, either at a kitchen table or in another room. This involves thinking (again) in zones, from the various preparatory stages (chopping the onion, cooking the onion, pouring the onion onto the platter, bringing the platter to the table) to final presentation. The best kitchens allow for all stages of interaction between cook and guest.

Often, too, this goes beyond simply making a family dinner. As we've started spending more and more time in kitchens, the uses and purposes of our kitchens have expanded: we pay bills there, so we need a small office space; we watch TV there, so we need a television conveniently placed (preferably not using up precious counter space) and a remote. Given a big enough bar or tabletop, children may do homework there. With so much activity, lighting, too, gets more attention than usual, and comfort—not just cuisine—becomes a priority.

### Design Don't

Don't let these rooms sink—or eat—your budget! Keep an eye out as you go: these two rooms can absorb an inordinate proportion of your planned costs.

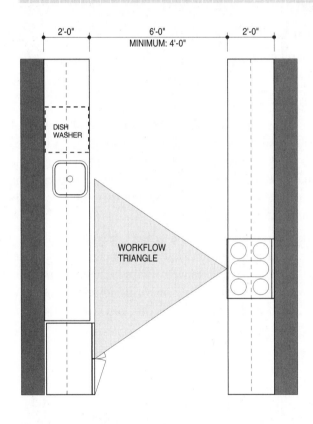

KITCHEN LAYOUT: GALLEY

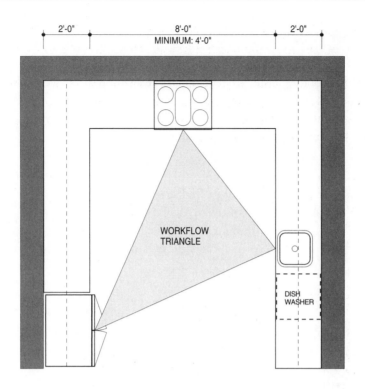

KITCHEN LAYOUT: 'C' SHAPE

*Kitchen layout options*

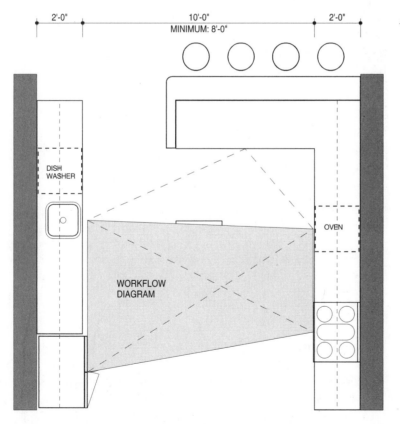

KITCHEN LAYOUT: 'C' SHAPE WITH BAR
ISLAND POSSIBLE

## Organizing Spaces

Once you understand the way your kitchen will work with your own lifestyle, it becomes easier to develop the design for the space itself. A shopping list of cabinets is only useful after you form a sense of the structural makeup of the kitchen. Ergonomics also may figure in: how high are the countertops? How low are the cupboards and shelves?

In fact, we're not the only people to point this out. The folks at Ikea make the same observation on their website and in their kitchen catalogues. If you have Internet access, you can find several valuable tips—even a program for kitchen design—at www.ikea.com. While we still would steer you away from prefab plans, understanding the basics and being able to try out different possibilities as you develop your design are invaluable in building a successful custom kitchen.

## Choosing Cabinets and Counters

In the end, what you want from your cabinets is pretty simple: they should provide the most possible storage space while allowing you the most possible space to work in and interact with guests. Typically, this means lining them along the walls, placing countertops beneath, and setting a second line of cabinets, resting on the floor, under that. (By and large, the heights and sizes of countertops and cabinets are standardized. If you or members of your family are particularly small or tall or wheelchair-bound, you will need to adjust accordingly, remembering that it is always easier to make a countertop *higher*, by adding vertical support, than it is to make it *lower*, by cutting down.)

You may want to add an island in your kitchen, or a "peninsula," so to speak— a countertop attached to the wall at one end. Strategically placed between the doorway and the stove, such bars are handy not just for placing prepared food to be carried into the dining area, but as informal gathering places for breakfast or snacks. Cabinets placed beneath the counter add to its usefulness, of course, since somehow kitchens never seem to have enough storage space.

> **Design Tip**
>
> Consider maximizing your use of lower (floor) cabinets rather than upper (wall) cabinets, which are more difficult to access. Anything above five feet high will require finding the ladder, then finding a place to store the ladder, and so on. Yes, you want storage, but if you have to jump through hoops to reach it, will you even use it?

Selecting cabinets that appeal to you aesthetically is, obviously, a decision only you can make. But with so much furniture in the kitchen (think about it: it's quite a lot), you might consider glass cabinet doors or doors with panel construction, breaking down the mass into small elements, visually. Too much going on along the walls can make you feel like you're sitting in a room with a big Mack truck parked there.

Cabinet height is another consideration, again partly based on design preferences, but also with your own day-to-day comforts in mind. For maximum storage, they should go straight to the ceiling, but, again, the upper shelves will be more difficult to reach. Alternatively, you can keep the space at the top of the cabinets free and open, maybe placing lights or displaying collections of tea pots, pitchers, antique cookie tins, and the like.

But it's the appearance of the cabinets (and counters) that will likely matter to you most, combined with their durability. To some extent, you may need to compromise between using the strongest material, like stainless steel, and those easiest to work with, like wood. Plywood with veneer (Formica, for example) works; solid wood looks terrific, but it warps. Countertops can be made of various materials, from Corian to marble, from butcher block to stainless steel. A recent development is the use of pressed paper and resin (Richlite) or lightweight concrete, which are considered "green." Concrete, however, can develop hairline cracks over time.

Whatever you use, you can add special touches by varying the hardware, using hinges and sliders that turn and twist and do all kinds of funny (and useful) things. Everyone knows about pulling out a drawer to find a garbage pail, for instance, but there are also inserts that can support dishes and cabinets that spin out like lazy susans for ease of use.

> **Flashpoint**
>
> An important safety tip: around the cooker, cabinets should be hung higher. If you do not use a hood above your stove, make sure overhead cabinets are lined underneath with a metal sheet to reduce the risk of fire.

> **Design Tip**
>
> You can save on materials while still maintaining luxury in your kitchen by combining counter surfaces. You might, for example, alternate between stone and butcher block. Butcher block should always be incorporated into the counter so that it can be replaced, if necessary. Place the drawer-with-trash-pail combo underneath the butcher block, too, so you can sweep the scrapings straight in while you work.

## Floor and Backsplash Finishes

Backsplashes are the vertical surfaces on the other end of the countertop, generally on the wall (except on a peninsula, where you have none). The idea is to catch splashes so they don't damage your walls, but as everyone knows, in real life things tend to fall and splash where you don't want them no matter what you do: between the stove and the counter, on the chair, on your shirt.

Nonetheless, good kitchen design demands a splash, and splashes we shall have. Pretty much anything water-resistant will do: stainless steel is sometimes used. One woman we know brought home handmade painted tiles from a trip to Italy; another, having purchased an antique Delft tile on a visit once to Amsterdam, years later e-mailed the shop and ordered several more, installing them alternately with ordinary white tiles throughout her newly remodeled kitchen. Adding a decorative pattern in this way brings a nice touch, be it in metal, stone, or ceramic, especially when hand-crafted.

That said, none of these additions—which can be costly—are absolutely necessary. High-gloss paint or highly polished plaster (though expensive) will also do the trick.

Of course, most splashes and spills land (if not on you) on the floor, which is why choosing the right floor finish in the kitchen can make a tremendous difference (and why wall-to-wall kitchen carpeting has never exactly been popular). If you're using tile or stone, underfloor heating is especially delicious and, if you can budget for it, worth the extra expense. Still, as oft-used as they are, such hard materials are not necessarily the best options, since kitchens contain numerous breakables and breakables shatter. This makes wood or linoleum (another "green" material) considerably more attractive particularly to families with young children. The downside here: wood is harder to keep clean and more difficult to heat from underneath (then again, it doesn't get as cold as stone or tile).

When choosing wood, look for stronger, denser sorts like Brazilian cherry, ipe (Brazilian walnut), and teak. Soft pine may be easier on your wallet but will sustain more than its share of dents and dings in such a high-trafficked area. For those who favor fancy, English-retro style, a reclaimed, submerged pine suits the bill nicely. Yellow pine, however, is a highly prized (and priced!) wood. Because it can be cut to fine detail, it is frequently used to make church organs and engineering patterns.

And no matter which wood you choose, make sure it is treated, and retreat it regularly. When items drop on a varnished wood floor, eventually they can chip the treatment. If water gets in, warping can occur. That said, there is something particularly cozy about the feel of bare wood against bare feet early in the morning when you and your faithful, floppy mutt are the only ones awake.

## Accommodating Appliances and Equipment

Determine early on in your kitchen planning where the plumbing will lie so that pipes will be near the sink, rather than having to draw a line through the cabinets. Figure these things in advance—once built, it's much harder to move these things around. It helps to make a list of items and activities, since electrical facilities must accommodate a great number of things. Be sure to include details, like exhaust hoods, feeds for your icemaker, and any unusual special equipment you may have.

**Flashpoint**

Remember to make space for pipes, which usually come from behind the cabinets, and for appliances like ovens and microwaves, which can be freestanding or built in to the cabinets or counter. And don't forget the $H_2O$ feed for the icemaker or the exhaust or hood over your stove! (Be sure to replace filters regularly.)

Overall, your stove, oven, refrigerator, sink, and microwave need to be in a certain relationship to one another. Think through the food preparation process: from fridge to counter, counter to stove, stove to sink. Do not, however, keep your fridge too close to the stove—remember, it emits heat, and with the stove nearby, will also have to work harder! Also bear in mind smaller appliances like food processor, toaster oven, and coffeemaker, which should either have a dedicated space on the countertop or be in convenient sliding storage. Other such items include …

- Espresso machine
- Coffee grinder
- Bottle warmer
- Fruit juicer
- Blender and food processor
- Bottle opener (can be mounted to the counter)
- Wine cooler
- Bread machine, popcorn popper, ice-cream maker, and the like
- Baby monitor
- Phone and intercom system

**Design Tip**

If planning to incorporate entertainment systems, remember, too, to include cabinets for TV and CD player. And keep computers and other electronic items far away from the water and heat source!

Put common sense to work here. It's worth the time spent now in the efficiency you'll be awarded as a result later.

## Plumbing

Plumbing in the kitchen is something you only want to do once; it is unspeakably inconvenient to have to rearrange these things during construction. Once the layout is clear and you know where appliances go, where the sink is and the dishwasher is, where the gas pipe is and the oven, set out the plumbing. Initial planning is important, so that the plumbing can be run in the wall, and not behind cabinets. Make sure your locations are correct, and it will follow that the plumbing is right behind it.

All gas pipes should *always* be installed by licensed plumbers.

## Lighting

Lighting in a kitchen is a lot more important than you probably think. People go there to have fun, so you want it to be upbeat. They go there to prepare food and to eat, so you want it to be color-true, while being bright enough to work by. (Dim light and sharp knives can be a painful combination!) While under-cabinet light is usually fluorescent (which, because it is cool, is safer when attached to a cabinet than other lights), halogen light actually provides the best possible light for a kitchen's needs. (Note that halogen overall, however, may be overkill; it is best used as an accent where it counts, to highlight the food.) If your family tends to dine in the kitchen, reserving the dining room for special occasions, you might consider a dimmer here, as well.

# Baths

Not everyone is prepared to install refrigerators and fireplaces in their baths as has become the trend among a certain set, but bathrooms can and should be given more thought and imagination than they've been getting. The standard setup is to stare smack at the john when you open a bathroom door—not necessarily the most elegant or enticing entry to a room. While this is perhaps the most economical and simple arrangement, a preferable alternative would be to see just a wall with a vanity and mirror at the entry, say, or a chair and table, with the toilet in a separate room or off to the side. And if views and privacy permit, perhaps you could place a large window beside the tub, clerestory lighting, or windows on the east wall to admit early morning light.

## Floor, Wall, and Ceiling Finishes

One rule prevails here: water must be contained—not just in the sink and shower, but also kept from penetrating the walls. Wall finishes should therefore be kept waterproof, and if possible, impermeable—which is why bathrooms are usually finished in ceramic tile. This, too, is one reason why ventilation is important, either via a window or an exhaust duct, preferably with fan attached, providing a minimum exhaust rate of 50 cubic square feet per minute. (For comparison's sake, a cooker hood can go from 300 to 1200 cubic feet per minute in terms of air exchange capacity.) The better your exhaust system and stronger the fan, the more flexibility you will have in your use of materials (though wallpaper in the shower is not a good idea no matter what). Alternatives to standard ceramic tile, however, do exist, such as stone tile, pressed tin, and (heavily treated) wood. (Some wood sorts, like ipe, do not require as much treatment.) Also try combining materials—tiles and paint, tiles and wood, wood and paint. Much of this will depend on the configuration of the actual room and location of bath and shower in your design.

Walls can also be put to functional use, combining decorative detail with practicality: niches can hold candles, decorative soaps, and perfumes. For ceilings, your best choice is probably paperless gypsum board (wallboard), which is less likely to attract mold.

Bathroom floors can actually be a lot of fun, since the small space permits you to use more luxurious materials than you might be able to include in, say, your living room or kitchen. Stone tiles (especially above a heated floor) are elegant and inviting; hand-painted ceramic tiles, often far too costly and fragile for use on an entire kitchen floor, can add a playful, colorful note, either used on the entire floor or combined with other, undecorated tiles. Do be careful regarding finishes, however: stone and some tiles can be dangerously slippery. Honed marble is a better idea than polished marble; tiles designed specifically for floors tend to be more abrasive than the glazed ones used on walls.

**Flashpoint**

Again, take care: bathrooms have a way of causing massive leaks in your wallet—draining as much as two times the amount any other room absorbs from your budget. Keep an eye on your costs as you go.

**Design Don't**

Although it's common to do so, we do not recommend using high-gloss paint on ceilings, as it exacerbates condensation. Your goal is to get rid of steam without transmitting moisture through the structure of the wall and ceiling. Windows or a fan (or both) will help.

**Design Tip**

Think of your bathroom as an inhabited space, with nice lighting, a window, and a bit of furniture, so it looks like someone lives in that room. It doesn't have to be simply tiles and faucets; the use of a few elements like accent lighting and a plant is quite beneficial.

## Cabinets and Equipment

Here's where you get to get a little crazy. Start with the basics—vanity, medicine chest, sinks (his and hers, if possible), towel bars, towel hooks, mirror. Cabinets will, of course, have waterproof surfaces. (Corian, Formica, stone, and ceramic are all standard options.) Then go from there. Do you have room to create two zones, his and hers? Is there space for a bathtub-built-for-two? A Jacuzzi? TV? Music, with loudspeakers installed into the ceiling or at top of walls? A mini-fridge? (Don't laugh; some people have them—perfect for chilling the Champagne and strawberries before a bubble bath *à deux*. Why not?)

Showers can be of all sorts, and you should check the possibilities before making a decision. These days, shower stalls can often be set at the same level as the floor, saving you from having to step over a threshold. They can also generally be built to size, in the event that you have an odd-shaped nook to fill, or include stone or tile seating. Will your shower be separate from the tub? Will you even *need* a bathtub or shower in every bathroom in the house?

Similarly, sinks come in countless shapes, types, sizes, and colors, and the options grow constantly. If you prefer a vintage look, you can even sometimes find antique wooden ones at flea markets, which can easily be adapted for modern use.

## Plumbing Fixtures and Fittings

Faucets and sinks tend to be standardized, and will come with information (usually printed on the box) describing the kind of space they need between pipes, and what kinds of mixers will be necessary. Undermounted sinks are glued under a hole in the countertop, with the advantage that water that spills over the edge can be pushed easily back in.) Others, made of artificial materials, are often cast as one with the countertop. Some manufacturers now offer glass sinks in jewel-like colors, and they are quite beautiful; however, some report that they are vulnerable to chips and cracks, and so best used (if at all) in a guest bath or powder room. Though we have not found that to be the case, it pays to be cautious.

As for faucets, the most affordable are the kind where you push one button that goes from very cold to very hot, and you can't set the water pressure. The more you are able to control, the higher the cost of the system. Do remember this is something you will be living with every day, dealing with constantly. Go for the best your budget can possibly take.

You can also buy fittings to match (tub, sink, shower of the same manufacturer and model, say). If you select these individually, do try to make sure they are visually related to maintain a uniform, smooth look in the room. (The same goes for towels, towel hooks, and light fixtures, by the way; if there's metal in the light fixture, try to coordinate it with the door handle or other metal accents). Whatever you decide, please use a temperature control button on the hot-water faucet. These lend valuable protection against scalding.

# Other Touches and Conveniences

Small things can make a big difference: adding wiring for a mirror defogger, a built-in blow-dryer, extra-large mirrors (especially in the master bath, where it's useful to situate a full-length mirror on the door and another opposite to permit front and back views, heated towel racks, and (because they always ring at the most inconvenient times), perhaps a telephone. This is, after all, one of the most important and most-used rooms in your house. Make it a place you like to be.

## The Least You Need To Know

- Kitchens and baths can absorb two times as much money as the rest of your house. Plan carefully!
- Plan your kitchen for efficiency: think in terms of purposes and creating "zones."
- The dangers in kitchens come from fire, in baths, from water. Protect surfaces accordingly and use the best materials you can afford.
- Think of your bathroom as a real *room*.
- Add personal touches to these rooms—a hand-painted tile, a favorite artwork—for an unexpected and pleasant surprise.

# Part **6**

# The Entrancing Details

Back to the fun, design part. In the next chapters, we will combine ideas and design suggestions with crucial information to help you create the little "extras" that will personalize your home: the windows, the fireplaces, the floors, the wall finishes, the built-ins, even the lighting. And don't forget the exterior: columns, porches, decks—all the features that make your house special. Gradually, having established the basics, you are now filling in the details. Let your imagination wander along the way.

# Design Elements

## In This Chapter

- ◆ Windows and dormers
- ◆ Getting through the doors
- ◆ Finishing walls and floors
- ◆ Shaping ceilings and roofs
- ◆ Sculpting the stairs

Remember the discussion of plans back in Chapter 8? Plans come into play in the most essential elements of a house: floors, ceilings, windows, walls, and doors. Strip the finishes, remove the moldings, empty the spaces, and these are what is left. Designing them with flair and personality is the core of architecture. Designing them to fit *your* personality is at the core of creating a custom home.

## Ideas for Windows and Dormers

Earlier, you set a plan for all your windows, incorporating them into your floor plans, elevations, and sections, and finally, your 3-D models. You know how many you will have and where, and probably how big you think they'll be, but do you know yet what they'll look like? Will they be taller than wide, wider than tall? Square, rectangular, round? Standard window options include these possibilities:

- ◆ Paned windows
- ◆ Double-hanging windows
- ◆ Bow windows
- ◆ Bay windows
- ◆ Sliding windows
- ◆ Casement windows
- ◆ Dormers (or dormer windows)
- ◆ French doors (for lower floors or to a balcony or terrace)

Architect Le Corbusier, who authored what is generally termed the "International Style" of architecture, advocated the use of horizontal windows, a signature typical of many buildings from the 1920s to the 1950s, especially in Europe. Such windows capture the best sunset views, creating a frame around the low horizon; but generally speaking, larger, vertical windows provide better proportions and more light. Study your site plans again to familiarize yourself with the orientation of your land and the way light falls. This is where any photographs you may have taken can be helpful, or if possible, revisit the site a few times, preferably at different hours of the day, to reacquaint yourself with what the views will reveal when looking out, and the placement and quality of light that will shine in.

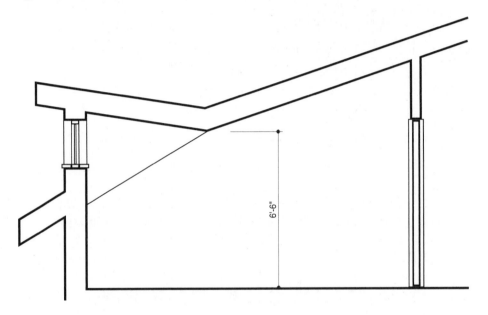

DORMER

ALLOWS MORE EFFICIENT
USE OF ATTIC SPACE.

*Dormer windows add a sculptural element to the house.*

**Design Tip**

Windows do not just allow you to look out. They let natural light in. Work with window size and shape and placement to coax and shape the light you want to have fall into each room.

Once you determine this, you will also want to consider window patterns and proportions, both in relation to the interior and exterior of your house and, again, their handling of light. The higher you are, for instance, the brighter the light. While these things are less noticeable in a two- or three-story house than in, say, a New York apartment building, what you will notice is how deeply the light reaches into the room.

Some tricks you can use include …

◆ Building a light shelf to reflect light further into a room.

◆ Varying window heights within a room to combine effects.

- Adding more or higher windows, in north-facing rooms, to compensate for the lack of available light.

- Placing seating near windows, or building in window seats.

- Using arched windows to suggest an important, even regal space when seen from the outside, and to allow you to extend the reach and openness of the window space from within.

- Using *dormers* to add a decorative, sculptural element to your exterior design.

### Architerms

**Dormers** are projecting windows built onto the roof. The need for a dormer arises when one wants to put a window at the normal size or height, but the roof is too low. So you make a cutout in the roof and extend it upward, creating a sculptural element. You can have a two-slope (gabled) roof intersecting the main roof, or a single slope that follows the direction of the rooftop from which it emerges. Sometimes it's an afterthought; what was supposed to be an attic becomes living quarters for the children, or you transform a now-grown child's clothes closet into an extra bath.

Windows mediate between the inside and outside spaces of your home, obviously, but there are ways to enhance that interaction beyond the standard hole-in-the-wall arrangement. Window boxes on the outside bring a garden directly into view, or you could try replicating an idea we spotted once in Bucharest, in which a full-sized planter, about a foot deep, nestled up to a bay window from the *inside* of the room. The result is almost a greenhouse effect, luring not just light but warmth inside amidst the flowers. This could be an especially nice feature for the kitchen, where you could grow fresh herbs throughout the year.

However, it isn't all good news: there is also a downside to windows (Frank Lloyd Wright reportedly said that architecture would be very easy if it didn't have to deal with windows). For starters, windows are expensive—the more you have, the more you'll spend. But more importantly (certainly for Wright), windows have to be placed in a certain composition on the wall. From a design perspective, this can be a particularly challenging exercise.

Also current energy codes demand certain levels of insulating ability. This makes it virtually impossible to create a glass house anymore. If that's what you've been planning, we suggest you return to Chapter 1 and start over. But at least you'll know a lot of this stuff already the second time through.

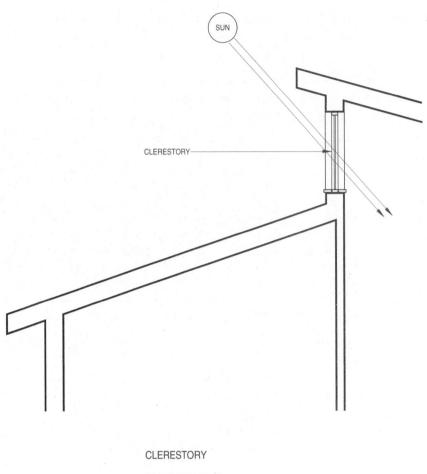

CLERESTORY

CLERESTORY

ALLOWS LIGHT AT TOP
OF WALLS AND OVER ROOFS.

*Bring light deep into the room with clerestory windows situated toward the top of the wall.*

# Designing Doors

Why do you have a door? To keep the rain out, burglars, cats, dogs. They are either for safety, to keep the elements out, or for privacy. Whenever you can dispense of these things, like living-to-dining room, you won't necessarily need a door. (Sometimes, in fact, you don't even need a wall.)

However, since lately energy is a concern, doors are becoming important not just for privacy, safety, or marking transitions, but for keeping room temperatures at the desired correct level. (In a sense, those wonderful designs of the open stairwell with space above and below could be said to be an energy concern. Unfortunately the best solution is to have a door at the top of the stair and bottom of the stair, though that becomes claustrophobic.)

As long as you can get things through it, you can make a door any size you want, custom or off-the-shelf. Closet doors tend to start at 20 inches wide. The bathroom door, which is generally the smallest in the house, is about 24 inches, though that can feel a bit submarine-like; 28 inches is preferable, and is another standard size quite popular for bathrooms, closets, and secondary spaces.

For entry doors and entrances to representative spaces such as the library or living room, 36 inches is an ideal width. (In addition, you may want to install 36-inch doors at the entry to garage and laundry rooms, as large items often have to go through these doors.)

*An example of custom double doors, with raised panels; the panels have a different finish than the frame.*

Styles? As with windows, you have several options. Doors can, for one thing, be either solid core or hollow-core, which is to say, made either with wood inside (solid) or two panels on framework (hollow). You can almost always see the difference, and you'll certainly know it by the price: about eight dollars for the hollow door or a few hundred for the solid one.

Once you get past that point, you'll be selecting among various doors, such as …

♦ Doors with windowpanes (from just a few at the top to basically the whole thing being wood-framed glass). All-glass doors are restricted to special cases, usually for sliding entrances to gardens or decks, but are another possibility.

♦ Paneled doors or smooth ones. Interestingly, some have suggested that when choosing between a paneled surface and something blank, like a plain wood door with nothing on it except a handle, people tend to prefer the paneled one, which has more "visual information." This may explain why some people consider modern, streamlined design "boring" and "cold."

♦ Dutch doors. Nothing more than a door sliced horizontally across the middle, these can be attractive both as interior and exterior options. An added, practical benefit is their ability to keep dogs and children out of a given room but still within eyesight.

◆ Double doors. Normally these are reserved for two extremes of the house—either formal rooms (dining, living) or pantries and closets.

◆ Pocket doors. These sliding doors that disappear into the wall somewhere are a fun feature and can be made to be especially decorative with stained glass accents.

◆ Antique doors (and windows) found from architecture salvage shops and flea markets. Please be sure to measure frames and doors carefully, however, and be aware the doors may be a size that is no longer considered standard, requiring additional custom-fitting. It is, however, appealing to bring something into a new house that has an older history behind it.

◆ Swinging doors (good for the kitchen/dining room egress), and sliding or folding doors, which take up minimal space. However, some sliding and folding door mechanisms are inherently fragile, so that somehow it inevitably happens that whenever you are in a hurry to get dressed in the morning, you take the closet door off its tracks. The sliders and the folders, often made from the flimsiest materials, have a tendency to get unhinged.

Don't forget about hardware—doorknobs, door handles—again, either custom ones made to order or purchased off the shelf. The range is vast: you can find cheap hardware made of tin or pressed metal for $1.98, or there is cast bronze for $100 and more. Any movement in the door will put a strain on the hardware, so for doors that are used regularly, it is better to invest in heavy-gauge hardware that will last longer, hold the door upright, and close it properly. Doors to rarely used areas can get away with light hardware. Decide which you prefer, door handles or knobs, which, for better or worse, children and people of a certain age can't open very easily. The Americans with Disabilities Act also favors handles. (Think of what happens when you apply hand cream and then try to open the bathroom door.)

Folding doors, which people usually hate, do save space. They're ugly as sin, but they do work.

**Flashpoint**

It's important that doors can open fully to more than 90°. Hardware can sometimes get in the way, so you think you're getting a 36-inch opening and you're not. Watch for this.

## Finishing Floors

It's hard to live in a house without a floor, since even the earth can act as one. Earthen floors, however, are less than optimal: they are fragile, they get damp, bugs crawl out of them. Hence you will probably want to consider other alternatives, from stone to steel, from artificial resin to mahogany.

Changes of level and patterns, both visual and textual, dominate the design elements of floors. Raised entryways, sunken living rooms, a podium to place a piano on … all add visual interest and frequently indicate a change of function or an emphasis within a room. But we generally select a floor on the basis of patterns, textures, and the use of materials to create them, from tiled kitchen to carpeted boudoir. (We discuss these in more detail in Chapter 20.) Is durability a concern, or are you looking for a floor for an infant's room that you will inevitably change when the child is a little older? Are you a wall-to-wall-carpet kind of person, or the type who sneezes at the sight of cloth placed on the floor? Are you prepared to splurge for wood inlay, where various colors and types of wood form a pattern like a mosaic in the floorboards?

## Floor Planning

The flooring you choose for each room should suit that room's main purpose: you don't want silk carpets in the kitchen. But don't fall into the "one material, one function" trap, either. There are countless possibilities and you have plenty of room to innovate. Consider what you will use the space for and plan accordingly, bearing in mind that it is also possible to mix materials, combining a wood floor with area rugs (or one large rug)—a classic design choice—or setting stone around a fireplace. A coco fiber insert placed in a wood or stone floor at the entrance way also helps keep people from tracking dirt into the house.

Think about sound, as well. Footsteps, especially when they're right above you, can be enormously irritating. Note that there are two kinds of noise—impact and the rest—and impact noise is the most difficult to muffle. Any hard surface (including wood) will transmit sound well; consequently, plan to install an insulating layer under any flooring surface. Mineral wool is usually installed in the ceiling cavity, but while it is indeed sound absorbent, is usually not enough. Adding a soundproofing mat beneath the finished flooring material will make a significant difference. These are usually made of foam, rubber, or felt, though another option is to add a second layer of plywood over the wood joists and under the finished floor.

## What Floor? Notes on Materials

Basic options for flooring are divided into four categories:

- Hard: Wood, stone, terra cotta.
- Resilient: Material that keeps or return to its shape during or after use, such as rubber, vinyl, vinyl composition tile, linoleum, or cork.
- Natural fibers: Wool, silk, flax, hemp, jute, sisal, sea grass, paper, coconut husk fibers (coir), linen, cotton. Wool is considered the standard for fibers.
- Synthetic fibers: Nylon, olefin, polyester, acrylic, rayon.

We've reviewed most of what you'll need to know about wood and stone in Chapter 13, but a few additional tips may be useful when thinking specifically of floors.

Stone floors, for instance, respond slowly to changes in temperature, which means, conversely, that they retain heat and cold extremely well. Consequently, these are not your best choice for insulation. We also suggest being wary of prices for stone flooring that seem too good to be true: when pricing by the square foot, make sure the stone is thick enough to withstand real wear. (This, by the way, also applies when pricing wood.) You want your floor to last, not chip away like nail polish. (More information about prices is coming up.)

And speaking of wood, think and investigate carefully before making your selections: aesthetics aren't the only factor here. Soft woods like knotted pine—currently in vogue—are less suitable for heavily trafficked areas. But don't assume this means you can't put a wood floor in your kitchen—you can. Just make sure, again, that you choose appropriately. Soft wood is easily dented and sucks water, and is not recommended.

Terra cotta is another good hard-flooring option, and one we especially like, especially for kitchens. Terra cotta is an unfinished baked clay manufactured in different-sized tiles, usually square, hexagonal, octagonal, or rectangular, and about $3/8$- to $1/2$-inch thick. Most that you encounter will be machine-made, but hand-made ones are also available. Well-produced terra cotta is rich looking and rough, like a wool sweater. When having it installed (or installing it yourself), the best method is still the ones artisans used 1,000 years ago: sand is placed across the under floor and terra cotta arranged on top. This separates the tiles from structural expansion and contraction due to temperature, preventing cracks.

Among resilient flooring options, we're particularly partial to cork, an easily renewable—hence, environmentally friendly—material that wears well and provides excellent insulation. It is also soft and yet supportive underfoot, making it great for chefs and others who spend a great deal of time standing. It is non-slippery, hypoallergenic, and does not generate static. (Although one of us suggested testing this by dragging the family cat across it, the other would prefer you didn't.)

Harvesting cork takes time: harvesters must wait until the tree is 25 years old before stripping its bark the first time—and they can't even use that batch. It takes twelve additional years to produce a usable bark; after that, the tree is stripped every nine years.

Cork is structured like honeycomb and is about 85 percent air. You buy it in $1/4$- to $3/8$-inch tiles and pretty much "as is," which is to say, in its natural color, which can range from pale, golden café au lait to a rich, dark chocolate brown. An alternative is "toasted" cork, which looks almost black; but the toasting process robs the material of some of its beneficial properties, including resiliency. Like wood, cork should be well sealed with two to three layers of a water-based polyurethane. (You can also try using butcher's wax, but this requires frequent renewing.)

Like most things, however, cork has its drawbacks. It is easily damaged by heat (such as from dropping a hot skillet), must be glued (with non-toxic glue, preferably) to the sub-flooring, and is prone to fading in sunlight. You may find, in fact, that the area near the window lightens significantly enough that it looks as if the window has cut a different color pattern into the floor—a kind of "square of sunlight" that doesn't disappear.

Of the fibers, one of our favorites is bamboo, another replenishable material that is also extremely economical: you'll find it for as little as $2.00-$4.00 per square foot, but we suggest you nod politely at the salesman and decline. A better quality stock can be had for a perfectly reasonable $8.00 per square. (Please note that bamboo is a grass, not a tree.)

Bamboo used for flooring and similar purposes is processed after cutting by boiling, which removes the sugar content. It is then cut into strips that provide a hard, strong surface. Be careful with the edges, though: like many fibers (think of those woven pot-holders you made in primary school), edges can fray. When installing a bamboo floor, add a strip of wood along the periphery as a preventive measure. (Note: Some will insist this is unnecessary. Do not listen to them.)

**Flooring Minimum Prices**

*Wood (per square foot)*

**Installation:** $4.50/sq. ft and up

**Ash, natural finish:** 2½" wide by ⁵⁄₁₆" thick, variable lengths = $4.25

**Maple, natural finish:** 2¼" wide by ⅜" thick = $5.00

**Maple, stained:** 3" wide by ⅜" thick = $6.30

**Maple, stained like cherry:** 2¼" wide by ⅜" thick = $7.35

**Oak, natural finish:** 3½" wide by ¾" thick = $5.30

**Oak, natural finish:** 5" wide by ¾" thick = $5.50

**Cherry, natural finish:** 3" wide by ⅜" thick = $4.70

**Walnut, stained:** 3" wide by ½" thick = $9.10

*Stone & Ceramic Tiles*

**Installation:** $7.00 and up; material prices per square foot (unless otherwise indicated)

**Ceramic tile:** 12"×12"×¼" = $1.50

**Ceramic tile:** 18"×18"×¼" = $3.00

**Porcelain tile:** 12"×12"×¼" = $2.00

**Marble tile:** 12"×12"×¼" = $2.00

**Granite, 'absolute black':** 12"×12"×⅜" = $7.00

**Stone trim of tiles:** 1"×1"×12", tumbled finish = $15.00 per linear foot

**White marble threshold:** 4"×36"×⅝" = $9.00

*Others*

**Carpet:** Starts at $1.50 per square foot, $3.38 with padding, $3.57 with better padding. Labor extra; plan on about $4.50/sq ft

**Cork:** $6.00/sq ft

**Bamboo:** $8.00/sq ft (can be had for $4, but not good)

# Holding the Floor

For some reason, people tend to fret a great deal about their floors, which, like the rest of a house, need regular care and upkeep to remain in optimal condition. Please do not get neurotic about this: it's not your wife and children we're talking about here. It's a house. It is meant to be lived in and used. Floors will get marred and scuffed, scratched and dirty. That's part of how a house becomes a home.

Still, we thought we'd pass you a few tips that may help in narrowing down your options as you explore the possibilities.

As a rule, the softer the material, the more work you'll need to do—though raw, unpolished marble demands particular attention. (If you're really looking for a maintenance-free floor, in fact, we suggest cement and stainless steel for that cozy prison look.) Stone floors like travertine and marble stain over time and need to be cleaned periodically and resealed. Wooden floors scratch and dent (high heeled shoes can be especially damaging) and will need to be sanded and, again, resealed. Soft woods will usually require this more often.

In addition, if installing stained wood floors, be aware that some stains do not penetrate as well as others. Consequently, when you hit the wood (or drop something onto it), the natural wood color becomes exposed. Be sure to use (or that your builder uses) stains that penetrate at least 1 millimeter into the wood.

Watch out for transitions between floors, as well: stone to wood, wood to carpet. Exposed edges risk becoming loose, and someone might trip. Changes in height between rooms (say, from a stone floor to a carpeted one) can be softened by adding thresholds to separate them.

Much of the task of selecting floors, though, is ultimately personal—and can become an enormous task; once you've settled on the material, there are all those colors and patterns still to choose from. Give it the time and deliberation that it deserves. You will be living with and looking at this every day for years to come.

# What to Do with Walls

You're probably inclined to think of walls as things architects place and designers decorate, but that is not always the case. Think of what can, in fact, be done with walls: they can have niches or cuts. They can be opaque, like sheetrock or plaster, or translucent, of glass—sandblasted in patterns or entirely, or with panels of color—or various forms of plastic. There are screen walls, shoji walls, half walls, divider walls, low walls, high walls, semi-low, semi-high, straight or curved, flat or rounded. (Please note, though, that curved and rounded walls are far more costly than straight, flat ones.)

Translucent walls appear to enlarge a space, and allow a sense of intermingling between rooms. Think about using a trellis, which allows light and air through, while still defining separate regions. Then there is the kind of glass that frosts with the flick of a switch, and LED panels, sometimes covered with milky glass so that the whole wall emanates light.

Also try looking at walls not just as structures that surround a room, but as elements that define it. By combining materials on a single, long wall, you can separate areas of a room into distinct regions—brick where the family room is, for instance, and plaster in the dining area— without actually placing another wall between them.

*Varying the finish on a long wall can define separate "rooms" without the need for dividing walls.*

# Shaping Ceilings and Roofs

When a certain fashion designer goes to sleep on summer nights, he can, with the push of a button, make the ceiling of his bedroom and the rooftop right above it simply disappear. (Fortunately, in case of sudden rain, the buttons work the opposite way, too.) A similar feature in a basement office space exposes the glass floor of a wading pool in the center of the enclosed courtyard up above. (There's another floor idea, come to think of it.) When the ceiling retracts, light comes through the glass brick pool as if it were a skylight.

Obviously, not every home will feature gadgets such as these, but the examples illustrate the wealth of possibilities that go beyond your standard triangular roof and rectangular ceiling configuration.

Ceilings indeed to serve as a metaphor for sky; people are naturally attracted to taller ceilings, to a sense of being elevated (which explains the vaulted ceilings of Gothic architecture and the spiritual effects of many Gothic and neo-Gothic churches). Domes, too, imbue elegance and majesty to a room or building, either as a ceiling, a roofline, or both.

Unfortunately, in terms of construction, it's easiest just to drop a flat ceiling everywhere: you simply line the structure above with sheetrock and you're done. On the other hand, many suburban areas ban flat roofs, which people find less attractive and so believe can reduce property values (a good point to keep in mind if you think you may ever want to sell your new home).

Rooftops do not, however, have to retract or curve to be architecturally interesting. Sculpt the sky above your home with multiple slopes, dormer windows, varying heights.

Again, it is also possible—and often desirable—to sculpt your ceiling to follow the roofline, but limitations, both budgetary and practical (not to mention personal taste) may prevent that. And in the event that open sky and the company of stars are also not part of the current plan, exploring the history of ceilings in art and architecture may lend inspiration. After all, one of the greatest ceilings of the world, at the Sistine Chapel, remains one of the greatest art works in the world almost 500 years after its completion. Some suggestions to get you started:

◆ Skylights, glass blocks, or recessed areas bring light and airiness to a room.

◆ Wood paneling, reminiscent of old English club rooms and libraries.

◆ Exposed wood beams, for a rustic look.

◆ Medallions, like the ones that decorated European homes in the seventeenth century, are now available at most home-supply shops made of various forms of plaster, foam, or polystyrene and look sufficiently like the real thing, which used to be made of marble or plaster. These can be stuck on to a flat ceiling, painted, and surrounded with painted frame (preferably wood) moldings. Of course, if you can spring for the plaster versions, all the better.

◆ Hire someone to create *trompe l'oeil* images on your ceiling, or to replicate the ceiling frescos of the great homes of yesteryear.

## Sculpting Stairs

Yes, we talked about stairs earlier, but that was the technical part. Now we're dealing with design: what will your staircase look like? Are you going for the sweeping, dramatic version, or the functional, just-get-me-from-one-place-to-the-other kind?

In staircases especially, materials and design work synergistically: if you're going the wide, sweeping route, linoleum is just going to look ridiculous. Think about the shape of your stairs and the importance you want them to have in your overall design. Generally, stairs are put on display, as it were, at the entryway of a home, a kind of calling card to visitors.

While it's not unusual to tuck the stairs into a stairwell, instead, why waste the chance to make a visual statement? (Such configurations are also often a waste of space, as well.) One possibility is to design the entrance with a double-height space. The staircase rises to a landing on the next floor where it meets a small balcony with a corridor that connects the upstairs rooms (bedrooms, mostly). True, this creates a larger space (zone) to heat, but it has tremendous impact visually.

Or you could spiral your stairs, a classic design choice. The key is to repeat a rhythm of steps and rises, cut the same way. If you cannot curve the wood (or

---

**Architerms**

Trompe l'oeil, literally "trick the eye," is a form of painting used often in interior decorating to make painted surfaces look like something else: marble, for instance, or even another, adjoining room where none actually exists.

whatever material you use), the spiral will look oddly faceted. Of course, it's possible to buy premade spiral stairs, but assuming you want something more customized for your custom home, look for a workshop that specializes in building staircases, or study images in books and magazines, noting the specific elements of the designs that appeal to you. If you're like most people, you'll find that the more generous the curve, the more pleasing the arabesque of stairs is to the eye.

Coordinate your layout with the materials you select. Wood is the most used and the easiest to work with. Try using different combinations of wood, either by wood type or treatment—stained wood, painted wood, natural wood, oiled wood; different finishes can be used either as accents or to create almost a zebra effect. Or try painting, though we advise you not to paint the actual treads (or handrail, really) so much as the risers. A few weeks of regular wear on a painted staircase shows. A lot.

Metal is popular, as well, though it creates a very different, more industrial look. The exception to this is the kind of tiny, cast-iron spiral staircase associated with English conservatories, but these are better used for secondary spaces, linking, say, a bedroom and downstairs garden, or a hobby room and kitchen. These come in kits, and are quite affordable.

**Design Tip**

Enhance your staircase with decorative balustrades and newels. You can try using different wood finishes for these than you do for the rest of the steps, for instance, setting up a contrast, or find designs that enhance the layout of your stair with outspoken contours and definition.

*An example of mixing materials when designing and building a staircase.*

**Design Don't**

Carpeting stairs of any material allows people to move up and down them quietly, leaving sleeping families undisturbed. Please be sure that if you do, you glue it down. Do not use staples! Children or pets could eat them.

If you are looking to build your main stairway in metal, however, be aware that it can be very slippery. You can either sandblast them or add material to make them non-slip. (It is also not an inexpensive option by any means.) Metal staircases also come as a kit, and the way they are assembled becomes part of the composition. (One added advantage of metal stairs is that they don't catch fire, though they will weaken in high temperatures.)

Concrete has long been associated with fire escapes and office buildings, but in fact, a spiral concrete stair can look like a sculpture if properly designed and poured. (Talk to a structural engineer if you think you want to go this route.) Customize the stair even more by casting it in place and topping it with the material of your choice—from crushed semiprecious stones to glass mosaic tiles to personal items. (Your high-school track medals? Coins you picked up during your honeymoon in Cuernavaca?)

Staircase designs in glass have a magical quality, kind of the reverse of Cinderella's slipper on the palace steps. The enchantment, however, may fade during the construction process, as this is not an easy material to work with: the pieces of a staircase have to be drilled, and for a glass staircase to be drilled, it has to be tempered, and when tempered glass shatters, it shatters into thousands of pieces. Instead of finding your feet on the stair, you're likely to find the stair at your feet. One solution to this is lamination, which holds the glass together (windshields are made in this fashion), but laminated glass takes on a greenish tint that may not quite be what you're looking for. However, glass artists and artisans are constantly stretching the possibilities for glass. Perhaps soon, the glass staircase (if not the slipper) will be yours.

## The Least You Need to Know

- Use doors to make a design statement, not just to separate rooms.
- Design your floors to suit your lifestyle as well as your aesthetic preference.
- Explore different ways to shape a wall—they don't have to be plain and flat—and different materials with which to build them.
- Use translucent walls to make spaces feel larger than they really are.
- A stair is an important architectural element and potentially powerful feature of your design—take advantage of the possibilities.

# Chapter 18

# Special Features

## In This Chapter

- ◆ Fireplaces and built-ins
- ◆ Adding a luxury touch
- ◆ If you work at home (or even if you don't)
- ◆ Audio-video, theaters, and other spectacular events

Stick a bunch of rooms together, throw a roof on top, and there you have it: a house. But it's the special features that make a house a home, and the way that you approach those features that make a house *your* home. Even when you've visited houses in the past while looking to buy—or even rent—these were usually the things that made the difference, that determined your decisions.

Ornament and proportion can have as much to do with this as amenities: from wainscoting to window seats, flower gardens to fireplaces, humans have an innate need not just for comfort in their surroundings, but for beauty. Designing your own home means creating exactly the house you want, and this is where you get to think about some of the things you've dreamed about the most.

## Fireplaces

Speaking of comfort and beauty, few things provide more of both than a fireplace. Images of the family gathered around the hearth, of a kiss by firelight, are part of our collective romantic culture, ingrained so deeply into our imaginations they've in fact become cliché. But a fireplace can be more than this: from a design perspective, it can become one of the decorative highlights of your home.

Originally, of course, fireplaces served a crucial purpose, providing heat to warm the house and prepare the meals. Nowadays, the familiar roaring fire is a luxury, not a necessity, and options have opened up in terms of what a fire-

**Flashpoint**

When planning fire-places, check local ordinances concerning what materials may be burned, as well as any physical requirements for the fireplace itself: how deep, how wide, how tall.

place can look like, how it functions, and, indeed, what it burns. In many areas, legislation has ruled out burning anything but cooking gas—methane. While this may crash all traditional notions you may have of the classic wood fire, it allows for all sorts of otherwise-impossible designs. Alternatively, the stalwartly old-fashioned could choose to install a long, low-lying tube at the base of the fireplace, surrounded by noncombustible, false "logs," combining the storybook experience of a wood-burning fire with the clean efficiency of methane. In any case, confirm what the laws are in your area before embarking on the actual design.

**Flashpoint**

As you think about each of the special features and details of your design, ask yourself …

◆ What does it need to do?

◆ What is the most attractive way to do it?

## Technical Requirements

If you plan on creating your own fireplace rather than purchasing a stock model, determine the technical requirements and allowances before actually creating your design. Proportions are critical in this: you want the smoke to stay inside, while still having a large enough space to heat the room effectively. Hence, in a small fireplace, for instance, you'd place the fire nearer to the top, where smoke can escape quickly upward. We advise strongly that you consult books on the subject—or an architect—to determine the best and safest way to position where the fire itself will burn. (This is a greater concern when dealing with wood fires; gas fires do not emit smoke and so there are fewer limitations and less stringent requirements are likely to apply.)

In the same vein, determine what kind of exhaust system you will use, if any: some people install fans at the top end of the flue.

Speaking of flues, a few other points:

◆ They must be constructed of noncombustible materials. Prefab, fireproof flues are also available.

◆ Your flue leads out to the roof, becoming the chimney. Check local regulations: generally, chimneys must clear the roof by four to five feet.

◆ Side openings at the top prevent sparks from flying out the top or to the roof.

◆ An open damper sucks hot air out and lets cold in. Make sure you select a flue that allows you to close the damper when the fireplace is not in use.

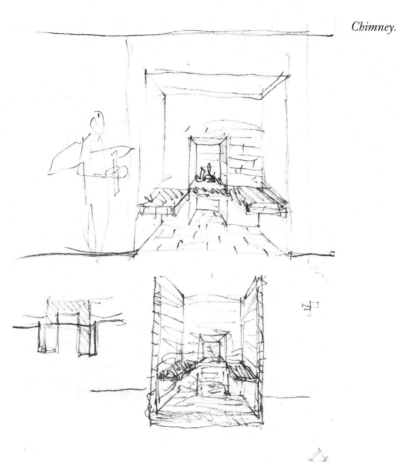

*Chimney.*

## Materials

It should go without saying that all materials used for or around a fireplace must be noncombustible: stone, brick, ceramic, or some metals. Wood and other less flameproof materials can be used as ornamental accents—think of old wooden mantelpieces—but must be placed sufficiently far from the flame and mounted onto the stone or brick (or other nonflammable surface). If you choose to have a raised fireplace, cover the hearth and platform with similarly inflammable materials; for a fireplace situated directly on the floor, be sure to allow for stone or tiling for at least 16 inches in front and 8 inches at the sides in case sparks fly out.

## Placement

Exactly how many fireplaces are we talking about, anyway? Does it make sense only to have one, or could it be used as a divider between two rooms? A stone wall separates the living room from the master bedroom in the Pocono Mountain vacation home of one family we know; a fireplace on each side keeps both rooms welcoming and warm. As an added bonus, and because of the overall

**Flashpoint**

Frank Lloyd Wright was famous for, among other things, his central fireplaces, from which as many as four rooms had access. Wright fans cite the architect's 1938 Hanna House and the 1904 Ward Willetts House (said to be the first "typical Wright house") as favored examples.

layout of the house, the two fires together generate enough heat to keep the rest of the house comfortable as well (though a central heating system helps on particularly cold February mornings).

Such a configuration works equally well between living and family rooms, living and dining rooms, or even upstairs bedrooms. While two separate fireplaces leading to a shared chimney (with separate flues) carved their way into the design of the Pocono house, you could as easily have just one, open on either side. While perhaps not appropriate, for privacy reasons, for the wall between the living room and master bedroom, this arrangement fosters a convivial sense of community and congeniality between individual public spaces in the house. (And nostalgic former scouts can re-create their campfire days with a toasted marshmallow duel or two from either side of the burning flame.)

## Design

And what exactly is this fireplace going to look like, anyway? Will it be arched or square, brick or metal, with mantel or without, large enough to cook in or small enough that it doesn't take up too much space? Does it project from the wall or burrow into it?

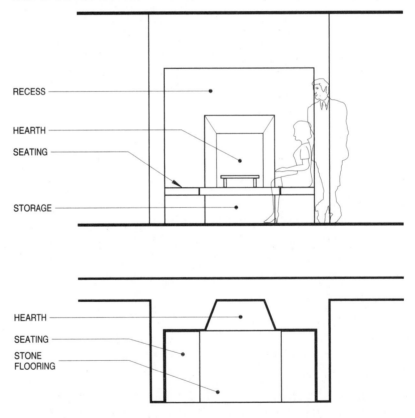

RECESS

HEARTH

SEATING

STORAGE

HEARTH

SEATING

STONE
FLOORING

FIREPLACE

SEATING IS INCORPORATED INTO FIREPLACE. THE HEARTH
IS RAISED AND STORAGE FOR WOOD UNDER THE SEATING.

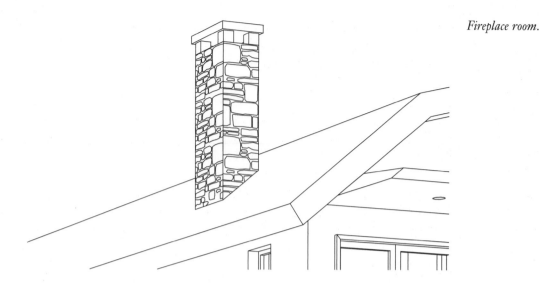

*Fireplace room.*

Designing a fireplace is one of the times you get to let your imagination run a bit. Think of it as a painting or a sculpture in the room, with shadows, highlights, even color: what about a fireplace of glazed brick in red and blue and yellow, or deep ebony with cobalt blue touches, like inlaid lapis lazuli? Let the materials be the decorative element: use veined marble panels, book-matched, as the face of the fireplace. Dealers in architectural ornaments and antiques often have magnificent early American mantel-pieces available to mount on the outside of simple brick or tile structures.

Or you could bypass all of this: prefab fireplaces are readily available, with a wealth of options easily found online.

But where's the fun in that?

> **Design Tip**
>
> How about a fireplace room? One architect's fireplace includes a seating area *within* it, with benches lined, intimately facing one another, on either wall—a sort of room within a room.

# Built-Ins

Built-ins continue the "personal touch" you bring to your home design. Remember that program list? You'll want to pull it out again, along with your clippings and other "ideas and inspirations" files, to remind yourself of what you wanted and to stimulate more ideas and possibilities of your own. Were there bookcases in your plan? Window seats? A wet bar or special cabinets? Do you need to sneak in extra storage in a minimum of space?

Generally speaking, built-ins can be less expensive than freestanding pieces, but their main advantage lies in the way they utilize space. Not only do they take up less room than ordinary furnishings, but they allow you to make efficient use of bits and pieces of wall and floor.

Of course, most built-ins aren't really even built in at all: they are assembled elsewhere and then screwed or bolted to the walls and floor. These can include many different elements:

- Bookcases and vitrines
- Countertops
- Banquettes

- ◆ Wall niches
- ◆ Kitchen cabinets
- ◆ Computer stations and desks
- ◆ Closet systems
- ◆ Window seats

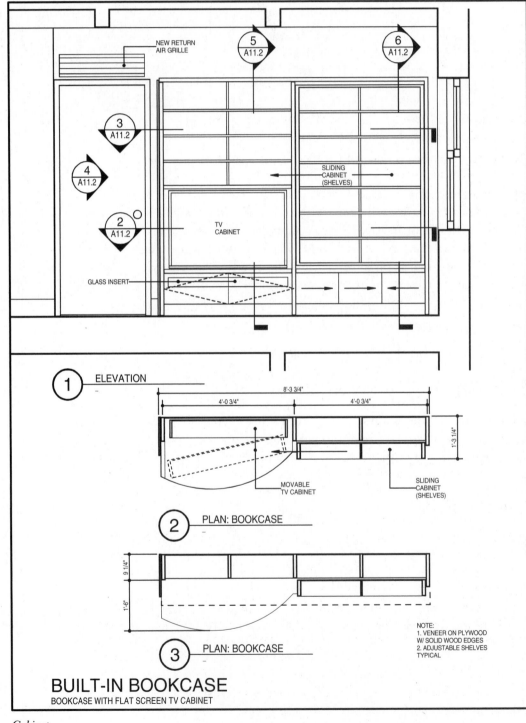

NEW RETURN
AIR GRILLE

5 / A11.2

6 / A11.2

3 / A11.2

4 / A11.2

2 / A11.2

SLIDING
CABINET
(SHELVES)

TV
CABINET

GLASS INSERT

1 ELEVATION

8'-3 3/4"

4'-0 3/4"    4'-0 3/4"

1'-3 1/4"

MOVABLE
TV CABINET

SLIDING
CABINET
(SHELVES)

2 PLAN: BOOKCASE

9 1/4"

1'-6"

NOTE:
1. VENEER ON PLYWOOD
W/ SOLID WOOD EDGES
2. ADJUSTABLE SHELVES
TYPICAL

3 PLAN: BOOKCASE

## BUILT-IN BOOKCASE
BOOKCASE WITH FLAT SCREEN TV CABINET

*Cabinet.*

## Bookcases and Cabinets

Be certain that walls are strong enough to carry the load! A friend lost an entire collection of heirloom china when her kitchen cabinets crashed to the floor following a large Thanksgiving dinner.

A familiar decorating trick revolves around the hidden television or stereo equipment, tucked behind an armoire door or behind two cabinet doors in a wall unit. Why not create a built-in, high-tech alternative, with a sliding door that parts along the wall to reveal a flat-screen TV behind it?

Built-in shelves are also not always just reserved for books. Feature a collection of ceramic vases, collector plates, colored glass, on shelves or nestled into an open cabinet atop a wall divider, or tucked safely behind the glass panels of a vitrine door. Position cabinets or bookcases along a window wall, around a doorway, even along a corridor—anywhere you might want to show off special items or photographs. That said, there are few things so enticing and so cozy as a room lined with bookcases on every wall.

> **Design Tip**
>
> Here as elsewhere, do not separate design from performance. Use the very best materials you can afford. Kitchen cabinets get used hundreds of times a year. Invest accordingly.

## Countertops, Seating, and Bars

These are all areas you will touch. The tactile quality of the materials you use should therefore be a consideration in your design: think of how it will feel in actual use. Are you the type who will enjoy the industrial cool of a steel table as you sip your morning coffee, or would you prefer the coziness of wood, or the icy, old-world elegance of granite or marble? Plastic seating can be aesthetically pleasing, but will you want to sit in a plastic chair in August? Are you willing to live with the hazards of furnishings with sharp corners?

Countertops and ledges can go almost anywhere, and be made part of the decoration of a room. Sometimes their actual purpose may only become apparent as you live with them: people tend to congregate instinctively wherever they find seating or a table, and so such touches can be particularly welcoming. This can be especially important to consider if you entertain a lot: think of all the post-cocktail party cleanup you have done, removing cups and glasses from various windowsills around the house.

Similarly, a high countertop in a kitchen can become a social spot, a breakfast table and a means of keeping the junk in the kitchen hidden from view. In the powder room, they can top a cabinet used for storing extra toiletries or provide casual seating for a mother supervising a child's bath (or both). And deeply recessed windows, of course, make for daydream-inspiring window seats.

## Wet Bar

Every self-respecting secret agent has a wet bar in his office, so why shouldn't you have one in your home? Actually, wet bars are becoming increasingly popular, perhaps in part because of the growing interest in home theaters (more on that later) or a renewed wave of hospitality. Here again is a chance to slip in another counter, too, along with other built-in needs. (And don't forget the plumbing for the sink and an outlet for the fridge!)

- Storage for glasses and dishes
- Drawers for napkins and utensils
- Rack for beverages that do not require refrigeration
- Don't forget the can opener!

Where you choose to place the bar is an individual decision, of course, but we recommend situating it either between the living and dining rooms or by the home theater (if you have one). Another more dramatic—and extravagant—option would be to create a bar that swivels so it can be accessed from, say, living room, dining room, or porch. Even a small alcove would work in a four-foot-wide pace, and still allow for a fridge, a cooler, and some counter and storage space. (Just remember to go back and adjust your drawings and models accordingly.)

*Wet bar.*

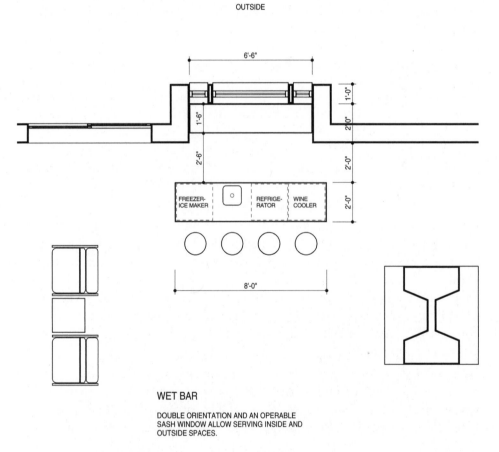

WET BAR

DOUBLE ORIENTATION AND AN OPERABLE
SASH WINDOW ALLOW SERVING INSIDE AND
OUTSIDE SPACES.

## Secret Storage Spaces

Here and there, nooks and crannies can be converted into surprisingly clever storage spaces: drawers can be incorporated into the treads of stairs, for instance, or inserted into the "dead space" that forms the base for your lower kitchen cabinets. (An alternative is to create sliding trays, either on wheels or tracks, rather than drawers, in this space.) Deep windowsills and window seats can easily hold toys, linens, or those boxes of letters from your best friend in childhood who moved away. (Be sure, though, that these spaces are well insulated against moisture!)

# Home Office

Depending on your needs, a home office can be as tiny as a closet or larger than your family room. Think of it as the command post of a submarine: even if you work at home, whatever the size, you want it to be as efficient as possible—a desk, a filing cabinet, a box, a lamp, a shelf, and an outlet. (Well, maybe several outlets.) Even tucked into a niche beneath the stairs, having a home office or study constructed of the most beautiful materials you can afford will add tremendous luxury to your home—and to your day.

Here again is where you may want to consider built-ins such as bookcases, *vitrines*, and various storage elements that will keep your office organized and save space. Do remember that even in a large office, equipment can take up valuable feet and inches—copiers and printers have paper feeds, require side and top access, and so on.

Of course, you may not need to get that fancy: perhaps a corner desk will do, a place to write letters, pay bills, draw sketches, compose your memoirs. Even then, we do suggest finding a way to close off your nook, particularly if you have placed yourself in a bedroom you share with someone else. (And besides that, a view of a cozy bed when you're supposed to be getting work done is a very dangerous thing, as any college student knows.)

**Design Tip**
One way to introduce extra richness and elegance to your home without busting your budget is to utilize top-tier materials in small spaces (like home offices), or for the occasional detail.

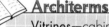
**Architerms**
Vitrines—cabinets with glass doors (and sometimes glass walls as well)—are a good way to showcase special collections and art objects, especially if they are fragile.

*Home office.*

At the other extreme is the study/guest-room combo, where a full-sized library or study converts for friends and family with a pull-out or Murphy bed. A common and practical configuration is to situate this room almost as if it were an extension from the main house, with a bathroom between. The privacy that this affords is likely to be appreciated by both guests and anyone who runs a business from home (or, for that matter, prefers to read and think in utter sanctuary). Wrap the walls, perhaps, with built-in bookcases or windows, and, depending on your taste, your budget, and the climate, add a fireplace for an extra-welcoming touch.

# Going Remote with Audiovisual and Other Electrical Equipment

Remember when remotes were used only for garage doors? Then TVs became the next hot thing, then lighting systems, and so on. Now, it's possible to hook the whole house to a computer, though this is beyond the scope of what we can cover here. Pretty much anything can be programmed, though, from lamps to music, climate to security systems and intercoms—all controlled from a single touchpad about the size of a personal digital assistant (PDA). (Though like any moveable part, remote-controlled garage doors involve certain dangers; an accidental brush with the remote button could cause the door to hit someone. Hence we tend to prefer the manual route.)

**Design Tip**

A-V consultants don't always have much of a background in engineering. An acoustic engineer can best calculate what the room's possibilities will be.

To complicate matters, extremely elaborate A-V systems spring up on the market regularly, usually conveniently around Christmastime, creating something of a dilemma for those looking to integrate these systems into the structure of their homes: by a year or two from now, you'll be ready to upgrade, frustrated that your remote control allows you to turn the TV, lights, and oven on and off, but not to operate the vacuum cleaner while reading the bestseller you simply can't put down. Never fear: most of these arrangements are easily adjusted for new developments. In any scenario, work out your audiovisual and other such systems with an electrician, and plan the wiring to run through the entire house. While equipment is best located in one area, it is possible (and advisable) to have several channels.

**Design Tip**

To get an idea of what's possible in *your* home, consider that a 3,500-square-foot home can accommodate a CD player and receiver, TiVo, and a printer, all set remotely, as well as a full sound system that will send music to all—or specially selected—corners of your abode.

A note of caution: If you're not that interested in these systems, do not install them thinking they will add to the value of your house. Experience indicates that they make no real difference.

# Home Theaters

Home theaters are also popular options these days, but can be tricky. The size of your screen will determine the size of your theater space as well as your sound system. Take care not to allow echoes, which can be disorienting, and to provide for windows to be darkened either by blinds or shutters when needed. Smooth walls will act like soundboards. Hard surfaces, like stone, are hard on the ear. Hence surfaces should be soft; one way to combine the need for darkness and quality sound is to hang heavy, lined curtains at the windows (and elsewhere, if you can). A rug and heavy fabrics on furniture also help.

Assuming you will be using this room to watch films, TV, or both, pay attention to ergonomic and health guidelines. TVs are best viewed at a distance of 10 feet with a three-degree downward slope. (We insist on this when designing media rooms for clients.) On the other hand, there is a distinction between home and a public space, such as a bar: if you want to have a place for all your buddies to gather 'round, you'll want the TV to be high—or, alternatively, to pitch the floor at an angle.

> **Architerms**
> **Echo** is perceived when the distance between the ear and a wall is equal to or greater than 16.5 meters, or about 54 feet. (The speed of sound is 34.3 meters per second, and the human ear needs 0.1 seconds to distinguish between two separate sound events.)

## The Least You Need To Know

- Add personally designed touches to your home with built-ins and extra features that make living there fun.
- Use fireplaces to create a feeling of tradition, community, and elegance to your home—while doing a kindness to the environment.
- Create a "private space" with a home office.
- Bring the entertainment to you with integrated A-V systems, a home theater, a wet bar—or all three.

# Chapter 19

# Lighting

## In This Chapter

- ◆ Working with natural light
- ◆ Lighting your life from within
- ◆ Designing your lighting systems

Let there be light. Light of my life. Lighting the way, shedding light on the subject, while you reach for the light at the end of the tunnel.

We are fascinated by light, obsessed with its magic. With the possible exception of bats and some bears in the wintertime, living creatures crave the light and direct themselves always toward it; studies have shown that a surfeit of daylight can even cause depression in some people.

At the same time, the eye is a sensitive organ. Too much light can be uncomfortable, and the wrong color light can distort your perception of what you see—a fact familiar to everyone who has ever set foot in a department-store dressing room.

In this chapter, we'll look at how to get it right.

## Natural Light

Windows, of course, bring the outside in; they allow us to enjoy the views of the world around us from sheltered safety, to watch the snow and rain fall, the seasons change, the sun set at the closing of the day. But they are also our main source of light and air. For this reason, code regulations in fact require you to install at least one window in every room of your home (baths, darkrooms, dressing rooms, and wine cellars being among the few exceptions).

How many you decide to have is up to you (and the building code), as are the sizes and shapes of each. Some people prefer to have as many windows as can fit in a room, though there are energy penalties for this, since glass (even insulated glass) does not insulate as well as wall. New laws have also established new energy ratings and requirements for walls called the "R value," which indicates the insulating value of the wall. You'll need to make sure your walls comply—

a task for which you would again be well advised to speak with an architect or engineer. Generally speaking, the bigger the room, the bigger the window: a 6-foot window in a 16×18-foot room, for instance, is fine.

### Architerms

You are now in the **design development phase.** Here, you will begin to elaborate and refine the floor plans and exterior and interior elevations; detail the plans for kitchen and baths; and select the various materials, finishes, and products for your home.

The other potential drawback to having overly large or too many windows is the reduction in wall space for furnishings and artwork. Unless you're willing to dispose of some of these when you move, review the furnishings for each room as you decide on the placement and shapes of your windows.

### Design Tip

Eaves, too, shape the shade and the light that come in your windows and skylights, creating cooler shadows in the summer months and, provided they are the right size, allowing light in winter. The idea is to deal with the sun *before* it hits the window.

Still, strategically placed windows create effects in your home nothing else can quite match in terms of function as well as form: transparency brings lightness (not only light) to a space and allows you to follow not just the sun but the changing shadows of the day. (A bedroom window facing east can be a particularly nice touch—the more if you can counterbalance it with another facing west. To see the first rays of the sun and watch the light and shadows dance across the earth begins the day with promise.

### Design Don't

Sunset views are universally appealing, but too many west-facing windows can foster too much warmth, especially in hotter regions. A smaller window (or *clerestory*) in an interesting shape can be more effective than a very large one.

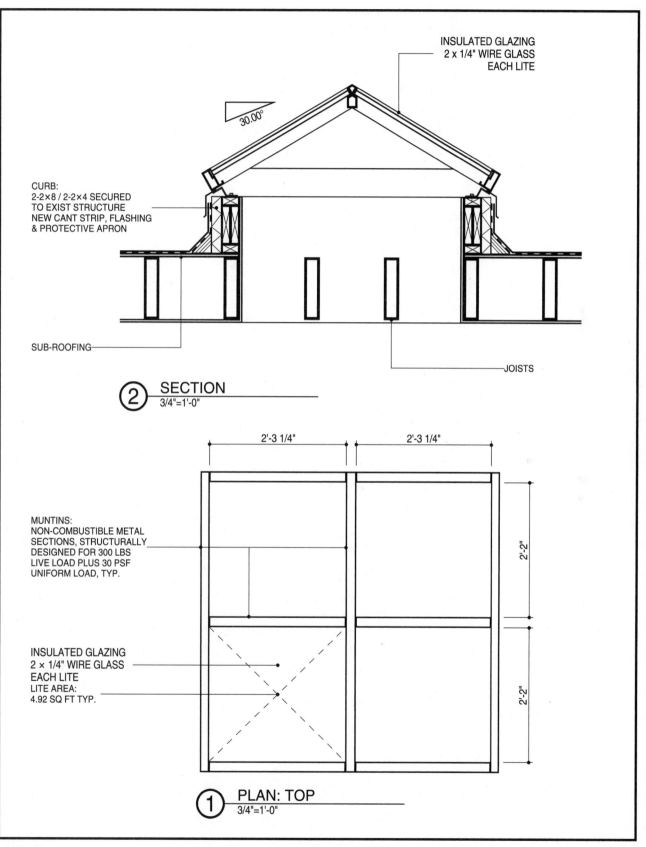

INSULATED GLAZING
2 x 1/4" WIRE GLASS
EACH LITE

30.00°

CURB:
2-2×8 / 2-2×4 SECURED
TO EXIST STRUCTURE
NEW CANT STRIP, FLASHING
& PROTECTIVE APRON

SUB-ROOFING

JOISTS

② **SECTION**
3/4"=1'-0"

2'-3 1/4"    2'-3 1/4"

MUNTINS:
NON-COMBUSTIBLE METAL
SECTIONS, STRUCTURALLY
DESIGNED FOR 300 LBS
LIVE LOAD PLUS 30 PSF
UNIFORM LOAD, TYP.

2'-2"

INSULATED GLAZING
2 × 1/4" WIRE GLASS
EACH LITE
LITE AREA:
4.92 SQ FT TYP.

2'-2"

① **PLAN: TOP**
3/4"=1'-0"

*A skylight.*

# Artificial Light

Artificial light does more than make things visible at night: it affects the color and quality of what you see, shapes the spaces with highlight and contour, creates atmosphere and mood. Variations are virtually infinite, based on one basic principle and its bad-news corollary, namely …

- Everything can be solved with dimmers.
- It is expensive to dim fluorescent lights.

The problem this presents is that it is not always possible to combine the best lighting for atmosphere with the most economical *lighting fixtures* (although it is worth noting that dimmers do prolong the life of incandescent bulbs). Consequently, it makes sense to establish from the beginning which rooms need dimmable light and which don't. Once you've done this, you can work out the details of what goes where, and how. The usual arrangement is to mix systems with the exception of garage, corridors, laundry, mudroom, closets, and other storage. Even baths and kitchens derive benefits from having a mixed lighting system: overall (ceiling) downlights for high general-level light, localized spots (mainly halogens) to provide accents.

Think of it as dusk lighting versus general lighting: concentrate light where it is used and needed most.

## Form in Light

Use lighting throughout your home in different ways, each to fulfill a different purpose:

- **General/overall:** For seeing the whole space
- **Task:** To see the area of interest: desk, corner of room
- **Accent:** To see a detail; use halogen lights, for instance, to accent choice objects and parts of the space (these may also be dimmed)
- **Special effects:** For amusement and decorative purposes

Much about your lighting scheme involves aesthetic rather than practical choices, mostly between using direct or indirect light. Direct light is your standard, light-bulb-in-the-ceiling overhead; indirect lighting sources include sconces, light coves, and most floor and table *lamps*. Indirect lighting, where illumination goes straight up and then descends back is especially effective for creating mood and sculpting a space; spots focus on an object, making them useful additions to studies, hobby rooms, and home offices.

### Architerms

Popular terminology doesn't always match professional terms. Technically, a **lamp** is what emits light—what most people call "bulbs." A light fixture is what most people call a "lamp"—the thing you screw the bulb (lamp) into. These overlap somewhat, but are not interchangeable.

When deciding on your lighting sources and fixtures, think about the practical and aesthetic qualities of each, and what it is you need in each room. Some tips:

Spotlights concentrate light; floodlights diffuse it. Spotlights (which focus on the object) can be installed as track lights strung across the ceiling. One considerable drawback to this option is that the light is best distributed by using multiple tracks—a look that harkens not-so-favorably back to the cheap lighting systems of the 1970s. Still, for those who enjoy a bit of nostalgia (or don't care), it is an effective, easy alternative. (There are, to be sure, museum-quality track lighting systems that are quite good-looking and technically outstanding, but they are expensive: about $90/head and up.)

### Flashpoint

Wattage actually has nothing to do with how much light you're getting from a bulb: it's a measure of power used (spent) and emanated as heat. This is another reason we recommend compact fluorescents, where a 14-watt bulb provides the light of a 90-watt regular bulb. For usable light, check the bulb's lumen output (for example, "800 lumens").

Recessed lighting requires finding space between the beams. Be certain that you know what you want when you install recessed lights, and that you don't plan to make major changes of any kind: once these systems are installed, you cannot move them without having to cut into (and repair) the ceiling. Note: use dedicated mounting bars for installation between wood joists.

Halogen lamps, chandeliers, or sconces (dimmable) are useful in dining rooms for occasions when candlelight may not quite be appropriate.

Sconces allow you to hide the fixture itself, transforming the light source into a decorative, sculptural accessory. It was a popular look in the 1930s and works well for Art Deco–style or alternatively, postmodern industrial interiors.

### Design Tip

Try to think creatively about spaces; lights are a wonderfully effective way of shaping a space.

Narrow beam light accents a small area or object; wide beam illuminates the space in general. Suspended lights function as an accent, but also have an intimate effect when directed over a dining table or small seating area.

Fluorescents are usually used for kitchens, both under the cabinets and as overheads. Fluorescent lamps (bulbs) have light color labels—cool white, warm white, daylight, or black—or the temperature of the light emitted, upward of 2,000° Kelvin.

Floor lamps, particularly halogen lamps combined with a dimmer, allow you to create virtually any lighting situation you can think of. They are one of the best design options—with one important caveat: we do not recommend having these in homes with small children. Children seem to be particularly attracted to the prismatic quality of halogen bulbs (or in some cases, get a kick out of shaking the stem), but these bulbs become extremely hot, as do their covers. While we hate to turn away from a great design option, we do believe in putting safety first.

*An example of indirect lighting.*

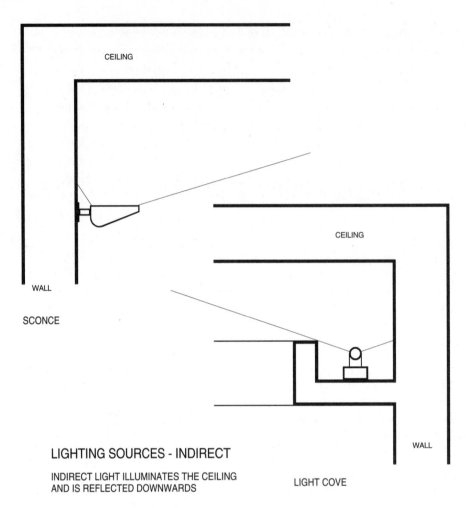

**LIGHTING SOURCES - INDIRECT**

INDIRECT LIGHT ILLUMINATES THE CEILING
AND IS REFLECTED DOWNWARDS

Experiment with fixed versus movable lighting. You may want to play around with the lighting possibilities in your current home, trying out different lamps in different rooms. Do not get hung up on whether the lampshade matches the drapes or if there's really enough room for that big lamp on that small table: this is about the quality of light.

## Color

**Design Tip**

For color, the best light is one that approximates sunlight.

Color matters more in light than you may realize. Misjudge the color of uncooked foods, and people could become ill: in fact, in the wrong light, good food can look spoiled and unappetizing, which is why restaurant lighting is always so carefully planned—yes, even at Burger King. (Small note: the Department of Agriculture advises against judging food by color, cooked or not.)

Green-blue light and cold fluorescents make people look pale or blanched or ill (hence "dressing-room syndrome"). Warm light, which we associate with candlelight, tends to be the most flattering, especially to faces. And any light that is close to replicating sunlight will show colors to their best advantage.

From an ecological (and economic) point of view, the color rendition of different lighting can also make a difference: the better the color rendition ability, the less light you need—and so, the less energy you use.

Using dimmers allows you to alter the contrast and gradation. By setting lighting "scenes" with different lighting in different spaces, you create varying affects throughout the house. Think of the difference between, say, a police interrogation and a wedding night.

**Flashpoint**

Compact fluorescents are not easy to dim, but it can be done. Consult a professional if you choose to go this route.

# LED Lighting and Other Special Lighting Effects

Lighting can also be used as a fully decorative device, alone or combined with the architectural elements of your home. Options might include creating a closet of sorts, some six inches deep, with a glass door panel at the front illuminated by a light within. This can be especially effective in small or narrow windowless spaces, such corridors, both providing light for the space and making it feel less cramped, less closed in. Dividers and walls of fabric (or thin sheets of onyx, alabaster, smoked glass, or other material) with a light placed behind them are also dramatic means of defining (or separating) spaces in a room.

Many homeowners are also now incorporating LED lights into their structural architecture for an industrial, trendy touch. LEDs can be managed through specialized controls that give each light a different color. Entire panels can be made to order and installed along walls or atop ceilings, again combining practical function with aesthetic fun.

# Creating Design Layouts

Included in your plan drawings will be a lighting plan and an electrical plan which indicate where the lights will be. When creating your plan, it helps to focus on the activity in the space.

- Remember that light has to support the function of the space.
- Consider all tasks likely to occur in that space. Do you use your dining table not just for dining but also for playing family games of Scrabble? For homework?
- When creating your plan, stay alert for those areas that tend to be forgotten: interiors of closets, stairwells, areas above mirrors, and so on.

Theoretically, a whole *soffit* could be just one light, just like the sky. The goal, though, is to manipulate and orchestrate the lighting, using it to make the best advantage of every room, every closet, every corner. By combining light's power to articulate, define, and shape the spaces of your home with its most basic function—illumination—you will produce the lighting system and design that works the best for you.

**Architerms**

The word **soffit** used to be reserved for the underside of the tops of archways and architraves. Now, it's generally used to refer to the upper space of a room.

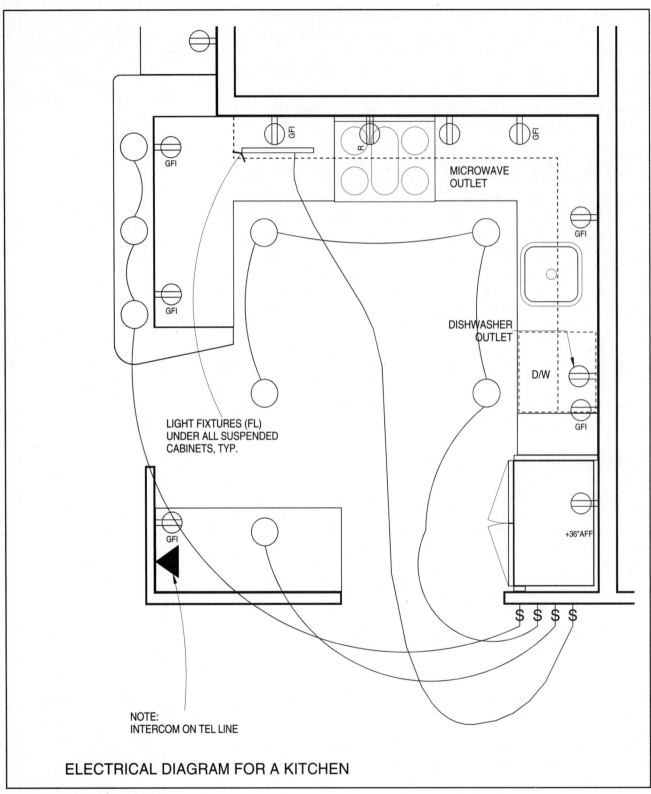

GFI

GFI

R

MICROWAVE
OUTLET

GFI

GFI

GFI

DISHWASHER
OUTLET

D/W

GFI

LIGHT FIXTURES (FL)
UNDER ALL SUSPENDED
CABINETS, TYP.

GFI

+36"AFF

$  $  $  $

NOTE:
INTERCOM ON TEL LINE

## ELECTRICAL DIAGRAM FOR A KITCHEN

*Lighting design layout (kitchen).*

## The Least You Need to Know

◆ Take advantage of natural light whenever possible.

◆ Shape windows to bring more light in winter and shade in summer by using eaves and light shelves.

◆ Combine lighting systems—overall, downlights, spotlights, accent lights— for optimal effect, but take care using halogen lights around children.

◆ Use dimmers: they create atmosphere in a room.

# Chapter 20

# Elaborating Your Interior Design

## In This Chapter

◆ Customizing your interior

◆ Ideas for walls, floors, and other basics

◆ Finding inspiration in materials

The architecture process, as you've doubtless noted by now, is not an isolated event. Rather, it intersects and even mixes with other areas of creating a home, from construction to decoration. *Interior architecture* is one of the most rewarding activities for many design-it-yourself-ers, as this is the part where you come closest to interior design and the "software" that goes into the "hardware" of your home.

It is not, however, quite the same. Interior designers chiefly work with the accessories, the parts of a room you can take with you when you go, like carpets and furnishings, upholstery and pillows. The architect combines form and function (and light and shadows), actually shaping the structural elements, like the shapes and sizes of walls and windows. And both interior design and interior architecture involve such things as flooring, built-ins, wall tiles—the stuff you could take with you if you wanted to, but that is really part of the house itself.

## Elaboration Basics

Any aesthetic choice is, in the end, subjective, and hence the ideas you incorporate into your own home and how you choose to do so is a decision we can't make for you. But when planning the accents and look of your home, try to keep your thoughts and eyes open to the possibilities. Where can you bring a decorative touch? How can you take the basics and, as it were, "take them up a notch"?

The idea is actually simple: from need arises opportunity. Everything you need in your home offers the opportunity to create an aesthetic statement, to go beyond the ordinary and banal to the personal and unique.

### Design Don't

Finishes are where the money is! A large portion of your budget will go towards your wall, floor, and other finishes, and towards other decorative details. Keep an eye on costs, balancing and rebalancing your budgetary, practical, and aesthetic priorities accordingly. Where you need to compensate, compromise, revise, or reconsider, do so. (Don't forget to mark your drawings and other documents along the way!)

| Room # | Floors | Base | Walls | | | | Moulding | Ceiling |
|---|---|---|---|---|---|---|---|---|
| | | | N | E | S | W | | |
| **LIVING RM** | HW 1 | WD 3 PTD | P1 | P1 | P1 | P2 | N/A | PC1 |
| **DINING RM** | HW 1 & 2 | WD 3 PTD | P2 | P2 | P2 | P2 | N/A | PC1 |
| **HALLWAY 1** | STONE 1 | WD 3 PTD | P3 | P3 | P3 | P3 | N/A | PC2 |
| **HALLWAY 2** | STONE 1, WD 1 | WD 3 PTD | P3 | P3 | P3 | P3 | N/A | PC2 |
| **KITCHEN** | STONE 2 | WD 3 PTD | P2 / CER2 | P2 / CER2 | P2 / CER2 | P2/CER2 | N/A | PC1 |
| **BATH RM 1** | STONE 3 | CER1 / WD3 | P4 / CER1 | P4 / CER1 | P4 / CER1 | P4 / CER1 | N/A | PC3 |
| **MEDIA RM** | HW 1 | WD 3 STN | P1 | P1 | P1 | P1 | N/A | PC1 |
| | | | | | | | | |
| | | | | | | | | |
| | | | | | | | | |

*Finish schedule example.*

## Working with Walls

Why should a wall be flat? We've talked already about some of the options for wall shapes—rounded, convex, concave, half-walls, walls with built-in niches, and so on. There are also various applications to consider: paint finishes, moldings, and wall paneling, for instance. We'll look at the specifics of paint and paneling later in this chapter, but for now, let's think about ways to elaborate on the actual shape and structure of the wall.

Moldings add textural interest, and can be designed to frame sections of the surface in such a way that they make, as it were, an art work of the wall itself. Chair rails, popular in the nineteenth century, serve both practical and decorative functions, preventing chairs from nuzzling up so close to the wall that they could scratch or stain it while articulating the periphery of the room itself— a good example, by the way, of the idea of allowing aesthetic opportunity to emerge from functional need. In general, you'll find ideas for molding possibilities in books on home decorating or "coffee-table" books that document important architectural monuments. The White House rooms and some mansions that have been converted to museums boast a wealth of wall moldings throughout, for instance.

Equally a combination of design and device, niches in a wall help shape the light across its surface, work as decorative elements in themselves, and serve as repositories for decorative objects, such as a sculpture or flower arrangement or

### Design Tip

"Form follows function" is an old adage in architecture and design, generally associated with Modernism but in fact a description of architectural inspirations from time immemorial—think of the Coliseum in Rome, designed in 70 C.E. so some 50,000 could see the stage at once.

plant. For one client, we built a niche into the wall opposite the front doorway, where fresh flower arrangements or planted orchids, nestled into the hollow add a touch of gentle color and a fragrant, calming welcome home.

You can also manipulate a wall as if it were a sculpture, creating unexpected forms. In the process, it's possible you will even save space. Let's say the side of a walk-in closet forms a curve or even squared alcove, where shoes or a chest of drawers will be kept. The part that protrudes into the bedroom can be given a rounded shape, like a drum, perhaps finished in a different material or painted or smoothed with an ochre-toned Venetian plaster. The room is white, the curve is ochre, and the light of the sunset catches the color and makes the room come alive. We produced a similar arrangement for another client where a bedroom and bath shared the wall where the bathtub was. Rather than take the footprint of the tub straight to the roof, as would be the customary design, we created a box around the tub, curving it, and adding a niche and a light. Again, the point is you have to deal with an obstacle anyway, so you may as well use it to please the eye.

This same technique can be used with built-ins as well, by the way: create a sort of niche for the bookcase with a little drop in the soffit so it has a space of its own.

Of course, as we mentioned earlier, the material itself, such as brick or stone or paneling, can serve as a decorative element.

> ### Design Tip
>
> Throughout your house, try to give elements a definition, a specifically designed shape, so that the whole house, with all these elements added together, becomes personal—yours.

> ### Design Don't
>
> Try to think from a tactile standpoint, as well—not just "what does it look like?" but "what will it feel like when you touch it?" When you turn a corner from room to room, what kind of corner is it? A sharp metal angle that looks like it's going to scrape your elbow or slash your thigh is not inviting. In fact, studies show that when an object is near someone's head, even if it is above head-height, he will duck his head in self-protection. Material, texture, and shape all influence the way you feel about an environment.

Be careful, though, in combining all these elements—niches and moldings, built-ins and specially shaped walls—that you don't go overboard. Just because you find it at Home Depot does not mean that you need to own it. Design organically. Some have a tendency to find the prefab object in the supply department and use it. Rather, do the opposite: if you need a five-foot column to house your freezer, then that has a purpose and becomes a legitimate element in your design. It looks like it belongs there. Don't get carried away with all the available options. Work with what you have, with what your needs are. Allow your design to grow organically. Throwing disparate objects together just because you can creates a McMansion effect, lacking integration, imagination, and design intent. Don't let that be *your* house.

## Embellishing Floors

We discussed floors in earlier chapters, but the idea of embellishing your floors with various materials is somewhat different. Do you need to use the same wood throughout a room? The same stone? What about combining a cream-colored marble with black, or with something really dramatic and eye-catching, like red travertine? Wood medallions and inlay suggest a rich, Victorian look, or you could get ultramodern with custom-cast tiles from aluminum or glass. As you might imagine, these are not the most budget-friendly options, but they imbue a room with definite panache.

## Registers, Grilles, and Other Unexpected Details

Here again, necessity engenders opportunity for adornment. Air, heat, cooling, even some appliances inevitably mean that ducts will show up somewhere in a room. You *could* cover them with standard metal grilles from your local hardware store—but why should you? Search out what else is available online or through catalogs, or even get recommendations from an HVAC professional. Think of the registers and grilles not as metal objects to be slapped against a wall or floor, but as the decorative buttons on a captain's uniform. They come in various metals, including steel, brass, copper, zinc, and even a few finishes that replicate pewter (though they aren't).

Air handling will vary from house to house. Be sure you know the size of the duct you want to cover so you can coordinate it with a specific grille.

Other places grilles show up include radiators, which are often covered with metal mesh or a decorative cut-metal insert into a wooden frame; and fireplaces, where screens prevent sparks from flying into a room. Heavier gauge metals are best here, but (no surprise) tend to be more expensive.

# Materials

The materials you select throughout your home establish the atmosphere of each room. Marble floors or wooden ones, a steel stair or one in travertine, glass walls or plaster ones or brick—each of these will bring a special spirit to your house. Exploring and experimenting with various options is a crucial—and fun—part of the design process.

## Metals

And on the subject of metals, decorative metals stretch the ornamental possibilities even further these days, with all kinds of new and innovative developments that go beyond the traditional wrought iron gates and balconies. The rustic look of heavy mesh in kitchen door panels dates back centuries, but think of utilizing the same concept in other areas of your house, like walls and room dividers, so the play of light creates a kind of visual duet between the two rooms.

Recently, someone cooked up an idea to create metal tiles, something like the ones you used to see on tin ceilings. These, however, are first stamped with a design and then mounted onto board for added reinforcement, making it possible to use them the way you would ceramic tiles, say, in the kitchen or a bath, maybe placed against a strip of stainless steel for contrast. What's especially fun about this new technique is that it can also be done with acid wash, so even a photograph can be replicated in the metal and reconstructed on a wall. Other options:

- A fireplace grating could be made of forged iron with a mesh applied to it.

- Brushed steel makes an impact where tiles would ordinarily be used—for kitchen backsplash or around a fireplace

- Metals also make for elegant handrails and balustrades, though you might want to think twice if you live in a colder climate (freezing metal on your hands first thing in the morning is a nasty way to wake up) or intend to carpet your stairs (static electricity isn't a whole lot of fun for most people, either).

## Stone and Tile Finishes

We also spoke a bit about stone in Chapter 13, but when selecting stone (or tile) finishes, it's useful to have a bit more detailed knowledge about the various kinds of stone available and how they can be used. Some stone is appropriate for indoors, others not. Some tile is appropriate for floors, others only for walls. Some stone can be polished, others won't shine no matter what you use to scrub them. A few pointers, we thought, might help to sort it all out.

- Many stone items are custom-made, like countertops or tubs. Others, like stone tile, are precut. Tile thickness will vary, with thinner tiles (about ¼-inch thick) for walls and thicker tile for floors (at least ⅝-inch), which require a heavier load.

- Because of the heaviness of stone, it has to be mounted on an extremely strong support. Best is to use double layers of plywood plus heavy-set mortar (rather than thin-set).

- Some stone is better suited for the outdoors. Marble, for instance, is a variety of chalk. Still, some types—Botticino, for instance—are hard enough for outdoor use. (This is also why countertops tend to be highly polished—they resist water better).

- Always find out the technical characteristics of the stone—hardness, permeability, ease of taking various finishes. If your stone seller cannot answer these questions, go elsewhere!

- Be careful of the lower-cost, ¼-inch tile, which literally can fall off the wall when used under the wrong circumstances. It's tempting to use interior-grade tile outdoors, but it simply isn't strong enough.

- Most stones can handle the same kinds of finish, though a hammer finish will not work on very thin tile. One option available is a very thin stone tile, which is glued to a honeycomb backing made from aluminum for lightness. (These are particularly good for decorating boats, should you decide to take on *that* dream project when your house is done!)

- ◆ Wood has a grain that is itself decorative. Similarly, the veins of color and various elements within a stone can be exquisite.

- ◆ Finish choices include polished, honed (mostly for marble & granite), tumbled (stone polished in a drum until it emerges honed, matte, and smooth, but non-reflective), and thermal finish, in which stone is passed under fire to attain a rougher appearance and texture. Thermal-finished stone provides a strong grip, so it's an ideal for pathways, especially around a swimming pool or pond.

- ◆ Marble, quartzite, and granite all take well to polishing. Other stone like slate does not. It's important to pay attention to which stone can do what.

Generally, when working with stone tile, you will want rougher surfaces on the floor than you use on the walls. (Though rough stone walls can have a certain power, casting an image of rough impregnability. Think of the way large banks are built, or the stone walls of Medieval castles.) Two popular choices are slate, which can be finished in "split face," and travertine, which could be filled or unfilled. Slate is composed of layers, which separate if hit at the right angle. The result is a slightly uneven surface with an intriguing, decorative texture. Travertine naturally has large pores left from the gases present when the stone formed. Most of the time, these pores are filled with a resin, making open travertine difficult to find on the market.

It is also not the most practical choice for certain environments: most of Rome is built of travertine, but you wouldn't want to do this in Anchorage or Minneapolis, where water could get into the pores, freeze, and cause the stone to crack.

### Design Don't

Be careful to select stone that is appropriate for the space and climate in which you plan to use it. Porous stone does not do well outside, though this is less of an issue in dry climates. Some stone also won't do well in tubs and showers, as the cycle of water, soap, and household cleaners can deteriorate the finish—or the stone itself. Ask for advice, and choose carefully.

## Glass

Glass and glass tiles can lend tremendous allure to a room, enriching it with a glistening, deep color or an icy, crystalline magic. You could use glass tiles, glass blocks, patterned glass, glass *mosaics*, stained glass, clear or frosted glass, opaque or translucent glass, etched glass—the options are nearly infinite.

The best tiles are spectacular, with real gold on the face of them, but even the more affordable choices offer tremendous variety: it is, for instance, even possible now to scan a photograph and render the image in mosaic tiles. The technique has limited possibilities, however. Because the tile is just two centimeters square, a small area, viewed from close distance, would appear as a pixilated pattern without meaning. Consequently, photograph tiles have to be installed on a large area; but it would be possible to have the bottom of your swimming pool, for instance, brightened by the image of your own portrait. Or you could place such an image on a wall: perhaps do away with all those little family snapshots and replace them with a single-family portrait across the main wall of your breakfast room.

Glass mosaic now often comes glued to a piece of fiberglass mesh, making installation much easier than it once was. Using small tiles, you can, with this method, make the tiles follow the actual shapes of the walls, so they can conform to a gentle curve—around, say, the rounded walls of a shower stall or shower seat.

In addition, most companies, like the Italian Trend Tile, offer pre-arranged patterns, from florals to Art Deco–inspired designs, which can be small or large enough to cover an entire 8×4-foot wall. It's an ingenious idea, really, a way of combining the concepts and installation technology, as it were, of wallpaper with tile.

Obviously, glass has other uses in a home, mainly wherever you want to benefit from its translucency and ability to transmit light. Glass shower doors make the tiny space of a shower stall or tub feel larger. Glass sliding doors to the deck or garden create the feeling of bringing the outside in, and allow you to enjoy the beauty of your view to its fullest, rather than through the small eye of a window in a wall. And glass doors to the house, even for entrances that face north, allow light through to give a feeling for the atmosphere of the day.

The downside: thermally, glass is inferior to wood. Heavy-duty glass is also advisable on doors, especially where panels are at hand level, to ensure that children and pets don't inadvertently walk into them.

**Architerms**

Mosaics are designs or images formed of stone, glass, or tiles glued to a surface. Historically, they were used to cover floors and walls in ancient Greek, Roman, and Byzantine architecture.

**Design Tip**

Working with glass includes, of course, working with mirrors. Our own preference is for mirrors with frames around them: optical illusions are interesting, but create confusion. It's preferable to see where a mirror stops or ends. Using a mirror at the end of a room is a cheap trick, though as a virtual opening, it may provide the same psychological effect that windows do. Nonetheless, we suggest using mirrors as decorative elements, like framed paintings, and not as visual sleights of hand (or eye).

## Paint

Most of the time, walls get painted. It's a task almost all of us have taken on at some point, usually with a bunch of friends and an extra-large pizza. So we know—or think we know—the basics: select a color from the color chart at the paint store, use high- or semi-gloss for kitchens and bathrooms (easier to clean, withstands moisture), pour the stuff into the tray, roll the roller through, and go.

Well, kind of. First, what paint where? Varieties of paint include …

 ◆ Basement paints (recommended for concrete blocks).

 ◆ Outdoor paints.

- ◆ Indoor paints.
- ◆ Paint for concrete (sidewalks, etc.).
- ◆ Gloss.
- ◆ Semi-gloss.
- ◆ Matte.

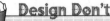

**Design Don't**

Use the right paint in the right places: doorframes should be gloss or semi-gloss, for instance. And be sure to follow the material until it meets another material. Do not paint the face of the molding in gloss and then the side of it in flat paint. Cover the material fully.

Unless you're using basic white (which makes life easy), it's worth employing a few trade tips along the way. Selecting a color, for instance, is not *really* as easy as grabbing a color chart and bringing it to the mixing person at the counter. The best way to select a color is actually to use it. Paint a piece of the wall and look at it in various daylight conditions (sunny, cloudy) and again at night. Colors do not appear the same under the fluorescent light of a paint supply store as they will on the wall of your room. Paint a few samples—say, a 2×4-foot section of wall in the room where the color will be used. Yes, it costs a bit more to buy a sample of paint than it does to stick a piece of printed paper against a corner. But it costs a *lot* more to make a color error.

Moreover, the same color paint can look completely different in different finishes. Eggshell white is not the same as white in matte finish. (Eggshell is a finish type like matte or glossy; therefore, the color white is available in matte/flat or eggshell finish, but these do not look the same.) Try both and compare the two, bearing in mind that if you plan to use both types of paint in the same room, you may need to order one of them in a color of a different name (though it will be, in fact, the same color).

**Design Tip**

Studies have shown that different colors can affect mood. Consider reading up on these as you decide on the colors of your interiors to help create the atmosphere you're looking for.

For our own clients, we recommend using as much white as possible. We'll leave the walls neutral and add a splash of color here and there, preferably in the orange-ochre range. It's a very warm color which works especially well with sunlight—and even more, perhaps, in the absence of sun, where it brings a certain pleasure and comfort. The idea is to keep the house itself neutral, allowing the objects, the furniture, the people, to appear at their best coloring.

But it's certainly not gospel. The fashion was exactly the opposite in the nineteenth century, for instance, and humanity seems to have survived those eras well enough. Follow what works best for you.

From a technical standpoint, paint can be applied practically anywhere, even on brick. However, in the interest of earth-friendly design, do your best to avoid using oil-based paints. Look instead for lime wash, milk paint, and other low-volatile compound, water-based paints without drying agents or formaldehyde. (See Chapter 14 for suggestions.)

# Paneling

Wall paneling was particularly popular in the 1960s, though it was first used in thirteenth-century England, when families living in forests paneled the insides of their homes to keep the wind at bay. Somehow, we suspect, over the course of historical transformation, the look became a status symbol, bringing to mind large chairs and Old Boys business conducted in hushed tones.

Good wood paneling is not a job to be taken lightly. It should be handled by a cabinet maker, someone whom you would hire to make a good, solid set of bookcases. Drawings have to be absolutely accurate, as labor and materials are pricey and errors, therefore, costly. Yes, you can use the chipboard and veneer stuff that was popular in the 1960s, but it's certainly not ideal. Slightly better is furniture-grade veneer; it's more durable than paint and like wallpaper, hides imperfections in the wall.

It's important to understand from the outset that creating a wood-paneled room is not as easy as it may seem. This is not a wallpaper job. There is inevitable shrinkage in any wood product, so there has to be some slippage, and joinery that will adjust to the seasons and humidity. Plywood tends to move less than solid wood.

Your paneling expert will start by laying out the joints and the moldings, following your design directions for the size of the panels and the kind and orientation of the wood veneer—right, left, up, down, radially, matched. Will it cover half the wall, all of the wall, part of the ceiling? will the finish be a simple lacquer, like polyurethane, or glossy? do you want various color stains or waxes, or do you prefer the wood be left so it can be painted, now or in the future? Smoother grains, like poplar or maple, lend themselves more easily to painting.

> **Design Tip**
>
> If you're considering wood paneling but might want to paint the wood at some point, stick to smooth-grain woods like poplar, which are more amenable to paint.

# Plaster

Plaster lends a smooth, even texture, and because it's handmade, carries a kind of old-world charm. Unlike paneling, it tends to be used on the entire wall, though not necessarily every wall in a room. You could, for instance, plaster a free-standing wall element, or plaster a fireplace around its opening. A thick, low wall between living and dining room adorned with niches and covered with plaster transforms from being a merely functional divider to a sculptural object.

Plastering is a skilled task—or should be. Usually, metal mesh is attached to a plywood or wallboard backing and the plaster applied over that. With the advent of wallboard, the use of plaster as a standard wall material has virtually disappeared, so that it's now become a high-end item, considered a fancy touch when used on the interior of a home (though it is still a common finish for exteriors).

Plaster also performs well as a decorative, ornamental material. Plaster ceiling medallions or wall moldings recall the grand mansions of the past. And Venetian plaster techniques bring a depth of color and illumination to the surface of a wall. Though some painting techniques can replicate the hand-finished, weathered look of painted plaster, they never quite achieve the same rich, polished effect.

But again, of course, these things are subjective and personal. And that was the point of designing your own home in the first place.

## The Least You Need to Know

♦ Use metal, stone, wood, tile, paint, plaster, and other materials to enhance and personalize the basic elements of your house.

♦ Allow the functions of various parts or elements of your house to shape their forms.

♦ Allow walls and floors to be as decorative as they are functional thorough the use of special finishes and shaping.

♦ Don't go overboard with ornaments, but don't scrimp on them either, or you'll feel like you're living in a sanitized box.

# Chapter 21

# Embellishing Your Exterior and Outdoor Spaces

## In This Chapter

◆ A look outside

◆ Adding exterior details

◆ …And the living is easy

One of the first rules of architecture is to "design from the inside out." So now that you've embellished the interior, let's take a walk outside. What's there? What isn't? A porch for your porch swing? A view for your window? How much time do you plan to spend outside, and what will you do there? What do you want people to see when they pass by your house? (Because, admit it, you wouldn't be doing all this if you didn't care!) What look do you want it to project? Your house should feel like "home" even before you open the front door.

# Exterior Spaces

Your home design could begin and end with the wall of your façade—but it doesn't have to. Extending your home with exterior spaces and paying attention to adjacent details (like your driveway, for instance) gives you more home to enjoy, and further accentuates your signature—your *self*—on the design.

## Porches and Pergolas

Baseball and apple pie, they say, are the great American traditions, but it's hard to imagine America without the trustworthy front *porch*. It is where we all plan to retire one day, sitting in our rockers, watching the neighbors go by, reading all the books we never had the time for earlier in life.

**Architerms**

A **porch** is an open space along the outside of a house, covered by a roof. It may also be enclosed by screen or glass. A low wall, like that surrounding a porch or balcony, is called a **parapet**.

Somehow, porches seem to hark back to bygone times, but they are very much a part of our present and can be one of the most delightful extra touches on a home. Screened-in porches allow for dining and entertaining without the nuisance of mosquitoes; open porches let you sit safely and still feel the rain when it falls, or chat with passers-by, or watch a sunset, and feel the day grow cool.

From a practical point, porches also provide shade indoors, keeping rooms cooler. If they include parapets, you gain extra seating and storage, planters for flowers, even a rail or thin countertop for a dinner plate and glass. Or you could surround them in wood lattice, covered in springtime by climbing plants—morning glories and wisteria, for instance. Grape vine also grows rather quickly.

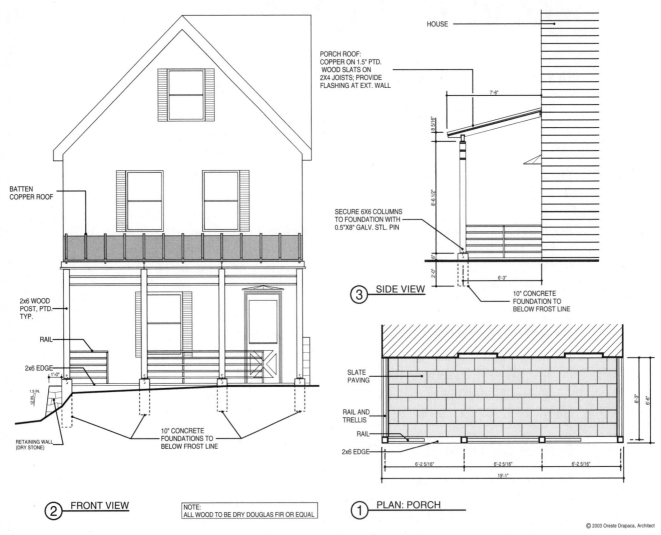

*Porch.*

© 2003 Oreste Drapaca, Architect

Porches are usually associated with the entrance of a home, and wrap themselves around the front of the house, mediating between outside and in.
*Pergolas*, too, work well at the entrance, perhaps between the street and the
front door, possibly leading up to the porch. They can also extend from it,
perhaps sheltering the path between the front of the house and the kitchen
entrance, or from the kitchen to a nearby herb garden. And they create a
romantic highlight to your landscape, bringing texture, shade, and light in
the view both to and from your house. While grapevines pour along the
top of the classic pergola, they're not mandatory; replace them with other
plants, or with an open wooden lattice. Although the columns can be made of
stone, wood, or brick, you will want to stick to wood for the beams, as beams
require bending stress.

> **Architerms**
>
> Pergolas, made from
> intersecting beams sup-
> ported by posts, provide
> shelter, usually along a walk-
> way. They are often covered
> with plants or vines.

*Pergola.*

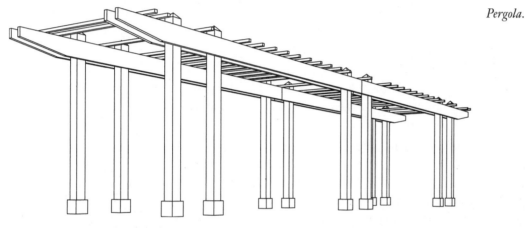

## Decks and Terraces

What's the difference between a *terrace* and a *deck*? (No, this is not a joke.) A
terrace rests on its entire footprint; a deck, usually built of wood (like on a ship,
hence the name), is an open platform, often raised. In building a deck, you'll
need to be sure that you use wood appropriate for the outdoors—treated wood
or wood that is resistant to outside elements, such as teak, cedar, ipe, or other
Brazilian woods. If you utilize the technology used in building ships, you can
have a whole different look, getting fancy with lots of lacquer to achieve the
highly polished look of a sailing boat. Terraces are more often built from brick
or stone, such as flagstone or slate.

But either is a welcome addition to a home, particularly in fair climates, like
an outdoor living room (though it's also nice to dine there). And either can be
cheerfully decorated with planters or a surrounding garden. Decks and terraces
tend to be located in the rear of the house for privacy, but decks, because they
are raised, can be anywhere—possibly from a bedroom—especially with a house
built on two levels.

How big? How will you use it? Most of the time, a deck or terrace should be big enough to put a table on, and the table, of course, depends on the size of your family, how often and how lavishly you entertain, and whether you plan to hold neighborhood barbeques from time to time. With the table, there should be space for outdoor armchairs, perhaps a grill, and enough room left over to walk around comfortably. You can even incorporate planters into the design: in the spirit of green design, think about using larger planters for small trees that add shade. (These could even be fruit trees, such as crabapple or cherry.)

Screened decks, like porches, allow for all-weather enjoyment of the space, as well. Planters are still nice here; the sun comes in laterally, so part of the shade created by large plants still cools the interior.

Other possible built-in additions include benches and storage for garden tools and barbeque, children's toys, Frisbees, and the like. Or combine them, building benches that lift to provide storage within.

## Walkways

To connect points of interest around your house—say, from the terrace to the swimming pool, or the garage to the front door—it's not a bad idea to have a *paved* walkway.

Moreover, paved walkways protect the foundations of your house from water (mostly in urban settings), and protect you and your family from slipping in wet weather: even dirt paths covered with crushed stone provide more traction than the bare earth or wet grass. (These are the kinds of things one perhaps appreciates less in the planning phase than in the course of real life, like the moment you realize you left your car outside with the sunroof open and suddenly it's pouring buckets.)

Pavers can be of many materials—concrete, stone, or even wood, which adds a rustic, quaint look—and joined with mortar or left "open-jointed" with grass growing between them. A memorable house boasted a fountain in the middle of a paved courtyard; in the summer, the water flowed from the fountain and cooled the pavers on hot afternoons and evenings.

## Driveways

In basic terms, driveways deliver your car and other vehicles from the street. They should be large enough to accommodate larger vehicles for workmen who will come to service your home (no matter how carefully you plan), such as landscapers, roofers, plumbers, or electricians. Consider going beyond the standard 12 to 15 feet, though it's not necessary.

Asphalt, gravel, and pavers provide traction, but since any such paved driveway tends to become hot, thereby contributing to the heat gain of the house, it's a good idea to keep some shading plants around it, as well. Pebbles do create less heat than asphalt (they are also less expensive); another option is concrete with crushed glass, which is actually more interesting than asphalt because of

**Architerms**

For most people, **paving** suggests asphalt. In architectural terms, however, anything lining a path that isn't earth can be paving: stone, tile, concrete, brick, etc.

the color. If you do choose asphalt, try painting it to reduce the amount of heat that it retains. Or limit the paving to just wheel tracks for the car, with grass between them, adding a small walkway, perhaps of stepping stones, from garage to the front door.

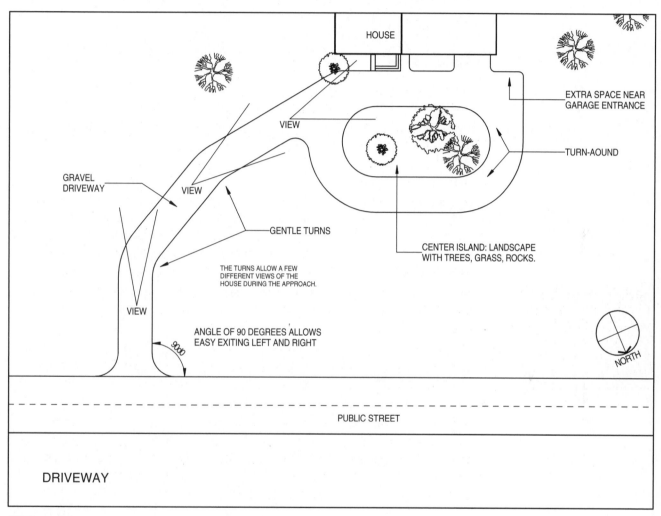

HOUSE

EXTRA SPACE NEAR
GARAGE ENTRANCE

TURN-AOUND

VIEW

GRAVEL
DRIVEWAY

VIEW

GENTLE TURNS

CENTER ISLAND: LANDSCAPE
WITH TREES, GRASS, ROCKS.

THE TURNS ALLOW A FEW
DIFFERENT VIEWS OF THE
HOUSE DURING THE APPROACH.

VIEW

ANGLE OF 90 DEGREES ALLOWS
EASY EXITING LEFT AND RIGHT

90 00

NORTH

PUBLIC STREET

DRIVEWAY

*Walkway/driveway.*

Whether your driveway sweeps and curves or simply carves a direct, short line from street to garage door is largely an aesthetic choice (depending on how far your house sits from the road). A gentle curve is always nice, but even though many people do find the sweeping appearance of a long, winding driveway beautiful, it both adds to the cost and decreases the amount of lawn available. Then again, a long line of poplars along a straight driveway can be quite impressive.

# Embellishments and Extras

Small things, too, can make a difference, as much on the exterior of your house as in the interior, as much in terms of the pleasure of daily living as in terms of the overall look of your new home. Don't be fooled by adages long out-of-date: it's *joy* that's in the details.

## Columns

Imagine, for instance, that at the end of the driveway, you step out of your car and onto a gray slate walkway, up a step and through a low garden of shade plants until you reach a colonnade—a procession of columns on either side of your front door.

In effect, a column is little more than a roof support, though a roof support with attitude. Some people find them stuffy and unfriendly, others think they add grandeur to a house. Either way, an entire row of columns imparts a repetitive rhythm to a façade, a form of decoration, while functioning as a support to the roof of a porch, say, or the *lintel* above the door Obviously, you want them to complement the style of the house—*classic revival* or *Southern antebellum*, usually, though not always: geometrical columns built of high-tech materials can add fun and zip to a more *postmodern* look.

### Architerms

**Classic revival** architecture dates to the early nineteenth century, mainly in the United States and England, inspired by the classical architecture of Greece and Rome.

**Southern antebellum** style is what you think of when you think of *Gone with the Wind*—large plantation homes with sweeping porches and columns. (The years prior to the American Civil War are known as the "antebellum period.")

**Postmodern** architecture emerged as a reaction to the bare forms of modernism. Postmodern architects return ornament and often wit to what they consider the "soullessness" of modernist design, while still making visual reference to industrial geometry. Michael Graves is perhaps the best known postmodern architect.

## Spigots

And just as you reach the door, something green and snakelike catches the corner of your eye: the garden hose. Right—you should water the garden now, so you don't have to deal with it later on.

A spigot is customary at the front of the house—for washing cars, for watering gardens, and for children to aim at parents. This latter is something they are prone to do no matter where the spigot is, however, and a spigot at the rear of the house is an added convenience, both in terms of garden care and washing muddy feet before entering the kitchen. (If you have a grilling area, you might choose to place the spigot there, insulating the pipe for safety.)

From there, you can elaborate further: an outdoor shower, sprinklers for the children to run through, a water irrigation system (more on this later).

## Electrical Outlets

Remember what we said about "never enough outlets"? It's not a bad idea to have some outdoor ones as well, for afternoons you'd like bring your laptop with you while you tan, or for recharging the phone of a guest who "just happens" to pop by for a swim. Most people mount exterior outlets on the exterior wall of the house, by the deck or terrace area. Code requirements demand that any outlet used outdoors be rated for exterior use, cased in an aluminum box with a cover and rubber gasket.

There might also be cases when you would like another outlet somewhere in the yard, though these require digging to run a cable, usually housed in an aluminum tube, called electrical conduit, from your house to where the contact point will be—and you may reasonably choose not to do that. Alternatively, you could put it above ground, along a fence or wall (people could trip over it if it runs through the middle of the yard). A lighting consultant might be able to help you work out how to light the garden to show it at its best. Keep in mind that there are lights that may have to be mounted high so they can shine down on a table, and others embedded in the ground to light the trees or other outstanding landscape elements from below. If your grilling area is not directly adjacent to the house (and the exterior outlet located there), add lights here, as well.

# Outdoor Living

So by now you've pretty much designed the house. You've designed the spaces adjacent to your house, like your deck or terraces or porch. But what about the rest of your property? Will you plant a garden, however small? Throw large outdoor parties? Dig a pool? Part of designing your home involves designing the space *around* your home: what you see as you approach, the view you've created all those windows for. A landscape architect or designer can help you with the flowers; let's just talk about the structures they surround.

# Gazebos

Traditionally, we have always adjusted the nature around us to fit our more specific human needs, like sitting down on something or walking on suitable ground. So it makes sense that, when we create a garden, we would bring touches to it that make it more comfortable: a walkway, a bench, a place where you can sit down and bring a book, your laptop—a kind of pavilion where you can commune with nature.

*Gazebo.*

The romantic, fairy-tale feeling that tends to come with the idea of a gazebo may have something to do with what must be the most famous gazebo of all time—the one in *The Sound of Music* that provides the backdrop for any number of love scenes, including Liesl von Trapp's discovery she is in love with Rolf, whereupon she sings "When You're Sixteen." (A bit of Hollywood trivia: evidently the actress playing Liesl, Charmian Carr, slipped while filming this scene and crashed her leg through one of the glass walls.)

Usually constructed of wood, gazebos take a multifaceted form, with at least a hexagonal or even octagonal building plan. They can also be round, like the Pantheon. Wooden railings and an open trellis surround the gazebo along the bottom, or in some instances, a gazebo might be completely open, almost an umbrella on stilts with a floor beneath. Still others—like the one in *The Sound of Music*—are glass enclosed, with French doors opening back out into the garden.

Like many things these days, gazebos can be had in ready-to-build kits from home building stores and catalogs. Use this method if you must, though we prefer the homemade variety, particularly when you've just gone to the trouble and expense of designing an entire custom house. A better option, we think, is to study images of gazebos in books or browse through build-your-own sets and premade floor plans until you find the style you like. You know this routine—it should remind you of the earliest phase of planning your house, when you were still working on the program for your design.

Typically, gazebos tend to be either white and Victorian looking, or the color of unfinished wood or bamboo, with an East Asian touch. Add electricity if you plan to entertain or dine there, or want to be able to use the gazebo in the evening. Built-in seating and storage (or benches with storage underneath) can also be useful. Or you might want to add a hot tub or a bar, or get truly decadent and have both.

**Flashpoint**

Speaking of the early phases of planning, you might just want to check with local ordinances to determine whether permits are needed for this, and to apply for one if required.

No matter how you choose to build it, however, keep in mind that this is not a toy house. The structure has to be built according to good practice. Columns should be set into concrete foundations with a foundation depth safely under the frost line (three and a half feet). Being open, gazebos are vulnerable to the force of upward winds; don't let *The Sound of Music* become *The Wizard of Oz*.

Orientation is not much of an issue in a symmetrical structure, of course. You have the same configuration all around the gazebo except the steps and entrance, which will relate to the pathway that leads there. (For safety, especially if you have small children, it's a good idea to keep the wall and railing high enough to discourage them from trying to jump on and over it, while still allowing a feeling of being out in the open air.) Again, depending on your planned use, your gazebo does not need to be all that large—eight feet is enough to allow four people to sit around a small table comfortably—or why not just have a gazebo built for two?

# Outdoor Dining—Open Air and Screened

It may be more efficient to create a rectangular space for outdoor dining, as this will allow you to accommodate a table for six or more, and could have an outdoor grill built under the same roof. Add a fireproof platform if possible, and perhaps a couple of low walls, so that you can keep the grill separate from the actual eating space. Or install a grill of bricks, a kind of built-in version, as another option.

It's also advisable to have walls, even if not all the way to the roof or all the way around, to screen the table from too much wind. Dining al fresco is no fun if you have to keep your hands on everything to keep it from being blown away! Japanese-style doors or columns situated several feet apart and joined by sliding panels would serve the purpose nicely, and will be particularly appreciated on damp or especially mosquito-filled evenings. Place bushes and small trees around the pavilion to keep the area cool in summer, and surround it with grass (or gravel as a second choice). Anything that is paved should be under the roof, keeping it shaded as much as possible. (Think of how hot a parking lot gets in summer.)

As for lighting, candles and gas lamps bring plenty of atmosphere and may be perfectly sufficient substitutes for electric lighting, which can get ugly and expensive. In organizing any lighting plans for both the interior space and any walks or pathways, remember (or review) the concepts we discussed in Chapter 19.

### Design Tip

Designing your outdoor dining area also gives you the chance to do some things you may not have been able to incorporate into your home, so long as the final design integrates with the main house. Try combining wood, brick, and timber; timber and brick; or timber and fieldstone, using, if possible, stone from your own site. The smaller size of this structure makes it possible—even desirable—to get a bit more creative and daring.

*Outdoor dining pavilion.*

Storage is also an advantage, as otherwise you will find yourself carting dishes and trays (not to mention forks and tables) from the house whenever you decide to eat here. The bench storage system suggested when we talked about decks and gazebos works fine. Add a counter with shelves as well, if you have the space.

# Pools, Ponds, and Pool Houses

If you have a pool on your property, first and foremost, make sure you have a fence to go around it. This is not just a matter of modesty—in most areas, it's the law, aimed at keeping children from wandering into your yard and swimming without supervision.

If you have a pool, pair it with a pool house. (And even if you don't have a pool, who's to say you can't have a pool house anyway?) Here again, your budget and your needs will be your guide: a pool house can be anything from a changing room and a space for the pool machinery to an entertainment center with full kitchen, stereo equipment, shower, toilet, and a spare room for holding parties poolside even in the rain. Add a phone, pool toys, and rafts, and climbing plants around the sides. (Avoid having too many flowers in order keep bees away from the pool; a wet bee is an angry bee.)

Even without a pool structure, a pool is a more than welcome added luxury. Make it look like a part of the landscape: a bit of earth work and careful selections of materials and stone go a long way to making the pool seem like it belongs there, naturally.

And if you prefer to keep things looking even more natural, consider building a pond, in place of (or in addition to) a pool. It doesn't have to be large—tiny garden-sized ponds filled with water plants, a frog or two, and an exquisitely shaped stone (from your own site, from a recent trip to the beach), impart a feeling of cool and tranquility on hot afternoons. Don't make the mistake of thinking that you can just fill a hole with water, though. You'll need a liner of some sort: concrete, gravel, wood timbers, rammed earth, rocks. Please, do not buy the plastic "pond" tubs available at home building supply shops. Please don't.

Or you could add a reflecting pool built of stone, slate, glass brick, or other material. According to green design principles, a reflecting pool, even one only two feet deep, tends to lower the temperature of the air around it. This is why such pools are traditionally used in Arab architecture. If you have a very fine mist of water on you, it lowers your body temperature. That is the idea of a reflecting pool.

## The Least You Need To Know

- Expand your home into the outdoors by adding a porch, deck, or terrace.
- Plan walkways and driveways so they best enhance your property and your house—but always put safety first.
- Using electric outlets and spigots to the exterior of your house can add to the pleasures of outdoor living.
- When planning and designing outdoor or adjacent structures, use the same principles you worked with when starting your house: program, budget, and so on.
- Work with nature to enhance the natural properties of your landscape.

# Chapter 22

# When Your Home Is an Apartment

## In This Chapter

- ◆ Dealing with the givens
- ◆ The law and your design
- ◆ Think of the neighbors
- ◆ Two apartments, one home
- ◆ How to handle stairs

Lives change. You get a new job that takes you from rural Arkansas to downtown Manhattan. Your Chicago aerie was fine when you were single, manageable when you wed, but with a child on the way, it's time for a bigger place. A family member becomes incapacitated, and multifloor living becomes difficult. For any of a number of reasons, your new home could mean a new apartment—but that doesn't mean you have to take whatever you find as-is. There is, after all, always room for improvement, and no reason you can't still live in the home of your dreams.

## It Could Happen to You

So for whatever reason, you need an apartment. You check the ads. You attend the open houses. You visit the agents. And then comes the sticker-shock: the value of your apartment has increased since you bought it, but is not enough to cover what you really need for a new place.

What to do? If you're lucky, you can just buy the apartment next door or directly above or below your current one—a situation we wish on all our clients. If not, you keep hunting. In both cases, chances are good that whatever you find will need to be redesigned, reorganized, and restructured to suit you, your life, your needs—all the things a custom house is made for.

So when you set out on your search, keep your imagination flowing and your mind open, but, as with planning a house, have at least the basics of a program in place before you start. Do you want a large kitchen and three bedrooms? Is the kitchen unimportant but a home office mandatory? How many square feet do you want? Does it really need to be larger than what you have now, or just configured differently? Are you willing to have smaller rooms in order to have enough of them—or do you prefer bigger but fewer rooms?

And outside the apartment itself, are there common areas, like a laundry room, a party room, or a gym? Do these cost extra, or are they included in the purchase price? Will you use them? If not, do you really want to pay for them? If outdoor space is important to you, you'll probably want a balcony or roof garden, or at least a park nearby.

You don't need us to tell you all this. Just remember, as you explore possibilities, that your "program" includes the nature of the building itself, too. The point is that the two-bedroom, river-view apartment with the health club in the penthouse and optional valet service is not necessarily going to cost you much more than a one-bedroom place that needs to be completely gutted and rebuilt. On the other hand, you can often easily convert a well-designed one-bedroom flat to two bedrooms, so don't rule it out just because it isn't exactly what you're looking for. In essence, you'll be remodeling it anyway.

## What to Look for When You Look

Essentially, the apartment *is* the site. It's only so big, and you can only do so much. Because urban and apartment living impose certain restrictions, you'll want to make the design process as easy and cost-effective as possible. From dealing with co-op boards to designing your way around fixed windows and pipes that accommodate not only your home, but your neighbors', you'll want to simplify the building task by starting out with something amenable to the renovations that you have in mind. You can't really make your ceilings higher, unless you've bought two floors, and even then, you can only raise one of them—and then the other will be lower! You can't make a post-war apartment look convincingly pre-war; it will only appear ridiculous. Be sensible.

That said, we encourage you to above all look for an apartment with good natural light. No, of course you don't want to stare into an auto-repair shop. And yes, a view of the river, the park, or a sweeping skyline panorama is desirable. But you will notice the lack of light more than you will notice the lack of a beautiful view, and more important, you will feel it. People simply are not happy without light. (Remember what we said earlier about the importance of light in creating mood!)

This may not, however, be as difficult as you think. In an urban environment, for instance, a building that faces north can pick up the reflection of sunlight from surrounding buildings. On a high floor, with open views and wide sky, any apartment will appear bright and well-lit. Higher ceilings further enhance this effect.

*A northern view is not necessarily dark and gloomy!*

Do, however, check the windows. Usually, they will be old, leak water or air (or both), and, if they haven't been replaced with double-glazed ones, will allow noise and drafts to come through. If they need replacing, good new double-paned ones with three-way openings could cost you over $2,500 a unit.

And as with choosing any building site, you'll want to investigate the neighborhood. In an apartment building, though, your real neighbors are the ones you'll run into in the elevator, the lobby, or the stairwell. What kinds of people live in the building? Who will be living on either side of you? Above? Below? Are they friendly and outgoing? Private but polite? Are they approximately your age? A building with lots of children can be wonderful if you have kids who'll be looking for playmates, or annoying as heck when they punch every button in the elevator and you're already running late. (And be assured, at least one kid will.)

Most of all, you want to look for a "healthy" building. Has the boiler been checked recently? Is there a report available on the conditions of the building's structure, the roof, the plumbing? Ask the seller for this information before you even bid on the apartment—the managing agent for the building has records. If the owner says they don't exist, he's probably covering something up. Do not risk purchasing an apartment without reviewing these papers carefully: if there is a major systems failure in the building, the owners will have to pay out-of-pocket or take a loan from the bank. (And the building's finances will reflect accordingly on the resale value of *your* apartment.)

# What You've Got Is What You Get

**Architerms**

The **soil stacks** are the vertical plumbing pipes (including vents) that run from the building drain through the roof of the building. These include vent stacks, which remove gases from septic systems, and soil stacks, which handle waste from toilets throughout the building.

There's a lot to be said for apartment design versus house design: you don't have to worry about striking rock when you dig, for instance, or about septic tanks, or finishes for the exterior. But you'll have other issues to think about, some similar to the designing of a house, others not.

The structure of a pre-existing building includes, naturally, the water disposal and *soil stacks*. This simple fact is going to drive much of your design. In order to remove waste from the toilet effectively, pipes have to be pitched, not straight. Obviously, the whereabouts of pitched pipes will determine where you place the bathrooms, which in turn will influence the general circulation (layout) of the entire space.

Consequently, in place of the site survey we described earlier, you'd be well advised to commission a survey of the existing conditions of the apartment, locating all pipes. Be aware that pipes are often hidden, and you may have to cut into the walls to find out exactly where they are. This will include determining the building's main, vertical pipes, which will tell you where the kitchen can go.

Then there are the windows. Local regulations may stipulate that every room other than a kitchen or bath *must* have a window. This means that if you were thinking of splitting one bedroom into two, you'll need to ensure that it's a two-windowed room to start with. Depending on your circumstances, though, there may be ways around this: in place of a wall, a sliding door could separate the rooms, or you might consider making the two rooms semi-private, with a large (open) archway cut into the dividing wall. If neither of these is possible, expect to completely reconfigure the room and adjacent spaces—or keep shopping for another apartment.

Additional restrictions apply when combining apartments: at least one door per flat must open into the public corridor and access the stairs. Fire regulations require that a single staircase connect no more than two floors of an apartment. That is, only two consecutive floor slabs may have an opening for the staircase to avoid a draft effect that would suck the flames upward.

Again, too, you will have to determine basic utility zones: although having two apartments allows you to choose which kitchen stays and which one goes—and if *both* go and an entirely new one takes their place—in the end, the rule to remember is that whatever has plumbing, keeps plumbing. Turning a living room into a kitchen simply will not work, unless the living room happens to share the wall where the plumbing lies with one of the kitchens, which isn't going to happen very often. And it's not just about the plumbing; usually such an arrangement simply doesn't work well with the sequence of spaces. You could, however, transform an eat-in kitchen into quite the dazzling bath—or, conversely, if you're the take-out type, a decently sized bath into a usable, if rather bare-bones, kitchen.

Be aware, too, that when plotting out kitchen and bath spaces, most building co-op boards and managers may impose limits on the number of bathrooms you can have to guard against overloading the system.

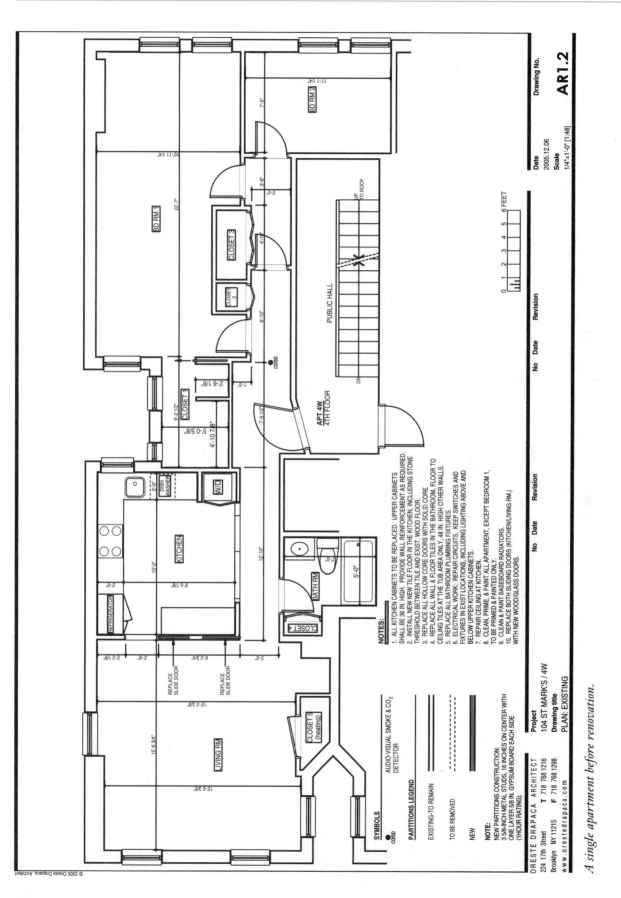

*A single apartment before renovation.*

**NOTES:**

1. ALL KITCHEN CABINETS TO BE REPLACED. UPPER CABINETS SHALL BE 36 IN. HIGH. PROVIDE WALL REINFORCEMENT AS REQUIRED.
2. INSTALL NEW NEW TILE FLOOR IN THE KITCHEN, INCLUDING STONE THRESHOLD BETWEEN TILE AND EXIST. WOOD FLOOR.
3. REPLACE ALL HOLLOW CORE DOORS WITH SOLID CORE.
4. REPLACE ALL WALL & FLOOR TILES IN THE BATHROOM, FLOOR TO CEILING TILES AT THE TUB AREA ONLY, 48 IN. HIGH OTHER WALLS.
5. REPLACE ALL BATHROOM PLUMBING FIXTURES.
6. ELECTRICAL WORK: REPAIR CIRCUITS, KEEP SWITCHES AND FIXTURES IN EXIST LOCATIONS, INCLUDING LIGHTING ABOVE AND BELOW UPPER KITCHEN CABINETS.
7. REPAIR CEILING AT KITCHEN.
8. CLEAN, PRIME, & PAINT ALL APARTMENT, EXCEPT BEDROOM 1, TO BE PRIMED & PAINTED ONLY.
9. CLEAN & PAINT BASEBOARD RADIATORS.
10. REPLACE BOTH SLIDING DOORS (KITCHEN/LIVING RM.) WITH NEW WOOD/GLASS DOORS.

**SYMBOLS**

CDSD    ●    AUDIO-VISUAL SMOKE & CO₂ DETECTOR

**PARTITIONS LEGEND**

EXISTING-TO REMAIN

TO BE REMOVED

NEW

**NOTE:**
NEW PARTITIONS CONSTRUCTION:
3 5/8-INCH METAL STUDS, 16 INCHES ON CENTER WITH
ONE LAYER 5/8 IN. GYPSUM BOARD EACH SIDE
(1 HOUR RATING).

**Project**
104 ST MARK'S / 4W

**Drawing title**
PLAN: EXISTING

| No | Date | Revision | | No | Date | Revision |

**Date** 2005.12.06
**Scale** 1/4"=1'-0" [1:48]

**Drawing No.**
**AR1.2**

ORESTE DRAPACA ARCHITECT
224 17th Street    **T** 718 768 1216
Brooklyn NY 11215    **F** 718 768 1298
www.orestedrapaca.com

© 2006 Oreste Drapaca, Architect

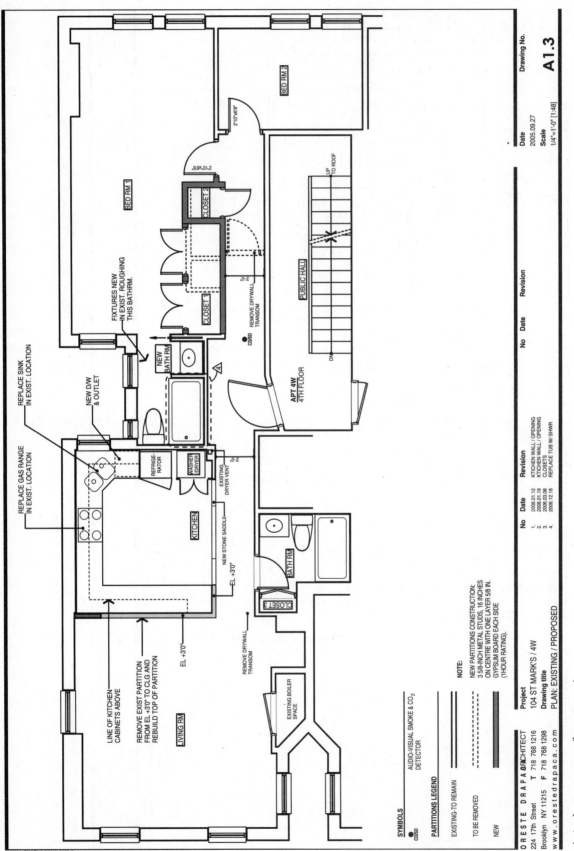

*A single apartment after renovation.*

# A Bit More on Kitchens and Baths

Although kitchens and bathrooms are exempt from the "window rule," ventilation systems are a must. Presumably heat and air conditioning are predetermined (a building either has central heat and air conditioning or it doesn't), but when working out the ventilation, you are as much on your own as the house-dweller. It may seem trivial and silly, but nonetheless you are going to have to find a way to install a duct (or vent) and fan in a reasonable and legal area. A kitchen vent has to be connected to a building's kitchen vent stack, and a bathroom vent to a stack dedicated to baths.

If you plan to have laundry facilities in your apartment, either in your kitchen or housed in a separate, designated laundry room, check in advance to be certain the building can handle the 220-volt requirements of most dryers. If not, you should be able to utilize a gas-fired dryer with a vent leading to the outside or to a legal, fireproofed vent stack dedicated to such use (not just any vent in the building; that would be a fire hazard).

A word about improvised and newly installed bathrooms: often, these may need to be raised in order to hide the pipes, placing the entire room on a sort of podium. Whatever your feelings may be regarding the aesthetics of this (some people can't tolerate it, others truly do not care), keep practicality in mind; it may not be a good option for someone with limited mobility.

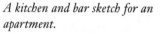

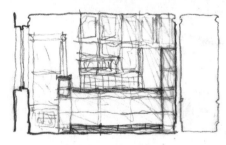

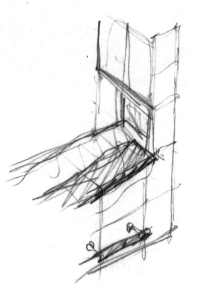

*A kitchen and bar sketch for an apartment.*

*This kitchen was built in the place of a former bedroom and shares a wall and plumbing lines with a bathroom.*

# Being Good Neighbors

You can be positively certain that your future neighbors are going to hate every minute of your renovation process, and no matter how kind and patient they are, there are going to be days they curse you under their breath. But these *are* going to be your neighbors, so you'll presumably want to keep any animosity to a minimum—both during the construction phase and after.

We've talked already about the need to keep the building pipelines clear. But the dust, the noise, the contractors dominating the elevator—these annoyances are almost unavoidable. Concern about them might, however, be among the things you ask about when seeking recommendations for a contractor: some builders are neater and generally more conscientious than others. Generally, the building management will have a manual with rules pertaining to renovations: powered jackhammers are not usually allowed, for instance, and construction workers may not interrupt water, gas, or electric supply throughout the building without advance notice.

We also advise you to check on construction as often as possible, as neighbors will be taking notes about noise, dust, dirt, and rubbish every time it annoys them. Make sure workers abide by all building rules regarding noise, use of service elevators and entrances where applicable, and so on, and that they respect building personnel—especially if you are moving to a new address rather than expanding your current apartment. Remember that any transgressions on their part are likely to be taken out on you—and most renovation contracts with the building will prescribe an entire menu of fines for various infractions.

Think, too, about your neighbors when selecting flooring and other materials, both for your own sake and for theirs. Generally speaking, the lighter the materials, the more they vibrate, ergo more noise, though lightweight or thin concrete and steel will also do little to absorb sound. We discuss this in part in Chapter 17. A 15-year-old drummer wearing Dutch clogs with steel heels, operating a traditional drum kit on a marble floor installed with thin-set on a concrete slab is going to be a nuisance. Walls made of studs and gypsum wallboard also do not insulate well, as they usually do not include insulating mineral wool filler and noise caulking, both of which we recommend (if funds permit).

**Design Tip**

Of course, if you really want to go the extra mile, you could do as one person we know did: set your downstairs neighbors up in a hotel for six months.

## Going Through the Phases

The actual design process, however, is pretty much the same, whether you are working with a house or an apartment. Although, again, you will have to consider the constraints imposed by pre-existing pipes and windows, you should still create an ideas file, write up a program, design your bubble drawing, and so on. While models are perhaps less important when designing apartments than houses (since you have no "exterior" to speak of), you could forego this stage if necessary. However, in some ways, the pre-existing conditions can make apartment redesign more complicated than designing a home.

If you do use a model, create one with a lid that makes it possible for you to look into and investigate small places, including odd spaces that might be created when combining two apartments. Consequently, we encourage you to create a model of the apartment, or at least some of the specific spaces. In the end, the more you do to make your design "real" in your mind, the easier it will be for you to make your selections, finalize your plans, and communicate your needs to your contractor later.

You will also handle things somewhat differently when it comes to permits, which are usually easier for apartment-dwellers to obtain, as the work is not construction so much as alteration This is true even when combining apartments, as long as the number of rooms does not increase. (If it does, you will need to update the certificate of occupancy.) Be sure to obtain a plumbing permit as well; although in practice a building's Board of Directors may ignore the legal requirement and allow work without a permit, we don't recommend it.

# When Two Is One

Almost everything we've said about home design applies to designing your apartment as well. But apartment living sometimes offers special opportunities (and challenges), particularly when it comes to designing the details.

It's easy enough, in theory, to combine two adjacent apartments: smash through the wall or floor between them, and there you are. But won't you end up with something that looks, well, like two apartments with a smashed wall between them?

Possibly, but not inevitably. Much will depend on how much you change the original layout. If you just make one kitchen into a closet and keep the rest, then yes, something about the flow and intrigue of the space will be lost, especially if the two apartments mirror one another exactly.

Of course, some people may *prefer* the idea of separate apartments: a young couple and their in-laws, for example. We know one couple who added an autonomous adjacent apartment for their son and his nanny.

But chances are, you're looking to combine the two apartments into a unified and integrated whole: you don't want two sunny-side up eggs side-by-side—you want an omelet. Yes, there are constraints: the design will be driven primarily by the pipe system of the building, as we've explained. But you'll still be reorganizing the spaces and finding new uses, even new shapes, for old rooms.

This may be especially true in newer buildings, where the generous space of pre-war apartments has lost out to efforts to cram as many apartments as possible into one vertical structure. Often, such apartments lack a real entryway or foyer, for instance—something you might consider adding into your design. Or you might carve a hallway through the center, reducing the size of some rooms but creating a sense of a larger, overall space. Or, by contrast, those who prefer wide open spaces may even choose to do without some dividing walls completely, using lighting and other devices to define individual areas. Combining materials along a single long wall, as described in Chapter 17, is a good trick to use for this.

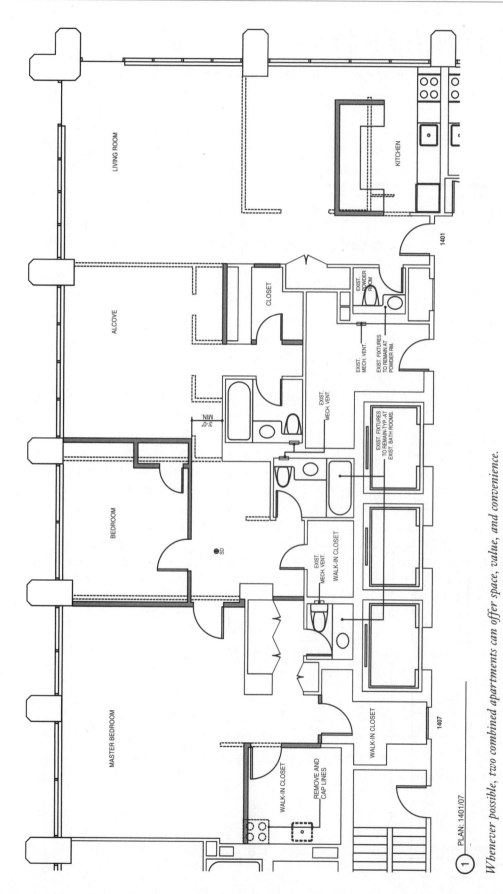

① PLAN: 1401/07

*Whenever possible, two combined apartments can offer space, value, and convenience.*

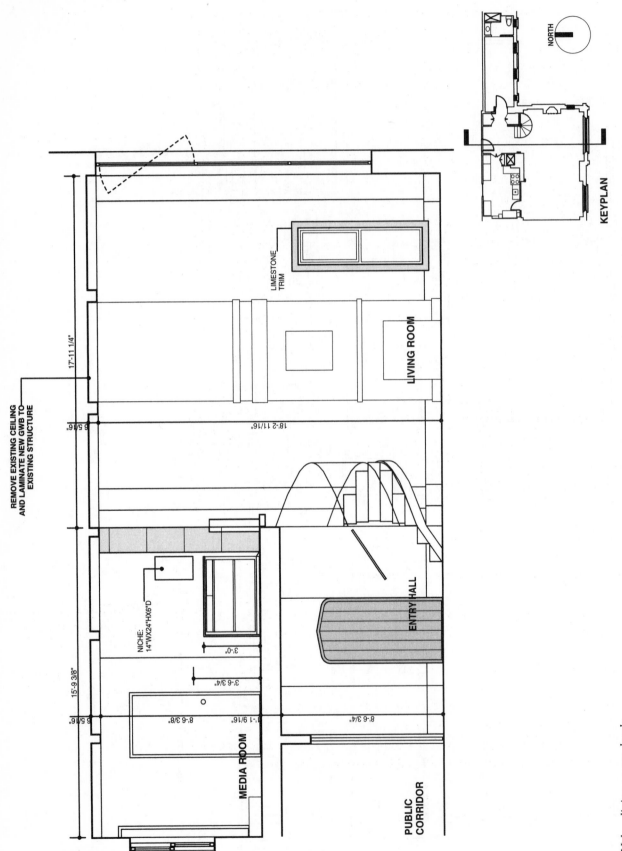

REMOVE EXISTING CEILING
AND LAMINATE NEW GWB TO
EXISTING STRUCTURE

17'-11 1/4"

LIMESTONE
TRIM

LIVING ROOM

18'-2 11/16"

6 5/16"

NICHE:
14"WX24"HX6"D

3'-0"

3'-6 3/4"

ENTRY HALL

15'-9 3/8"

6 5/16"

MEDIA ROOM

11'-1 9/16"

8'-6 3/8"

8'-6 3/4"

PUBLIC
CORRIDOR

NORTH

KEYPLAN

*Urban living on two levels.*

This applies, too, if you're expanding vertically, not laterally: if you are building a duplex—and space allows—try expanding the opening for the central stair beyond the staircase itself. True, you will lose most of a room, though you can still use the balcony-mezzanine created in the process as a library, for instance, encircled by built-in bookcases set along an outer wall; add a bistro table and a couple of chairs, and a tea or cocktail nook is born.

*A way to open the visual connection between floors and spaces.*

By connecting the two levels visually in this way, you are able to see not only the stairs, but the designs above and below: in essence, you remove the ceiling from the lower room, effectively doubling its height.

The result is dramatic, both in form and light. To further enhance the effect, consider running glass parapets and rails around the upper landing and along the stair. Or you could introduce a staircase without vertical risers, which then allows you to see through the steps; this again brings the two spaces into visual harmony, and maximizes light—especially on the lower level. An added feature is its near-invisibility in what is often an otherwise crowded space. (Such stairs may not, however, be suitable for homes with small children.)

As for the steps themselves, we recommend using as generous a width as possible, with a generous ratio between riser and tread to make them less steep.

**Design Tip**

Duplex apartments will, by and large, maintain the same configurations you'd find in a house: public spaces downstairs, private spaces above.

*What to do with spaces and where to place a staircase.*

*If possible, strive for visual connection between levels.*

*The finished design.*

# Dumbwaiters, Elevators, and Other Apartment Delights

Very few buildings still have active dumbwaiters these days—most have been shut down and boarded over. But if nostalgia (or whimsy) inspire you, it is certainly possible to build one, providing the building management agrees. (Having such a contraption running from the upstairs bath to the downstairs laundry room could be handy.) Count on it taking about 4 square feet from each room.

People, however, require a more solid form of transportation: elevators. If you're lucky enough to have an entire floor to yourself, you could design the entryway so that the elevator brings visitors from the building lobby directly into your apartment, rather than to an outer vestibule. (The private elevator door should, however, still open into a vestibule within the apartment.) Security precautions would, however, be in order here. You could have a second door, just outside the elevator door, which bolts from the inside. Alternatively, such elevators often allow you to lock the elevator door itself from the apartment, or even set it to bypass your floor entirely.

And about that fireplace: If it's there and it works, you're in luck. Don't try to build one. Or consider a "fake" fireplace, one that works with gas flames—the kind you frequently see in hotels. If a home without a hearth is not a home for you, it is certainly worth asking the building manager/engineer if conditions allow for adding a fireplace.

And if you're lucky enough to have landed yourself a penthouse, don't forget the outdoor luxuries: terraces, greenhouses, pergolas, and trellises are also possible for city dwellers.

## The Least You Need To Know

◆ Think of your apartment as your site, and plan accordingly; you can change the configurations of the total space, but not the size.

◆ Be sure to commission a site survey of your apartment and make sure the building is in good condition before you even consider buying in.

◆ Pipelines and other existing conditions will determine much of your design; be prepared to make adjustments as needed.

◆ Being considerate of neighbors during the construction phase will make life more pleasant for everyone once you've finally moved in.

◆ Reconfiguring spaces and combining rooms (especially those adjoining the apartments) allows what was formerly two spaces to harmonize neatly into one.

# Part 7

## Making It Real

There. You've done it. You've designed your own home. Congratulations!

In this last part, we will guide you through the process of getting your plans approved, your permits signed, your contractors hired—in short, everything that's left before you start on the road to making your dream home, your real home.

# Chapter 23

# Testing Your Developed Design

## In This Chapter

- ◆ Time for decisions!
- ◆ Estimating costs
- ◆ What are the alternatives?
- ◆ Finalizing it all—on paper

Put down your pencils. The designing part is finished. Yes, you will still do some retouching, some playing around, but at this point, basically, you're done. What's next is to start estimating in more precise terms what this is going to cost you, and start searching for the person (or team) that will take all the paperwork you've produced and gradually accumulated, and turn it into something you can actually live in: your house.

## Finalizing Major Systems and Materials

Time to start making decisions, and some of them aren't easy. But after the paging through catalogues, the late-night discussions, the consulting with friends, it all comes down to this: can you afford it? Be realistic. There is only so much negotiating you can do, only so many freebies you can hope for. You simply are not going to get a 10,000-square-foot fieldstone house on a 5,000-square-foot aluminum-siding budget. Of course, you know this, and you've been through the whole series of steps enough times by now (because we keep reminding you) that you have a general idea of where things stand.

But there are probably a few things you haven't quite calculated into the equation, and this is where you are going to have to start narrowing things down. Because ultimately, you need to get this house on paper. You can't build it until then. You can't really even start negotiating with a contractor until then.

(see Appendix B)

**Design Tip**

A note of caution here: nothing, in fact, is finalized until the front door opens and you set your first suitcase in the entry hall. You will finalize your *intentions* now, but expect circumstances to force (or if you're lucky, to enable) changes throughout the cost estimation, bidding, and building processes.

So how do things get finalized? Again, and obviously, money has a lot to do with it. There are resources (see Appendix B) that will tell you prices for various materials (and a few services) in different parts of the country. They're expensive books, but they do provide the information you need—within certain limits. Nothing can be completely accurate in this industry. There are always unknowns. The only thing that's a certainty lies with the builder, and that is that things have to fit: the microwave has to fit in the cabinet, the car has to fit in the garage. But timing and pricing are, to a large degree, out of your control.

If, once you've been through the financials, you continue to have doubts, look at the availability, look at aesthetics, consider potential installation problems.

Narrow down your choices by reviewing …

- Price.
- Availability of the material.
- Aesthetics.
- Potential difficulties with installation.
- Durability.
- How the materials fit in with any long-term plans.
- Cost and ease of use.

What's necessary is that at a given point, you are clear about your choices. You will never get the cabinets cut to size or the electrical wiring in place until you make decisions about whether, for instance, to use a gas or electric stove. Similarly, questions like "What size cooker should I get?" and "How much cabinet space do I need?" should have been answered while you were planning your kitchen to begin with. Within those parameters you can still play around with brands or models, but you will have to confirm the how and where in order to go forward.

# Entering Phase Four

At this point you have reached Phase Four—Contract Documents. Based on the final drawings, you (or most likely, a professional for you) will create the following documents:

- **Drawings:** Clear, accurate, scaled and thorough architectural drawings. These drawings (commonly known as blueprints) will have sufficient detail to communicate the requirements for the construction of your house to your builder.
- **Schedules:** Project materials, products and finish schedules. Schedules are detailed indexes listing the parts of the house by category. You have already selected various window and door types, light fixture types, grill and register types, and so on. The schedules will clearly identify the characteristics, model numbers, and any other important information about each one.

♦ **Specifications:** These are the written requirements for the parts of the house including quality of various materials, equipment and systems, workmanship.

These contract documents are complementary, and together include and describe all the ingredients needed to build your house. They will guide your contractor and subcontractors, who will refer to them constantly during the building process.

In addition, these documents form a major part of the actual contracts you will execute with the construction professionals you select. By making sure the contract documents are highly detailed and thorough, you can avoid additional costs after you have started construction—the "Oh, I didn't know you wanted *that*—that will be $10,000 extra" routine from the contractor.

# Creating a Cost Estimate

The next part of the process is going to take a bit more juggling as you put things into place. On the one hand, you can try to figure out what it is you've decided you want, work out the cost yourself, and go from there. Or you can hire a *cost estimator*, check his estimate against your budget, regroup as necessary, and recalculate. Your answers lie somewhere between "what do I want?" and "what can I afford?" Not until you work those out will you have determined and finalized the materials and finishes you will put into your home.

Hence there will be a lot of back-and-forth going on for a while as you move between Plan A costs and Plan B costs, determining financials and materials over and over again. Your cost estimator cannot provide you a reasonable figure without your having made at least tentative Plan A decisions; but you will want to be prepared with alternatives, which means that while the decisions you bring to him are *basically* final, they may not be *completely* final.

But start with Plan A. Decide what you want, budget it out, and then see where you land. Do you need to go to Plan B? Work it through and check with your estimator. All set? Then you've finalized your plans. Not yet? On to Plan C. And so on.

Your cost estimator will work out your numbers by performing what is called an "area takeoff," counting the square feet of sheetrock, of lumber, of tile, and so forth, and making informed adjustments and allowances. He will then suggest that you try taking away the marble baseboard and replacing it with vinyl, or something along those lines, promising it will save you $50,000 off the cost. Well, maybe it will. But is it the best way to do it? These suggestions are only monetary, and do not take into account the long-term, and living with those decisions.

Consequently, we recommend consulting an architect at this point. Not everyone can know everything, and in building a home the number of variables is significant. Some things are given: there has to be heat. There has to be light.

> **Architerms**
> An independent **cost estimator** will review your measured drawings and give you a general idea of what you will pay, from sheetrock to threshold, to build. Using what is called "value engineering," he can then make suggestions for ways to revise your plans to save costs.

**Design Don't**

Do not rely on your cost estimator for all your decision making. His job is to deal with numbers. He cannot tell you whether a certain modification will be wise from a structural or other point of view. Remember also that his figures are only an estimate.

There has to be a foundation and walls and beams. But the part you can take money from is the part you touch—the fantastic stones, the eight-burner stove, the appliances, the finishes. You don't necessarily need cherry-wood cabinets. You can get a custom kitchen with stained maple instead, which will save you a huge chunk of money right there.

Yet at the same time, the cost estimator's suggestion to replace marble with vinyl is a poorer solution, because unlike the substitution of maple for cherry wood, using vinyl in place of marble will actually devalue the house. It doesn't matter if you won't hate the vinyl every time you look at it. Don't do it. Other alternatives, like wood, will be better for you and for your investment. An architect can help you evaluate these choices.

Some cost estimators or other consultants might recommend doing away with your central AC as well. We're less convinced. As we've noted elsewhere in this book, doing this may save you money now, but if you end up with window-mounted air conditioning in its place, high energy bills may mean it will cost you more in the long run. And this, too, will lower the resale value of your house.

## Obtaining Further Cost Estimates

Whatever revisions you make, you still will have further cost estimates ahead—these from your builders, the ones who really count. These are the guys who live in the area, who know what things cost: the time, the materials, the labor. And they want to make a decent profit.

Occasionally, you may even find some contractors who will look at your rougher drawings, which is not a bad idea. Though many will be hesitant to do this because they fear setting too low a bid, at least you can get an idea of the price range, the scale of magnitude of your project.

Of course, that range will vary: the cost of building a house isn't just the price paid for nailing a wall into place: it's also the invisible hand of the market. Your builder can tell you what he will do and what he'll ask for it. These are the estimates that matter. Among the tasks you can expect him to price will be …

**Design Tip**

If possible, try to find a contractor to review your drawings early on—not sketches, but early scaled, measured drawings—and give you a general range of what he might bid for the project. This will give you a sense of what your costs will be, however tentative. You can then go back to this same contractor later for more definite prices and a binding contract.

- Cleanup of the site.
- Excavation.
- Arranging a Dumpster.
- Building the foundation.
- Rough carpentry (the two-by-fours, really).
- Roofing.
- Plumbing.
- Electrical work.
- Drywall.
- Doors.

- ◆ Windows.
- ◆ Painting.
- ◆ Various finishes.
- ◆ Trims, moldings, and baseboards.

Don't settle for the estimate of just one builder, either. Get several. You want to compare costs for building the way you would for any large purchase, such as a car or, for that matter, a new home.

This is where your cost estimator's independent calculations will prove invaluable: compare the builders' figures with what your estimator tells you it should cost. The numbers may not be the same (they probably won't be) but hopefully, they will be close enough.

## Adding or Deducting Alternatives

All those Plan A's and Plan B's you came up with while working with a cost estimator (or the ones you're about to come up with now if you skipped that step) will come in handy again while talking to your potential contractors. Again, there are elements that are fixed and elements that are not. You can explore various systems of heating the house, heating the water, the size of the garage, the kind of wood in the kitchen. You can explore different roofing stems, from asphalt shingles to copper, though the underlying part of the roof is there anyway, to stay.

Consequently, if the initial estimates are too high, you might ask your contractor candidates to price two different heating systems, two roofing options—even two foundations.

This can also be tricky, however. On occasion, a scenario in which all the components are not quite known can only be finalized according to whatever prices or procedures are available. Let's say a new heating-pump system on the market will handle both air conditioning and heating, be very efficient, easy on the environment, and potentially add excellent technical value to the house.

But because the product is new, your builder may not know exactly how long it will take to install. He may want to factor in a "learning curve." Nonetheless, this system could work to your advantage: you get a base price for the immutables, and separate prices for the various gizmos. For each new, untested gizmo, you agree on an estimate for the known version with the option to use the alternative when the details become more available. (Be sure that if the alternative winds up costing you less, your contractor credits you for the difference!)

You can also ask for final contract prices on three different versions of an element of the house—say, three contract prices for floors, two for HVAC, two for roofing. Agree to make a decision among these options once the foundations are down and the walls are up. The point is that once you've come to a tentative agreement on the price, by discussing specific parts of the project individually, you may be able to figure out ways to add or deduct things accordingly.

**Design Tip**

The cost estimator is the first you're likely to consult, but he may or may not be the best guide. The estimates that really matter are the ones that come from the builder (or from a group of competing builders), who is the final authority: he, after all, is where you get the thing done.

**Design Tip**

Unfortunately, some builders don't feel comfortable with the idea of changing anything. They will charge for any changes, even within the same categories. Find out from the beginning if the builders and contractors you are talking to are willing to deal with alternatives, or are the kinds of people who will charge you for every change you make. On the other hand, some product changes may require the builder to put in more installation time, and you can't expect him to do this for free.

And if not, you can begin the round again. Check back with the architect about changing the size of the house. Getting rid of 500 square feet can save a bunch of money. Is the basement really necessary? The guest bath? Then go back to the contractors for a more detailed round of estimates.

Again, consulting an architect can help, not just in terms of making dramatic design changes, but also replacing the costly finishes with others. A good architect will help you make the correct choices. And always remember that you can go back to your cost estimator, who can be consulted at various points in the process, independently of the others.

And round and round you'll go this way, until a certain point when everything finally comes together, decisions are made, and you are ready to begin.

## The Least You Need To Know

- Have a cost estimator review your drawings and plans to give you a general idea of the total costs.

- Should you choose to make changes based on the cost estimator's calculations, discuss his suggestions first with an architect, builder, or other expert.

- Contact contractors for general estimates.

- Continue exploring alternatives until you have finalized your plans and matched them to your budget.

# Chapter 24

# The Nitty-Gritty

## In This Chapter

- A final reality check
- Contractors and bids
- Getting ready to build—your new home, at last

Drawings in hand, plans in place, estimates lined up neatly in a row, you're ready to narrow down your selection and find the people who are going to make this thing really happen. As with everything else you've done so far, putting the right team together may take a certain amount of time and diligence, but it's something you want to be sure to do right.

Building your custom home should be fun and exciting, not littered with arguments, misunderstandings, frustrations, and—worst of all—things just not getting done the way they should. Work with your builder, create an atmosphere of mutual trust and respect, and sooner than you think, you'll be moving in.

## Reviewing Your Work

Let's go back to that program you wrote up—the lists of ideas, the "he wants/ she wants" debates. If there are items you've forgotten or omitted, put them in now. If there are arguments to settle, settle them. If there's a wall finish you never quite selected, a window size you never quite determined, select them and determine them. If you're still unsure about how to reconcile the cost estimator's assessment with any second or third opinions, see if reading through your program helps to clarify things. How important was that marble floor when you started out? Is it still? Did you have a second choice in mind that you've forgotten that would be perfectly satisfactory, after all?

Compare your floor plans with your bubble diagram. You've made a few changes along the way—be certain all rooms still flow the way they should.

Also check, once more, your final drawings and plans against your site map or plan and double-check applicable zoning laws. We know you've done this already, but this is where a little obsessive-compulsiveness can be a good thing.

You really, really don't want to find yourself slapping your forehead in a dramatic "I can't believe I forgot…" moment after your contractor has already started work. Even worse will be to discover after the building is nearly finished that the windows are out of line.

So once more: *Did you remember everything?*

*Do the numbers match your budget?*

*Will life be bearable without that indoor putting green you'd had your heart set on when you first started out?*

*Are the corners swept, i's dotted, t's crossed?*

Then onward.

# Finding—and Choosing—Your Contractor

Planting a tree, raising a child, building a house—these are important activities to most people. Those who do them best work collaboratively—and this applies to builders, as well. Because of their many years of experience—or sometimes just through brainstorming—you can find solutions working together. Good craftsmanship is something many builders hold dear. They want your house to be something they, too, can be proud of.

To a certain extent, finding the right contractor is not unlike finding the right custom clothing designer or plastic surgeon or hairstylist: if you see something that seems to have been done well, find out who did it. Unlike plastic surgery and hairstyling, however, you can sometimes even find these guys in the process of a job. If you do, stop. Talk to them. In fact, even if you go through a referral, try to see a work in progress. How organized is it? How much are the workers actually working? How orchestrated are they? Are they friendly? Manners count.

Moreover, whether found via word-of-mouth, picked up by the side of the road, or by playing "pin the tail on the donkey" with the Yellow Pages, any contractor or builder should be willing and able not just to pass you estimates for your future project, but to show you both a completed and uncompleted site—a record of past achievements. You may not need this before getting an estimate, but you will want to investigate thoroughly as you prepare to make your selections for the bidding process—essentially the last test before you make your choice.

If you possibly can, meet with previous clients independently and find out what the experience was like. Did it come in on time? On budget? Analyze what the client tells you: a few days or weeks late isn't important. Six months late is a problem. Was the contractor reasonable when asking about extras that weren't included in the original plans? Were his questions and suggestions sensible, or were they frivolous? Was he asking good questions, or trying to squeeze more money out of the client?

Dealing with the time and money issues of working with a contractor isn't always easy, but it helps if you are able to translate the estimates and promises into real terms. In real life, a short-term project that takes 50 percent longer is not that big a deal. If your contractor says your project will take eight months, expect a year; if he says it will take a year, allow for 15 months. If a one-year project takes longer than 16 months, you probably have reason for concern.

Even so, every house is different, and things happen: you could face a month of thunderstorms. Market conditions could change. Someone could buy the entire world supply of steel one month, and you're out of luck. It may be tempting to take your frustrations out on your contractor, but it isn't always his fault, and telling him it is isn't going to make him your best friend.

Does that matter? Do you want this guy to be your best friend? Well … kind of, yes. It's important to stay on good terms with the person who is putting your house up. Remember, he'd like to finish quickly, too. The sooner he's done with your house, the sooner he can go do a job somewhere else. The better you get along, the more likely he is to handle delays, possible errors, and unexpected complications amicably, cordially, and fairly. We'll talk more about this when we talk about schedules later in this chapter.

Pricing can also be tricky. A good builder can give a rough estimate on the basis of very rough drawings, as we've already discussed. But at the same time, we've found that good builders prefer not to give actual bid prices "just like that." A good builder knows that there are many ways to do the same thing, and consequently, a firm price offer—or bid—can depend on the final decisions made. The important thing is that he respects your budget and doesn't try to take advantage.

Still, in the end, because yours is a custom product, there is no guarantee that what you finally get is going to be exactly what you wanted. There's an unknown factor in here that requires you to make a leap of trust: you have to be willing to say, "I think this guy can work, the price seems okay," and take a chance.

# Learning About Base Bids

At this point, you have collected the names of various contractors, asked for estimates, researched their qualifications, and determined who among them is a serious potential candidate for the job. You're ready for the first round of bidding.

Working from the list of items you cannot do without (the foundation, walls, roofs, and so on), seek out bids from the various contractors you've been dealing with—the ones whose estimates seemed most sensible to you, the ones with whom you thought you'd feel most comfortable working.

## Understanding the Bid Process

Organize your papers, your drawings, the specifications that show what systems will be installed and what materials will be used, and send them to various candidates selected from among those who provided your estimates earlier.

Yes, they've seen them. Send them again. Be aware, though, that just because someone has agreed to look at your drawings, it doesn't mean that he's going to bid on them. However, people will want to see the drawings before they even spend the time to calculate a bid, so they can work out the materials and labor knowledgeably.

> ### Design Tip
> Remember that the round of bids from the contractors is obtained *before* signing a contract, which allows time and opportunity to revise the design drastically—even by removing a room—as you did during the estimate phase. Then rebid and see whether these alterations have lowered the cost sufficiently. This may happen one, two, even three times, though some builders may give up along the way.

Obtaining bids means, essentially, finding the contractors who are interested in building your house, making a profit, and making you happy with the product. One of your best tactics in this is to make sure that all bidders know that there are others involved in the process, that it's a competitive situation, but that you're looking not just for the cheapest, but for the best relationship and value.

## Sealed Bids, Open Bids, and Collusion Bids

When you're ready to accept bids, you have two possible routes: *sealed* and *open*. (We'll get to the "collusion" stuff later.) They are essentially what they sound like: in open bidding, the competing companies all know about one another and bid approximately the same figure, though perhaps with different breakdowns: contractor A charges more for the foundation than Contractor B does, but Contractor B charges more for building the roof.

Or you can also make this a time-fixed process in which you get a sealed bid delivered by so-and-so at such-and-such a location, all anonymously (though in a small community, word gets around). How you choose to do this is based really on your own preference.

*Collusion bidding* is rare, but it happens, so you should be prepared: occasionally, all potential contractors will present identical bids. This is an aggressive, antagonistic move, aimed at making things difficult for the owner for any of a number of reasons, such as perceived arrogance toward bidders. As the saying goes, don't let it happen to you.

There are also no hard-and-fast rules about how to choose the winning candidate. A good rule of thumb, mentioned in Chapter 7, is to knock the top and bottom two bids out of the running—the highest because he's probably padding the estimate, and the lowest because it is possible this low a bid means he doesn't know what he's doing, or that he will try to compensate by asking for extra money on things that aren't in the drawings. (And there will be things omitted from the drawings; it's simply not possible to include everything there.) Or worse, he runs out of money and simply stops work.

## Architerms

**Sealed bids** are received from various potential contractors, in sealed envelopes, usually delivered at or before a certain deadline, to be opened all at the same time. In principle, none of the contending contractors knows who else is bidding, or what the bids turn out to be (though in smaller communities, such things are hard to keep secret).

**Open bids** are essentially the reverse of an auction: everyone tries to outbid the other, but downward. All the contenders know who the competition is, and what the competing bids are. Some will bid higher, but offer more services or better work; others will bid the lowest number they can calculate.

**Collusion bids** take place when the competing contractors work together to produce identical bids for a client, essentially giving him no possible choice at all.

Once you've reviewed your options and made your selections, you can call the happy winner and say, "I'd like to discuss further how we can work together." Even then, there's still some room to discuss his bid further, and we recommend doing so. The outcomes of such discussions and more detailed arrangements can not only help clarify aspects of the project (and budget), but help you trust that any unanticipated conditions (such as uncovering a huge rock in the middle of digging that you hadn't known was lurking there) will result in an honest charge.

Somewhere around this point, your contractor will provide a contract based on the terms you've already agreed to verbally. Check it carefully. Examples of contracts and a list of local distributors can be downloaded from aia.org. Drawings and specs should be referenced into the contract, along with delivery time frame, payment schedules, and various responsibilities. (Be sure to include clauses in your contract that will cover continuances for unforeseen conditions, cancellations, and other nuisances. We suggest also adding penalties for being late.)

And naturally, you would also be well advised to have a lawyer review the document before signing.

## Design Tip

Contracts are there to protect both sides of a deal. You, the owner, are afraid the contractor won't deliver on time, on budget, to quality. You want to be sure you're not paying for something that won't get built. Your contractor is afraid he'll be asked to do too many things for free, not get paid in full at the end of the job, or that you'll otherwise take advantage of him and his work. Trust is crucial here. A lawyer isn't a replacement for that, but it's very good insurance.

# Establishing Schedules

So about those schedules: again, build in some flexibility. And no, it won't be different with your house just because it's yours. Schedules exist in this business as a guideline; they cannot tell you the actual future. You have to realize that

**Design Don't**

It's a good idea to build a timeline in to the contract, but don't get nitpicky about schedules. Anticipate delays, recognizing that these are a *normal* part of the process, not some conspiracy cooked up to make you crazy. On the other hand, don't accept the absurd. Communicate with your contractor, and keep this project a collaborative effort.

things will change, that decisions will have to be made. If you try to be too literal about it, everyone will be unhappy at the end.

Understanding what is involved in the process can also help both owner and builder come to an agreement about scheduling. What does it mean "to build a roof"? Do both builder and owner have the same perspective on this? Does the owner understand that this means selecting the roofing tiles, arranging delivery, all the smaller steps that make up the process? For his part, does the contractor know that you, as owner, are more than willing to choose a different brand, a different color, if it means sparing a three-week wait?

In the end, you and your contractor are actually more on the same page than you may realize. He wants enough time to do a good job, but not so long that he has too many people tied up in things that aren't making money. You want to move in as soon as possible, but you don't want a rushed, half-baked job done on your home. So negotiate.

And if we haven't said it enough, be flexible. The fact is, builders rarely come in on time. They want to please people so they say they'll be ready before they really can be. Too much pressure just makes everyone unhappy—your family, your workers, you. Rush a job too much and you risk errors that can't be fixed: a repair will look like it is being patched, and you will not be happy with it. Take a perspective view, and everyone will survive this a lot better.

# Arranging Permits

Building permits are handled by the owner, armed with a complete set of certified drawings that have been stamped by a licensed architect or engineer. (In some cases, the builder may be able to apply in your stead, but he will still need to show the stamped drawings.) If you have not consulted with either up to this point, your newly contracted contractor will probably be able to guide you to someone who can handle this for you.

Please note that this does not mean you have to have your drawings professionally remade. It's entirely possible that your own drawings are perfectly fine (with small adjustments), but they still need an expert's stamped seal of approval. Expect this to cost a few hundred dollars, though this can vary greatly by region.

In some areas, you can also hire people to do the legwork for you, so-called expeditors. The buildings department, like most bureaucracies, has created a complex web of paperwork that is not the easiest thing to navigate: there are applications for various things, the boiler needs a license, the boiler number and model number get filed, they want to know how many tubs, how many showers, how many sinks. An expeditor will file the paperwork on your behalf. (The idea, and of course it's a good one, is to make sure that no one can say "I don't know" or build something illegal.) Again, it comes at a cost (it should run you couple of thousand dollars) but these people can save you a tremendous amount of work and frustration.

And that's it. You've made your plans. You've completed your drawings. You've selected your materials, the details, the designs. You've hired your workers, signed your contracts, and arranged your permits to build.

Welcome to your new home!

## The Least You Need To Know

- If possible, visit completed sites and "works in progress," and talk to previous clients to get a sense of the real quality and style of a contractor's work.

- Remember that timing can be affected by outside influences; builders rarely actually come in on time.

- Keep a cordial relationship with your contractor; it will make the entire experience much better for everyone—and most of all, for you.

- When selecting from submitted bids, rule out the lowest and the highest offers and explore those that still remain.

- Have a licensed architect or engineer review and stamp your drawings for approval; you will need this when applying for your building permit.

# Glossary

**architect**   A designer of buildings (or websites or other elements). A building architect also oversees the construction process, integrating and coordinating everything from the first site survey through the laying of electrical systems to ensuring that the kitchen floor doesn't land in the master bedroom.

**cavity wall**   A technique of building an exterior wall out of two walls—a structural wall on the interior side, followed by an air cavity, then a wall on the exterior side, which acts as air and water screen.

**cement block**   *See* concrete masonry unit.

**cladding**   A protective or insulating coating fixed to metal, usually under high pressure. Cladding can also means siding or covering, as in "glass-clad façade".

**classic revival**   Architecture of the early nineteenth century, mainly in the United States and England, inspired by the classical architecture of Greece and Rome.

**collusion bids**   Collusion bids take place when the competing contractors work together to produce identical bids for a client, essentially giving him no possible choice at all.

**concrete masonry unit (CMU)**   A small block made of Portland cement, aggregates, and water; can be solid or hollow; also called "cement block," which is incorrect.

**contract documents**   The architectural phase in which final documents are developed on the basis of architectural renderings. These include drawings (floor plans or blueprints), schedules, and specifications.

**crawl space**   Generally a low (under three feet), unfinished, and unheated space under a house; it allows access to plumbing and electrical work.

**crown molding**   A molding applied at the top of an element (wall, eave), which has acquired the meaning of top molding in a room.

**design development phase**   The architectural phase in which one begins to elaborate and refine the floor plans and the exterior and interior elevations, and begins to select the various materials and finishes.

**documents** The detailed drawings, diagrams, lists, and information about the site on which a building is built.

**dormers** Projecting windows built into the roof.

**easement** The right of a third party to access your land. Usually this applies to utility companies, though it can also relate to a neighbor's home or public access ways.

**elevations** *See* floor plans.

**floor plans** Previously called blueprints, floor plans are scaled drawings, like a map, of your a building or part of a building. Elevations are almost the vertical equivalent; they show the vertical interior and exterior walls, without suggesting three-dimensionality, as if you had drawn a line around the house after it had been built.

**footing** The bottom of the foundation.

**footprint** The exact space a building occupies on the land—literally as if it had left a "footprint" in the soil.

**foundation wall** The vertical part of a foundation.

**HVAC** A standard term referring to heating, ventilation, and air-conditioning systems.

**lamp** In architectural terms, what emits light. Most people call them bulbs. A "light fixture" is what most people call a lamp—the thing you screw the bulb (lamp) into. These overlap somewhat, but are not interchangeable.

**lath** A metal mesh or wood strip, usually installed in rows as a support for tiles or plaster.

**light fixture** *See* lamp.

**lintel** A beam, usually wood, steel, or stone, above a door or window.

**lumber** Timber (wood) that has been sawed (usually into planks) or otherwise prepared for building.

**lumens** A measure of how much light actually falls on a given area.

**mosaics** Designs or images formed of stone, glass, or tiles glued to a surface.

**mullion** The vertical element of a window (or curtain wall), which supports the adjacent glass panes.

**newels** The decorative banister (railing) supports at the top and bottom of a stair.

**niche** A recess into a wall, of various shapes and sizes, usually built to display a three-dimensional object; may have lighting above.

**open bids** A form of bidding in which all the contenders know who the competition is and what the competing bids are. Some will bid higher but offer more services or better work; others will bid the lowest number they can calculate.

**open plan** Refers to designing a building in such a way that the floors (or stories) have few internal walls.

**opus incertum** The technique of building a wall out of rough stones set in an irregular pattern and set in mortar.

**order** In architecture may refer to an arrangement of columns and the elements above them; in classical architecture it refers to a particular type of column and the rules of using it (Doric, Ionic, Corinthian, Tuscan, etc.) In a more general contemporary context, it refers to the clarity of an architectural design.

**parapet** A low wall, like that surrounding a porch or balcony.

**parquet** A way of installing wood flooring, usually in small squares or simple patterns.

**paving** In architectural terms, anything lining a path that isn't earth—stone, tile, concrete, brick, and so on.

**pergola** A shelter made from intersecting beams supported by posts, usually along a walkway. They are often covered with plants or vines.

**porch** An open space along the outside of a house, covered by a roof. It may also be enclosed by screen or glass.

**postmodernism** A design style that emerged as a reaction to the bare forms of modernism. Postmodern architects return ornament and often wit to what they consider the "soullessness" of modernist design, while still making visual reference to industrial geometry. Michael Graves is perhaps the best-known postmodern architect.

**predesign phase** The first architectural phase, in which one selects and documents a site, gathering ideas for what the building will be.

**schedules** Detailed indexes listing the parts of the house by category.

**schematic design** The architectural phase in which, through the use of floor plans, elevations, and budget calculations, a building begins to take form.

**sealed bids** Bids received from various potential contractors, in sealed envelopes, usually delivered at or before a certain deadline, to be opened all at the same time.

**sections** Drawings of a building (or a section of the building) rendered as if the building (or section) had been cut vertically to show the interior.

**setback regulations** Stipulate the minimum distance from which you may place your home from the lot line of your property.

**sheathing** The covering material over the exterior studs of a building.

**Six Phases of Architectural Design** Architects have systematized the design process into six phases. You will need to follow these phases in sequence, as each one builds on the one before it.

- Pre-Design
- Schematic Design
- Design Development
- Contract Documents
- Bidding and Negotiation
- Construction

**soffit** Once reserved to describe the underside of the tops of archways and architraves. Now, it's generally used to refer to the upper space of a room.

**solving the circulation** A term architects use to describe finding solutions for connecting spaces efficiently and elegantly (including between inside and outside).

**Southern antebellum** An architectural style characterized by sweeping porches and columns. (The years prior to the American Civil War are known as the "antebellum period.")

**specifications** The written requirements for the parts of a building, including quality of various materials, equipment, systems, and workmanship.

**structural glued laminated timber (glulam)** A manmade product similar in general size and uses to a large piece of timber It is made of pieces of wood not exceeding two inches thick, glued in parallel strips one over another, with the grain running longitudinally. It is made to almost any size and specifications, and it is used to span larger openings, where normal size timber is not large enough. Depth can reach 72 inches and more for special orders, and length can reach 60 feet, with special orders to 175 feet.

**sustainable architecture** Architecture that seeks to create a minimum impact on the environment through the use of selected, minimally polluting, or recycled materials and moderated energy expenditure.

**timber** Wood used for building; also refers to trees or logs suitable for converting to lumber.

**wainscot** A panel, usually wood, installed at the lower part of an interior wall.

# Resources

## Books

Andres, Peter. "Daylight Planning with an Artificial Sky." *Detail* 2006.

Ballard, Scott T. *The Complete Guide to Designing Your Own Home*. Cincinnati, OH: Betterway Books, 1995.

*The BOCA National Building Code*. Country Club Hills, IL: Building Officials & Code Administrators International, Inc., 1996.

Bramwell, Martyn, ed. *The International Book of Wood*, New York: Simon and Schuster, 1976.

*Building Code of the City of New York*. Binghampton, NY: USA Gould Publishers, 2006.

Harris, Cyril M., ed. *Dictionary of Architecture and Construction*. New York: McGraw-Hill, Inc., 1975.

Jetzt, Christian. "Light Without Heat? The Complex Task of Daylight Planning" *Detail* 2006 (425-427).

Masello, David. *Architecture Without Rules: The Houses of Marcel Breuer and Herbert Beckhard*. New York: W. W. Norton, 1993.

Neufert, Ernst. *Architect's Data*. 2nd intl. English ed. Great Britain & New York: Granada/Halsted Press/John Wiley & Sons, Inc, 1980.

Ramsey, Charles G., and Harold R. Sleeper. *Architectural Graphic Standards, Tenth Edition*. New York: John Wiley & Sons, 2000.

Ramsey, Dan. *The Complete Idiot's Guide to Building Your Own Home, Second Edition*. Indianapolis: Alpha Books, 2004.

Studio Marmo, text by Frederick Bradley. *Natural Stone: A Guide to Selection*. 1st American ed. New York: Norton, 1998.

# Magazines

*Abitare*— Available as hard copy, English text, at various locations in the United States.

*Architectural Record*

*Architectural Review*

*Detail* (www.detail.de, look for the English language button) available as hard copy, English text, at various locations in the United States. Provides elegant technical solutions to design problems and showcases elegant designs.

*Domus*

*Dwell*

*Elle Decor*

*Metropolitan Home*

# Resources

*Means Building Construction Cost Data 2007 Book*, 65th Edition, published by RS Means Company (www.rsmeans.com).

*Sweets Residential Cost Guide 2007*, published by McGraw-Hill Construction, available at www.bnibooks.com.

*Sweets Unit Cost Guide 2007*, published by McGraw-Hill Construction, available at www.bnibooks.com.

# Index

# X–Y–Z

# Create your dream home with these Complete Idiot's Guides®

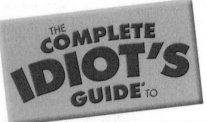

"Before you take another step toward building your home, sit down and read *The Complete Idiot's Guide® to Building Your Own Home* cover to cover."

—Dean Johnson, *Hometime* executive producer and co-host

# Building Your Own Home

### SECOND EDITION

♦ **Concrete information** on finding the resources to construct your house from foundation to roof

♦ **The lowdown** on housing options including conventional, manufactured, and kit homes

♦ **Budget-wise tips** to help you negotiate the lowest fees and get the most for your money

**Dan Ramsey**

978-1-59257-314-1
**New edition coming November 2007**

**New edition!**

Sunny solutions to your home's energy needs

# Solar Power for Your Home

### SECOND EDITION

**Dan Ramsey with David Hughes**

978-1-59257-643-2

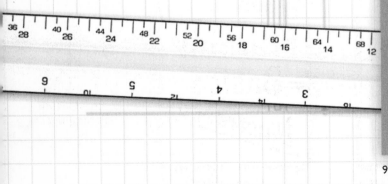

Innovative ideas for creating a truly useful space

New!

# Garage Solutions *Illustrated*

Robert and Theresa Russell

978-1-59257-620-3

"Elizabeth Moran and Masters Joseph Yu and Val Biktashev have produced an excellent and detailed book."
—Stephen Skinner, founder of *Feng Shui for Modern Living* magazine

# Feng Shui

### THIRD EDITION

♦ **A simple introduction** to classical feng shui

♦ **Expert advice** on improving your health, wealth, home, and relationships

♦ **Before-and-after illustrations** of real-life feng shui makeovers

Elizabeth Moran, Master Joseph Yu, and Master Val Biktashev

978-1-59257-344-8

# Green Living

978-1-59257-662-3
Available September 2007

# Simple Home Repair

978-1-59257-665-4
Available September 2007

# Framing Basics *Illustrated*

978-1-59257-668-5
Available October 2007

**ALPHA**
Idiotsguides.com

# Check Out These
# Best-Sellers

## Read by millions!

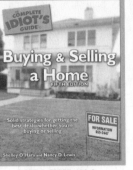
**Grammar and Style**
SECOND EDITION
978-1-59257-115-4
$16.95

**Buying & Selling a Home**
FIFTH EDITION
978-1-59257-458-2
$19.95

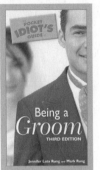
**Being a Groom**
THIRD EDITION
978-1-59257-451-3
$9.95

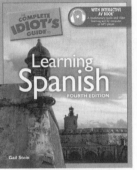
**Learning Spanish**
FOURTH EDITION
978-1-59257-485-8
$24.95

**Investing**
THIRD EDITION
978-1-59257-480-3
$19.95

**Baby Sign Language**
978-1-59257-469-8
$14.95

**Total Nutrition**
FOURTH EDITION
978-1-59257-439-1
$18.95

**Positive Dog Training**
SECOND EDITION
978-1-59257-483-4
$14.95

**The Bible**
THIRD EDITION
978-1-59257-389-9
$18.95

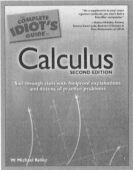
**Calculus**
SECOND EDITION
978-1-59257-471-1
$18.95

**Music Theory**
SECOND EDITION
978-1-59257-437-7
$19.95

**The Perfect Resume**
FOURTH EDITION
978-1-59257-463-6
$14.95

**Playing the Guitar**
SECOND EDITION
978-0-02864244-4
$21.95

**Manga Illustrated**
978-1-59257-335-6
$19.95

**Knitting & Crocheting**
THIRD EDITION
978-1-59257-491-9
$19.95

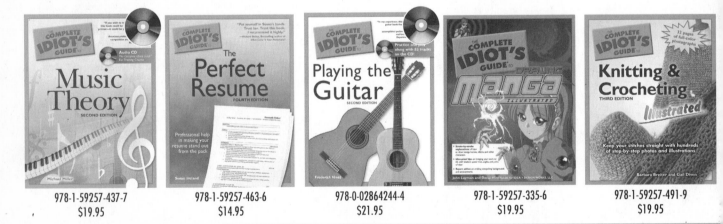

## More than *450 titles* available at booksellers and online retailers everywhere

www.idiotsguides.com

ALPHA